The Bedside
Guardian 2011

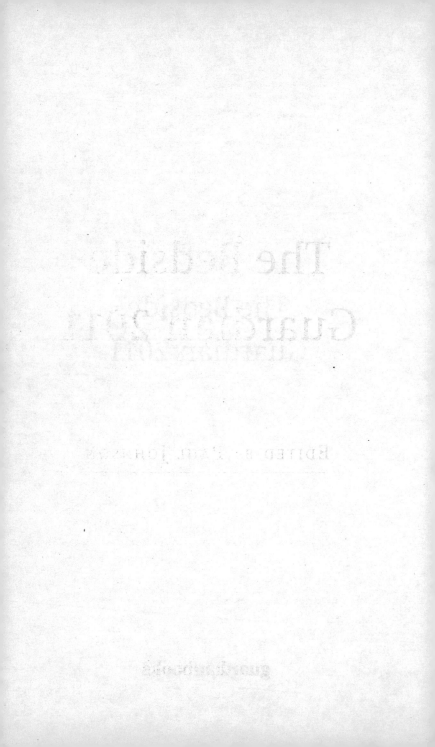

The Bedside Guardian 2011

EDITED BY PAUL JOHNSON

guardianbooks

Published by Guardian Books 2011

2 4 6 8 10 9 7 5 3 1

Copyright © Guardian News and Media Ltd 2011

Paul Johnson has asserted his right under the Copyright,
Designs and Patents Act 1988 to be identified as the editor of this work

First published in Great Britain in 2011 by
Guardian Books
Kings Place, 90 York Way
London N1 9GU

www.guardianbooks.co.uk

A CIP catalogue record for this book
is available from the British Library

ISBN 978-0852-65265-7

Cover design by Two Associates
Typeset by seagulls.net

Printed and bound in Great Britain by Clays Ltd, St Ives PLC

Contents

SPRING

Foreword

STEVE COOGAN

Two events above all others gave the Guardian newspaper much to report and analyse this last year. The Arab spring exposed ugly truths for western leaders. The west champions not any old democracy, just western democracy. Better the devil you know. The collective post-9/11 siege mentality means we seem to have jettisoned the Geneva conventions. A bit of torture, a few human rights violations by a friendly dictator, and denying the due process of law by using drones to kill suspects. When Barack Obama was elected, he said "we reject as false the choice between our safety and our ideals". Well done on that one, Mr President. The doublethink of "we will throw away our values to defend our values" was eloquently expressed in George Orwell's 1984. The inconsistent, hesitant, nervous response to the Arab spring by western leaders eloquently expresses it today.

The Guardian has never provided easy answers; it has always asked difficult questions. "Subscribe to our paper and feel a little uneasy about the world" is a tough sell, but it is the only honourable way. Probity and the thorough calling to account of those who exercise power is what it does best. Leave the comfortable oversimplification to the Daily Mail. The danger for the Guardian is of becoming cynical and sliding into a deep well of negativity. It can, though, shake off the curse of postmodernism, leading the charge into a future where we aspire to be more ethically rigorous with ourselves and others. Some journalists are better at this than others (a good challenge is to try being humorous and uncynical; it is possible).

The second big story is the phone-hacking scandal: the Guardian at its best. The newspaper's dogged tenacity is as heroic as News International's foot-dragging was utterly shameful. The Times in particular has yet to recover from the most naked example of proprietorial interference when it repeatedly refused to cover the story until that position became untenable. It was either that or abject fear of its owners, and I don't know which is worse. But the Guardian's Nick Davies, along with other journalists and a few individuals with balls and cash, saw things differently. Together they pulled at a snag in the thread of the Savile Row suit which clad News International and, bit by bit, inch by inch, it started to reveal the naked truth. The more it tried to run in the other direction, the more quickly it unravelled (you see, the snagged-thread analogy really does work). And it's still unravelling, although News International are quickly trying to measure themselves up for another bespoke suit to clad themselves in and attempt another oily assault on the British public. We cannot let that happen, and anyway, thanks to the non-cowards in this saga, we have already seen NI's naked body, and it's no Page 3 girl (OK, I'll stop the clothed/naked analogy now).

No amount of respectable, well-modulated management-speak from James Murdoch can disguise the direct link between increased circulation and literally going through people's rubbish bins. This intrusion into people's lives has been the way of things for the past 40 years. History teaches us that it doesn't matter how plainly wrong something is, if you do it systematically, unblinkingly and for long enough then it becomes accepted, part of the zeitgeist. That is Rupert Murdoch's toxic legacy. We should not allow his son to carry forward the mantle. We have an opportunity for a fundamental cultural change. It happened in the way MPs claim their expenses and it can happen with the more unscrupulous members of the tabloid press, and that includes Mr Paul Dacre. How we achieve this is yet to be determined, but it is about ethics, common decency and treating people with respect, not press freedom. That myth is propagated by those who have no interest in exposing corruption in high places, and the broadsheet journalists who encourage the simplistic polarisation of this argument become the unwitting stooges of Murdoch Inc.

Freedom and responsibility go hand in hand. The tabloid press have enjoyed all the freedoms but exercise few of the responsibilities. If the freedom they loftily espouse is not to do with titillation and tawdry fascination and everything to do with exposing duplicity and corruption, then why were they so slow to expose the whole hacking scandal or its questionable relationship with the Met police? Because it doesn't suit their interests. I became involved in this saga because, apart from a few notable exceptions, including this newspaper, no one was giving NI as hard a time as they give everyone else.

The more sinister aspect of intrusion into people's personal lives goes beyond respect for an individual's right to privacy. It is used as a weapon against those who get in the way of News International. Its behaviour is not unlike a protection racket: be nice to us – that is, let us conduct our business unencumbered by scrutiny or indeed regulation – and we will return the favour by publicly supporting your political campaign. Be nasty to us – ie subject us to too many checks and balances, or curtail our plans to expand our empire – and you will feel our wrath. Of course senior management don't get their hands dirty. No one gets beaten up; they just drag your name through the mud. It's a word in an ear and a life is ruined.

Beneath this scandal is a more important debate about morality, ethics and the notion of public service. None of these things really register very highly with a company like News International. Their priority is their shareholders. The reason James Murdoch would like to see the demise of the BBC is because its very existence gives succour to those who champion the idea of an institution that serves the people first. This sticks in his craw because by contrast his worldview, driven purely by commercial interest, looks, well, a bit depressing. At the MediaGuardian Edinburgh International Television Festival in 2009 he said the only way to guarantee independence is the market. No, Mr Murdoch, the unchecked market leads to the hacking of Milly Dowler's phone. Your god should be treated with a little less reverence.

At the heart of this scandal is the wholly undemocratic alliance between newspaper proprietors and government. In a hundred years, the relationship will be seen as corrupt as the Corn Laws and Rotten Boroughs of the 19th century. Make sure you are on the right side of the debate. The Guardian is.

Introduction

PAUL JOHNSON

Editing the Bedside Guardian is daunting and delightful in equal measure. First, there is the history: this year's volume marks 60 years of continuous publication – although there was a period between 1994 and 2006 when the modernists gained the upper hand and dropped the word Bedside from the title, on the grounds, presumably, that it smacked too much of drinking-chocolate and hot water bottles. Back in 1951, the editor of that first edition, Ivor Brown, talked about the virtues of vigour, wit, clarity and humanity, and added: "Good readers are natural addicts of good writing and the Manchester Guardian has a long tradition of excellence in this kind." Omit the word Manchester and those words hold as good today as they did then – even as, in the age of the web, journalism is being transformed at a stunning pace.

Then there is the hopelessly subjective task of choosing one outstanding piece over another, squeezing some in at the last moment, throwing others out with a wince. It is an exercise which dramatically brings home the sheer scale of what the Guardian, in its many forms, produces in the course of a year: about 54 million words in about 140,000 separate pieces (not to mention the ever-expanding range of audio, video, photography and interactive content). Integration of web and paper means that the news cycle is now 24 hours a day, seven days a week, with

London passing the baton to New York and New York passing it on to Sydney before it comes around to London once more; the lexicon has been extended to include live blogs, tweets, minute-by-minutes, over-by-overs; and exclusives, more often than not, are broken first on the web. Looking back over that mass of material, it is clear that 2011 was a remarkable year. And the Guardian played a remarkable and central part in the year in two significant ways: creating the news agenda (phone hacking, WikiLeaks, undercover policing) and redefining the range of reporting through inventive use of new tools (Twitter-assisted coverage of the summer riots, and live blogging of the Arab spring – partly in Arabic, columnists asking the audience what inspired/angered them and what they wanted to see written about).

The story that supplied the spine to the year was, of course, phone hacking. As you will see, we've changed the design of the book this year to chart the saga through headlines, pausing at the most significant stories. Nick Davies had been working with persistence and skill on this investigation since July 2009, but it was the publication two years later of his and Amelia Hill's story of how the telephone of missing schoolgirl Milly Dowler had been targeted by the News of the World that triggered an astonishing and unprecedented sequence of seismic events. The widespread public revulsion it caused was followed within weeks by a series of resignations at the top of News International, the sudden closure of the toxic 168-year-old News of the World, the collapse of Rupert Murdoch's bid for outright ownership of BSkyB, the departure of the Metropolitan commissioner, Sir Paul Stephenson, soon followed by his most high-profile officer, assistant commissioner John Yates, and the announcement of a judicial inquiry, two parliamentary inquiries and two more police investigations. Any trials that may result are yet to take place, and we can only speculate what the outcome of the multiple investigations will be, but it is accurate to say that editor-in-chief Alan Rusbridger and Nick Davies, along with David Leigh, Amelia Hill and James Robinson, have forced, for the better, a complete re-evaluation of the relationship between the media, politicians and police in this country.

The book opens, though, with the Guardian-led international publication of 250,000 leaked US diplomatic cables and David Leigh's graphic account of the passing of a tiny memory stick to one of the paper's reporters. What followed was one of the Guardian's most testing projects ever: a team of print and web editors, investigative journalists, foreign correspondents, data experts and technologists led by Guardian deputy editor Ian Katz combed through the documents for a series of jaw-dropping stories – while ensuring that the name of anyone vulnerable or open to retaliation was redacted. Timothy Garton Ash summed it up as "the historian's dream ... the diplomat's nightmare". Chris Elliott, the readers' editor, concluded: "The simple journalistic truth ... is that all the stories emerging from the WikiLeaks material would have been important public-interest stories in any circumstances."

It was a year when one incredible story followed another. The Arab spring was documented by our own reporters – see Chris McGreal's graphic observations from the shifting frontlines of Libya and Jack Shenker's calm, almost laconic account, from the height of the protests in Cairo, of being teargassed, beaten by plainclothes police, put in the back of an armoured van but then freed by a group of determined protesters. There were also direct participants: see Ahdaf Soueif's account from Tahrir Square among the crowds sharing water and dates, hopes and fears, and Nawara Najem's moving description of dignity in the face of brutality and even death. In the same vein was Ghaith Abdul-Ahad's account of being held by the Taliban, suspected of being a spy. "'Walk!' hissed one of the shadows behind us," he wrote. "I heard the metallic click of the safety catch being released and the clank of a bullet being pulled into the chamber. I waited for the shot to come, but it never did." In the event the Taliban let him go, offering him a hundred dollars for his trouble. In the tradition of the Guardian, he refused the money.

The London riots saw the Guardian's team at its best: close-in, intelligent reporting in difficult and sometimes dangerous circumstances. Contained here are two very different examples by one reporter, Paul Lewis. Using Twitter to enormous effect (gaining 35,000 followers in five days), he sought help and information directly from those on the ground who were similarly plugged in. This is the first time an extended extract from a Twitter feed – it covers about two and a half hours – has appeared in the Bedside Guardian. But it is accompanied by Lewis's 2,600-word write-through of the week, chronicling his travels across the country, a fine piece of long-form journalism. And all through the year, the threat of financial catastrophe hung in the wind. Larry Elliott's August essay, "We've been warned: the system is ready to blow", is both scary and sagacious.

Amid the drama of 12 months there was also wonderfully empathetic writing: Richard Williams on the premature death of Seve Ballesteros; Amelia Gentleman on the human cost of multi-generational unemployment in Middlesbrough; Decca Aitkenhead on how Ann Widdecombe discovered her frivolous side; Simon Armitage's tricky time with his hero Morrissey.

And the fun: Catherine Bennett's cry-with-laughter spoof Middleton letters. Kate writes home, beginning at university. "Dear Mummy ... HE almost ran me over on his bicycle! Goodness knows how, I just happened to be resting in the road in that little skirt you sent." The peerless Simon Hoggart (who appears for the 18th consecutive year) on the bizarre performance of Andy

Hayman before a parliamentary committee, and also his account of rule-breaking love rats on the benches of the Commons. Other gems include Marina Hyde on the royal wedding and Tim Dowling (banjo) playing Glastonbury: "After their third song I get introduced, I walk out, I sit down and, well, I'm afraid I don't remember too much after that."

The delight has come with the realisation that everything has changed and yet nothing has changed. Vigour, wit, clarity and humanity, the four virtues identified by Ivor Brown 60 years ago, remain boisterously alive and well in the Guardian of today – however and wherever in the world you read it.

Autumn

The United States was catapulted into a worldwide diplomatic crisis today, with the leaking to the Guardian and other international media of more than 250,000 classified cables from its embassies, many sent as recently as February this year.

At the start of a series of daily extracts from the US embassy cables – many designated "secret" – the Guardian can disclose that Arab leaders are privately urging an air strike on Iran and that US officials have been instructed to spy on the UN leadership.

One tiny memory stick, one big headache for the United States

DAVID LEIGH

An innocuous-looking memory stick, no longer than a couple of fingernails, came into the hands of a Guardian reporter earlier this year. The device is so small it will hang easily on a keyring. But its contents will send shockwaves through the world's chancelleries and deliver what one official described as "an epic blow" to US diplomacy.

The 1.6 gigabytes of text files on the memory stick ran to millions of words: the contents of more than 250,000 leaked state department cables, sent from, or to, US embassies around the world.

What will emerge in the days and weeks ahead is an unprecedented picture of secret diplomacy as conducted by the planet's sole superpower. There are 251,287 dispatches in all, from more than 250 US embassies and consulates. They reveal how the US deals with both its allies and its enemies – negotiating, pressuring and sometimes brusquely denigrating foreign leaders, all behind the firewalls of ciphers and secrecy classifications that diplomats assume to be secure. The leaked cables range up to the "secret noforn" level, which means they are meant never to be shown to non-US citizens.

As well as conventional political analyses, some of the cables contain detailed accounts of corruption by foreign regimes, as well as intelligence on undercover arms shipments, human trafficking and sanction-busting efforts by would-be nuclear states such as Iran and Libya. Some are based on interviews with local sources while others are general impressions and briefings written for top state department visitors who may be unfamiliar with local nuances.

Intended to be read by officials in Washington up to the level of the secretary of state, the cables are generally drafted by the ambassador or subordinates. Although their contents are often startling and troubling, the cables are unlikely to gratify conspiracy theorists. They do not contain evidence of assassination plots, CIA bribery or such criminal enterprises as the Iran-Contra scandal in the Reagan years, when anti-Nicaraguan guerrillas were covertly financed.

One reason may be that America's most sensitive "top secret" and above foreign intelligence files cannot be accessed from Siprnet, the defence department network involved.

The US military believes it knows where the leak originated. A soldier, Bradley Manning, 22, has been held in solitary confinement for the last seven months and is facing a court martial in the new year. The former intelligence analyst is charged with unauthorised downloads of classified material while serving on an army base outside Baghdad. He is suspected of taking copies not only of the state department archive, but also of video of an Apache helicopter crew gunning down civilians in Baghdad, and hundreds of thousands of daily war logs from military operations in Afghanistan and Iraq.

It was childishly easy, according to the published chatlog of a conversation Manning had with a fellow hacker. "I would come in with music on a CD-RW labelled with something like 'Lady Gaga' ... erase the music ... then write a compressed split file. No one suspected a thing ... [I] listened and lip-synched to Lady Gaga's Telephone while exfiltrating possibly the largest data spillage in American history." He said that he "had unprecedented access to classified networks 14 hours a day 7 days a week for 8+ months".

Manning told his correspondent Adrian Lamo, who subsequently denounced him to the authorities: "Hillary Clinton and several thousand diplomats around the world are going to have a heart attack when they wake up one morning and find an entire repository of classified foreign policy is available, in searchable format, to the public ... Everywhere there's a US post, there's a diplomatic scandal that will be revealed. Worldwide anarchy in CSV format ... It's beautiful, and horrifying."

He added: "Information should be free. It belongs in the public domain."

Manning, according to the chatlogs, says he uploaded the copies to WikiLeaks, the "freedom of information activists" as he called them, led by Australian former hacker Julian Assange.

Assange and his circle apparently decided against immediately making the cables public. Instead they embarked on a staged disclosure of the other material – aimed, as they put it on their website, at "maximising political impact".

In April at a Washington press conference the group released the Apache helicopter video, titling it Collateral Murder.

The Guardian's Nick Davies brokered an agreement with Assange to hand over in advance two further sets of military field reports on Iraq and Afghanistan so professional journalists could analyse them. Published earlier this year simultaneously with the New York Times and Der Spiegel in Germany, the analyses revealed that coalition forces killed civilians in previously unreported shootings and handed over prisoners to be tortured.

The revelations shot Assange and WikiLeaks to global prominence but led to angry denunciations from the Pentagon and calls from extreme rightwingers in the US that Assange be arrested or even assassinated. This month Sweden issued an international warrant for Assange, for questioning about alleged sexual assaults. His lawyer says the allegations spring from unprotected but otherwise consensual sex with two women.

WikiLeaks says it is now planning to post a selection of the cables. Meanwhile, a Guardian team of expert writers has been spending months combing through the data. Freedom of information campaigner Heather Brooke obtained a copy of the database through her own contacts and joined the Guardian team. The paper is to publish independently, but simultaneously with the New York Times and Der Spiegel, along with Le Monde in Paris and El País in Madrid. As on previous occasions the Guardian is redacting information likely to cause reprisals against vulnerable individuals.

29 NOVEMBER 2010

WikiLeaks: Open secrets

GUARDIAN LEADER

How secret is "secret"? That is the first question posed by the publication yesterday of material derived from the leak of a quarter of a million US state department cables in the Guardian and a number of other newspapers. Much of the material is certainly very private. When people around the world tell sensitive things to American diplomats they do so in the expectation that there is a high degree of implicit confidentiality about the conversations. But "private" is not the same as "secret". It now transpires that these confidences were posted on a US government intranet, SIPDIS, for a very wide distribution among diplomatic, government and military circles. They may have been marked "secret" but all secrets are relative: there are around 3 million Americans cleared to read material thus classified.

The American authorities evidently suspect that the cables – as with the already-published Iraqi and Afghan war logs – were leaked by Private Bradley Manning, a 22-year-old soldier who was able to access them from his post as a junior intelligence officer based in Baghdad. Never in their wildest nightmares could politicians, bankers, dissidents, world leaders, government officials and other sources have imagined that their confidences would be thus distributed to the four corners of the American map. Before US government officials point accusing fingers at others, they might first have the humility to reflect on their own role in scattering "secrets" around a global intranet.

The next question: what is a secret? It is worth remembering the words Max Frankel, a former editor of the New York Times, wrote to his paper's own lawyers as they were fighting off the litigation around the 1971 publication of the Pentagon Papers, a comparable leak to the present one. He wrote: "Practically everything that our government does, plans, thinks, hears and contemplates in the realm of foreign policy is stamped and treated as secret – and then unravelled by that same government, by the Congress and by the press in one continuing round of professional and social contacts and co-operative exchanges of information."

The information sent to WikiLeaks falls into different categories. There are things that were widely known, but which acquire special significance by virtue of the quality of the source or analysis. It will hardly come as a surprise to President Ahmadinejad, for instance, that he is not flavour of the month in many Arab states. But it is interesting, and significant, to learn what the leaders of Gulf states have said in private; to hear how vehemently they expressed their views; and to compare those private expressions with their public positions. There are things that were not widely known outside a tight circle: the true position on controversial issues of repressive regimes, for instance, or the unguarded remarks of world leaders who imagined they were in safe company. Finally, there are matters which were not known by the wider world – one example being a directive in Hillary Clinton's name for diplomats to gather personal intelligence, including biometric information and email addresses, on the UN leadership. This was one of a number of "human intelligence directives" sent out by the state department across SIPDIS to diplomats across the world, instructing them to gather such information on a wide variety of people.

Once the material fell into the hands of WikiLeaks, an organisation dedicated to publishing information of all kinds, there was no realistic chance of it being suppressed. While opposing publication, the US administration has acknowledged that the involvement of news organisations has not only given protection to many sources, but has also given a context to information which, had it been simply dumped, would have been both overwhelming and free of any such context. As Timothy Garton Ash puts it: it is both a historian's dream and a diplomat's nightmare.

4 SEPTEMBER 2010

'What kind of bland, insipid question is that?'

SIMON ARMITAGE

It's a bit like being on a date. It's not a blind date exactly; poet meets songwriter seems to be the general idea. But I've no idea if he knows who I am, and for all that I've stalked the man and his music over the years, I can't say with any confidence that I know who Morrissey is either. Can anyone? So when the door opens and he strides into the room, neither of us seems sure of the protocol. I am meeting him of course, that's a given, but is he meeting me? I shake his hand, a square and solid hand, more in keeping with the mobster and bare-knuckle boxer image he's cultivated of late than the stick-thin, knock-me-over-with-a-feather campness of yesteryear. Then he gives a little bow, a modified version of the one I've seen him give about a thousand times on stage, one foot forward and the other behind, head low, eyes to the floor. It's a bit like being greeted by a matador: the gesture of respect is genuine, but we all know what happens to the bull. I cast my eyes downward as well, and notice that he's wearing cute gold trainers, like those football boots reserved for the world's greatest players. They look like they should have wings on the side.

We're in the ballroom of a swanky hotel in a swanky street near London's swankiest department store, and while he's ushered away in the direction of an ornately upholstered chair for a portrait photograph, I head towards the hospitality trolley. Rock'n'roll riders are famously lavish or idiosyncratic, but I am in the company of a man who is famously abstemious. So where there might have been gallons of Jack Daniel's and chopped pharmaceuticals offered on the bare breasts of Filipino slave girls, it comes down to a straight choice between hand-stitched tea bags and several cans of Fanta orange, Morrissey's fizzy drink of choice.

I sidle over to the action. Morrissey is swivelling his head as instructed, registering one pose, then another. The light falls on his rugby-ball chin, then picks out his quiff, somewhat thin these days but still capable of standing a couple of inches above his scalp when given a bit of a finger-massage. He wears a red polo shirt, knuckle-duster rings and the general high-definition radiance of his celebrity. When the camera flashes, there's the occasional glimpse of the younger man within the 51-year-old face, then it fades. Somewhat implausibly in these decorous surroundings, I notice a push-bike leaning against the wall behind the photographer's screen, so I wheel it out and suggest we could do a remake of the This Charming Man video.

"It's been done," he says, with a kind of theatrical dismissal.

I was only kidding.

"Now both of you together," says the photographer.

"Cameron and Clegg," quips Morrissey.

"Which one am I?"

"You're Vince Cable."

The photographer positions us in front of a full-length mirror, not more than three feet apart. It's a me-looking-at-him-looking-at-me-looking-at-him sort of idea.

"Bit closer, please," says the photographer, so I edge a little nearer.

Morrissey: "Am I looking in the mirror?"

Photographer: "Yes, please."

Morrissey: "'Twas ever thus."

Photographer (to me): "A bit closer."

I do what I'm told, until my nose is no further than six inches from his cheek. I can't remember the last time I got within this range of another man's face, and this man is Morrissey, and we've only just met. I notice the grey hairs in his sideburns, his indoor complexion, the cool quartz of his eyes. I inhale the atomised confection of what I assume is an expensive cologne.

For me, this close encounter could be described as the arrival point of a journey that started over a quarter of a century ago. I won't go into the exact circumstances, except to say I was lying in a bath in a house on the south coast of England shared with five geography students and several members of the Nigerian navy. On the windowsill was a battery-operated transistor radio, and out of its tinny speaker, John Peel was talking about a band called the Smiths. Peel was never one for hype or eulogy, but somewhere within the lugubrious voice and deadpan delivery, I thought I heard a little note of excitement and perhaps even an adjective of praise. I dipped below the waterline to rinse the last of the Fairy Liquid out of my hair, and once the water had drained from my ears, I found myself listening to Hand in Glove. And to a homesick northerner honed on alternative guitar music, it was love at first hearing: everything came together with the Smiths, a band whose very name suggested both the every-man nature of their attitude and the fashioned, crafted nature of their output. When Morrissey sported Jack Duckworth-style prescription glasses mended with Elastoplast I went looking for a pair in the market. When he wore blouses and beads, I waited until my mother had gone to a parochial church council meeting then had a flick through her wardrobe and jewellery box. And once he had appeared on Top of the Pops with a bunch of gladi-oli rammed in his back pocket, any garden or allotment became a collection point on the way to the disco, and the dance floor, come the end of the night, would look like the aftermath of the Chelsea Flower Show. The Smiths split up in 1987 but Morrissey threw himself into a solo career, going on to produce – in my estimation – an unrivalled body of work, one that confirms him as the pre-eminent singer-songwriter of his generation. I listen to the albums ceaselessly. Despite which, I have never particularly wanted to meet Morrissey. A high court judge famously branded him as "devious, truculent and unreliable", and in interviews he has always appeared diffident, a touch arrogant and always uncomfortable. In fact, I've always wondered why someone who seems so painfully awkward in the company of others would want to punish himself with the agonies of public performance?

"Because as a very small child I found recorded noise and the solitary singer beneath the spotlight so dramatic and so brave... walking the plank... willingly... It was sink or swim. The very notion of standing there, alone, I found beautiful. It makes you extremely vulnerable, but everything taking place in the hall is down to you. That's an incredible strength, especially for someone who had always felt insignificant and disregarded. Coupled with the fact that you could also be assassinated..."

We're now sitting in diagonally positioned chairs with a table between us, Morrissey with his stockpile of Fanta, me with my list of questions.

"Where's home?"

"I'm very comfortable in three or four places. When the world was a smaller place, Manchester was the boundary. But it's a relief to feel relaxed in more places than just one. I know LA well, but it's a police state. I frequent Rome and a certain part of Switzerland. And I know this city very well."

"And presumably it would be a problem now, walking down Deansgate. Because of the fame?"

"Yes, but I don't really do all the things that famous people do."

"You don't dip your bread in, you mean?"

"Yes. That's very well put. I can see why Faber jumped on you."

It's quickly apparent that Morrissey's wit, articulacy and all-round smartness is always going to mark him out as an oddity in the music business. It's also clear that the sharpness of his tongue will make him more enemies than friends, and his list of dislikes is long. Morrissey on other singers: "They have two or three melodies and they repeat them ad nauseam over the course of 28 albums." Morrissey on people: "They are problems." And on the charts: "Nothing any more to do with talent or gift or cleverness or originality. Every new artist flies in at number one, but in terms of live music they couldn't fill a telephone box." And shockingly, on the Chinese: "Did you see the thing on the news about their treatment of animals and animal welfare? Absolutely horrific. You can't help but feel that the Chinese are a subspecies." Neither is he impressed with Arctic Monkeys' Alex Turner ("an NME creation") or George Alagiah (an unspecified complaint signalled with a roll of the eyes), and his views on the royal family would have seen him hanged in former times. He even has a low opinion of our poet laureate, and when I refuse to be drawn into the sniping, pointing out that she happens to be a friend of mine, this seems to encourage his desire to disparage. Like many who've gone before me, as the conversation rolls on I find I can't unpick the contradictions. The charm, but also the barbed comments. The effeminate gestures, then the surly machismo. The desire to be centre stage coupled with the lack of social ease. The obvious trappings of success, fame and fortune, but the repeated complaints of victimisation and neglect. What I am certain of is that nobody is more aware of being in the company of Morrissey than Morrissey himself. Call it self-consciousness, call it self-absorption, call it self-defence, but every gesture seems carefully designed, and every syllable weighed and measured for the ripples it will produce when lobbed into the pond. Sometimes it's in the form of a brilliant, Wildean retort, sometimes it's a self-deprecating comment of suicidal intensity, sometimes it's a shameless remark about the indisputable nature of his own brilliance, and sometimes it's a claim so mystifying that at first I think he's taking the piss.

"I'm cursed with the gift of foresight," he says. Then a few minutes later, he says it again.

"You don't mean in a crystal ball kind of way, do you?"

"That's exactly what I mean. Cross my palm with silver."

I smile at the thought of one of life's renowned social realists staring into the tea leaves, and I'm on the point of asking him to prove his assertion by forecasting the winner of this afternoon's 3.30 at Market Rasen when I notice he isn't joking.

"Do you find that you've accumulated cash?" he asks me, apropos of nothing.

"I get by."

"Is that a way of saying you've got loads but you're too embarrassed to admit it?"

"How would you like it if I asked you how much you earned?"

"Not an answer."

"I earn more than I thought I would when I became a poet."

"When did you know you were a poet?"

"Not until other people said I was."

Referring to his own experience, he tells me, "Once you feel it and other people feel it, too, you stand and are authorised as a poet. I was the boy least likely to, in many ways. I was staunchly antisocial. It was a question of being a poet at the expense of being anything else, and that includes physical relationships, strong bonds with people. I think you discover you are a poet; someone doesn't walk up to you, tap you on the shoulder and say, 'Excuse me, you are a poet.'"

In fact, Morrissey isn't a poet. He's a very witty emailer ("Bring me several yards of heavy rope and a small stool," he wrote, when I'd asked him if he'd like anything fetching from the north), and a convincing correspondent, especially on the subject of bearskin hats, as his recent letter to the Times testified ("There is no sanity in making life difficult for the Canadian brown bear, especially for guards' hats that look absurd in the first place"). He has also penned an autobiography, which he assures me is "almost concluded". But poets write poems, requiring no backbeat, no melody, and no performance. Being the author of There is a Light That Never Goes Out and other such works of genius doesn't make him WH Auden, any more than singing in a band called the Scaremongers at weekends makes me an Elvis Presley.

"Are you a violent person?" I ask. "You flirt with violent images in your work. Guns, knives..."

"All useful implements. As you must know, living where you live. Do you go out much, into those Leeds side streets?"

"No."

"You're missing everything."

I say, "At this moment in time you have no contractual obligations, do you?"

"That's right."

"I thought labels would be queueing to sign you."

"Believe me, there is no queue." Surprisingly, a rant about the music industry develops into a very touching statement about his band, talking almost paternalistically about his responsibilities and loyalties. The tone of voice reminds me of a recent email he posted to a Mozzer website, a tender and poignant citation for a girl who wasn't much more than a regular face in the crowd at his concerts, but whose devotion and death had clearly touched him. In fact, he talks movingly about all his fans, as if they were blood relatives, or even something more intimate. Which, rightly or wrongly, I take as my cue to ask him about his love life, or his alleged celibacy. Not because I want to know if he's gay or bi or straight, but because I can't understand how a man who apparently shuns emotional involvement and physical proximity of any kind can write with such passion and desire. If it isn't personal, is he simply making it all up?

"Well, it is personal because I have written it. But I don't believe you need to be stuck in the cut and thrust of flesh-and-blood relationships to understand them. Because if that was the case, everyone on the planet who had been married or in a relationship would be a prophet of some kind, and they're not. You don't need to be immersed to understand. And if you do take on a relationship you have to take on another person's family and friends and it's... really too much. I'd rather not. You find yourself working overtime at a factory to buy a present for a niece you can't stand. That's what happens when you become entangled with other people."

"But aren't you lonely?"

"We're all lonely, but I'd rather be lonely by myself than with a long list of duties and obligations. I think that's why people kill themselves, really. Or at least that's why they think, 'Thank heaven for death.'"

"How would you describe your level of contentment?"

He muses on the question for a moment. "Even."

"Does that mean your writing is a cold and clinical activity?"

"No, never clinical. I feel I don't have any choice. It's constant and overpowering. It has to happen. Even at the expense of anything else. Relentless. I know it's... insanity. An illness in a way, one you can't shake off."

"Will you keep on doing this till you fall over, or will there come a time when you decide to pack it in and paint pictures or plant an orchard instead?"

"The ageing process isn't terribly pretty... and you don't want yourself splattered all over the place if you look pitiful. You can't go on for ever, and those that do really shouldn't."

"Any names?"

"No names. Why mock the elderly?"

While trying not to lose eye contact, I glance at the list of remaining questions in my notebook.

"Do you own a valid driving licence?"

"What kind of bland, insipid question is that?"

"It's a good question, isn't it? Has anyone asked you it before?"

"No. But that's hardly a surprise, is it?"

"I thought it was a beauty."

"Why? Because you consider me incapable of operating such large and complex pieces of engineering?"

"OK, how about, 'Do you have any pets?'"

"Yes. Cats. I've had lots of cats. But also many bereavements."

A prescient remark, as it turns out, and one that suggests I should have taken Morrissey's powers of prediction more seriously. Because a week or so later I get a message to say he hates the photographs so much he has insisted they will never see the light of day. The bereavement, it seems, is mine, in the sense that he won't be seen dead with me. And I am to be replaced in the images by a cat. Thirty years of admiration bordering on the obsessive, then a date, then dumped. Jilted for a fucking moggy.

Back at the hotel, he doesn't seem to be in any sort of hurry, but the conversation has run its course, and as a way of winding things up I embark on some ill-conceived sentence that begins as a heartfelt compliment but escalates into some lavish toast of gratitude on behalf of the nation. With no obvious end to the burgeoning tribute in sight, I cut to the chase and simply say thank you.

"And I have a little gift for you," I add, pulling my latest slim volume out of my bag.

"Will you write something in it?"

"I already did."

"Two r's and two s's," he says. And I think, don't worry, Morrissey; if anyone knows how to spell your name, it's me.

He spins around on the thick carpet and walks towards the staircase. Except halfway down the corridor he opens the book of poems and pulls out – forgive me, people, but who wouldn't have? – a Scaremongers CD.

"Did you know you'd left this in here?" he asks.

"Er, sort of," I admit.

His eyebrows lift and fall, uncomprehendingly. Then the little wings on his golden shoes flutter about his ankles, and he ascends into heaven.

9 SEPTEMBER 2010

New witness: hacking was rife at tabloid

Ex-News of the World executive says Coulson must have known of practice

15 OCTOBER 2010

Comment is free readers on... their salaries

THE PEOPLE'S PANEL

As the fairness debate intensifies, four readers discuss whether they deserve what they earn

STUDENT SUPERVISOR *(Posts on Cif as bookfay; earns £17,000 per year)*
When I left university, I worked in a bar on a minimum wage – then about £4.50 an hour. Five years later, my salary is more than I have ever seen in my life, in fact it is too high.

As supervisor in the city centre bar, I worked 12- to 13-hour shifts, on my feet all the time, constantly dealing with information, change and customers' requests. I was assaulted, harassed constantly and every day had to say sorry for mistakes that were often not mine. I should have been paid then what I'm paid now. I love my current job and enjoy helping the students. It probably is "harder" in terms of using my brains – but there is no reason to pay me so much more than people working in bars.

I would never ask for a raise, not because I don't think I deserve one, but because I work in the public sector. I'm single, don't have a family and don't need more money. I would be ashamed to earn much more than I do, especially when I go to pubs and see people working such tiring hours for nothing.

THE HOUSING WORKER *(Posts as loudribs; earns £21,000)*

I work for a mental health charity in Leeds. The work we do is highly skilled and often traumatic. We talk people out of killing themselves and we're often in dangerous situations. We sometimes find bodies and deal with things that are horrific. We fill the gaps left by an under-resourced and undervalued mental health system. But most of all, we are invisible. The changes we make to people's lives are made quietly. Right now, there is a quiet chuntering that wages are going to be cut. We dread the phrase "big society".

While I survive adequately, this has mainly been due to some beneficent circumstances and some deliberate sacrifices. For example, my partner and I have no children, we rent and we don't drive. Any cut will mean that many of the things we have hoped to do (kids, house, etc) will remain out of reach, despite a life of deferred gratification. It also makes me wonder about the value that we, as a society, put on caring for the most vulnerable.

THE REWARD ANALYST *(Posts as OneinTen; earns £30,000)*
As well as my basic salary, my company allocates an additional £3,000, which can either be spent on benefits or taken as taxable cash. I am also eligible for a bonus of 10-15% of base salary, and am awarded a further 5% of salary in long-term incentives (shares).

Working in remuneration, I'm probably more aware of the process behind determination of salaries than most. My value to the company is measured in my team managing to offer competitive salary and bonus packages to attract and retain the best people in their field. I also believe that extremely high salaries come with the caveat that the company is buying into your life and that a desire to be "the boss", at any expense, is a necessary trait for an executive.

I'm considered rich by my friends, most of whom work in retail or admin. Very few earn more than £20k, yet because I have invested in a flat I actually have less disposable income, which they fail to understand: they see one's salary as the measure of wealth.

THE CITY LAWYER *(Posts as antifrank; Earns £512,000)*
For many Guardian readers, my salary will seem obscene for a job that isn't any use to society. How can I justify that? Well, I'm more useful than I sound. So far this year I've saved two companies from insolvency and helped to save several thousand jobs.

I'm not going to pretend I get paid for my social value though. I'm responsible for a team of 75 people and am on duty from when I wake up until I go to sleep. The value of what I do, for my clients and my firm, far exceeds my cost. Very few people indeed can do my job. Nurses, soldiers and policemen do important jobs I could not do. The respect I have for them doesn't mean I think they should be paid multiples more when the country finds it easy to recruit them.

The way to get the money back from me is via tax. My firm's tax reserve for me this year will be £260,000. I expect lots of public sector workers will be indignant about how much I earn. But they might want to consider how many of them my tax bill covers.

16 OCTOBER 2010

Murdoch denies wholesale News of the World phone-hacking

23 OCTOBER 2010

Britain's not working

AMELIA GENTLEMAN

Wally Taylor has powerful memories of the picket line his father helped to man outside the steelworks that used to stand behind the estate where he grew up. For months, a line of men stood outside the gates, warming themselves at fires burning inside 45-gallon oil drums, holding banners on sticks, and chanting protests against Thatcher's government and the steelworks' owners. The estate children weren't allowed near, but they watched their fathers' anger from the corner of a nearby street.

The protest failed and the South Bank branch of the Dorman Long steelworks shut down. Some time later the owners began to demolish the site where his father, Walter, had worked. "Every Sunday afternoon there was explosion after explosion," Wally says. He used to climb the slag heaps at the end of his row with friends to see the blasts. "We knew it was bad news for the area. Thousands of them lost their jobs. But for us kids, watching from the top of the tip, it was exciting. I'd never seen an explosion before."

Wally, now 42, and the eighth of 10 children, doesn't remember his father ever talking about how he felt about losing his job, but he sensed that something devastating had happened. "You pick things up, don't you? I think he was mortified. He had that job until the steelyards closed down and he never got another job after that.

"He and his cousin used to go out every day looking for work," Wally says, "but the shipyards were closing at the same time. There was no work. It destroyed him. He didn't think he could keep the family together. It kills you off. He kept his emotions back. He always had a smile on his face, even though you knew he was not happy." He died 10 years later of cancer of the pancreas.

These memories of the industrial action of the 1980s feel like fragile records from the distant past, recalled as if through slow-moving archival film, fodder for a late-night documentary on a little-watched digital channel, a subject far removed from modern life. Only, if you spend time in South Bank, a grid-shaped development of brick terraced housing on the edges of Middlesbrough, it soon becomes clear that the destruction unleashed by the closures remains raw, the trauma passed down the generations, barely dulled by the passing of each decade.

Walter's wife Winnie, 75 and no longer inclined or able to string together more than the occasional sentence, still lives in South Bank, in a two-storey brick house overlooked by the looming grey silhouettes of now-redundant industrial architecture. Most of her large and tight-knit family live in the area, a network of sons and daughters, grandchildren and great-grandchildren all within walking distance. Among her 10 children, only two have work; the rest long ago adapted themselves to a lifetime of unemployment. Of the grandchildren who are on the estate, none has managed to find a permanent job, and most have given up looking. The vast majority of her neighbours have no work. Many former residents have moved away, leaving homes that no one wants to move into, their windows and doors swiftly nailed over with grey sheets of metal by the council. Gradually, whole streets have been demolished, and replaced by nothing. Wally says that of the six different houses he has lived in since leaving home at 16, all but the one he currently occupies have been destroyed. "They're pulling the place down around us," he says.

Inside each home there is a peaceful calm born of years of inactivity. At 11.30am in Winnie's home, she is watching an antiques programme with one of her sons, Mark, 46, and a grandson, Leon, left for the day by another son. The child plays on the floor with the puppy, scribbles a bit on the wall with green crayon and asks for biscuits. Mark, who is his mother's full-time carer, gets up from his chair by the television to help her to the loo and to open the door to the gas man.

Outside, a CCTV camera twists silently, monitoring the movements of residents, its lens protected from bricks and stones by metal grilles. It has not had much preventive success. A few weeks ago, beneath its watch, some teenagers stole the new roundabout, recently installed in the playground. The seats of the swings have also been stolen, replaced, stolen again and, a few weeks ago, replaced again.

Around the corner, Mark's brother Wally is helping his wife fold the washing, his pregnant teenage daughter, Natalie, sitting on the floor, feeding her baby mashed potato and gravy, one eye on Midsomer Murders, another on the window to the overcast streets outside. Natalie is used to being at home. She stopped going to school at 11 or 12, and had her first child at 16. She has coped well, she says, better, she thinks, than her younger sister Charlotte, who was 14 when she got pregnant. Natalie would like to work in a care home for the elderly, but thinks the fact that she has no qualifications may make that an unrealistic ambition. "I didn't sit any exams. I never got entered for any."

She gives a half-laugh when I ask if it is hard to find work; being unemployed in South Bank is a fact of life. "It's been something that has been there all my life. It makes people depressed," she says. She pulls herself up to answer the door to a man from the local young offenders' team, who has come to talk to her father about arrangements for her younger brother's imminent return home from his first spell in prison.

The story of the extended Taylor family is the story of what can happen when whole communities are flicked in an instant into unemployment. The fourth generation of the family, still babies on their teenage mothers' knees, will in turn soon be affected by the unemployment that has been passed, an unhappy inheritance, from parent to child down the family line. Government figures show that by the age of 22 months, a child living beneath the poverty line, as these infants do, begins to fall behind children from richer families; by the time they turn six, previously less able children from wealthier backgrounds will be ahead. Children living in poverty are only a third as likely to get five good GCSEs as their richer classmates. Ripples from the industrial collapse of the 1970s are still thwarting the chances of those born three decades later.

The enduring hardship of South Bank residents is dispiriting to witness, but the trickling of adversity through the generations provides a salutary example of what happens when recession bites into a community, one that politicians should not ignore as the current economic crisis tips new patches of the country into high-level unemployment. On average, more than four unemployed people are chasing every job vacancy across the UK, rising to 12 in Middlesbrough. In its final year, the outgoing government repeatedly said it would not allow a new set of young people to be pushed into permanent obsolescence. "Never again should we lose a generation to unemployment," Yvette Cooper said, promising measures to ensure that the new jobless should not be written off as they were in the recessions of the 80s and 90s.

Before he came to power, Iain Duncan Smith, the new welfare secretary, commissioned his thinkthank, the Centre for Social Justice, to study areas where several generations were unable to find work. The proposals announced by the new government, however, do not yet promise much for residents of South Bank. Duncan Smith is committed to reforming the welfare system to ensure that work will pay better than benefits, and that fraud will be targeted. Neither proposal offers much prospect of change in places such as South Bank, where jobs have simply vanished.

Despite the Conservatives' much-repeated commitment to fairness, the three-year freeze on child benefit announced earlier this year, and the cuts to public services that will be the inevitable consequence of this week's comprehensive spending review, will affect the Taylors more than most.

Gruff and not prone to introspection, even less to self-pity or to presenting himself as a victim, Wally nevertheless concedes that there is a link between the closure of all the nearby industries that had employed his father's generation and his own troubled life. Around the time Wally's father lost his job, his mother began to find it hard to cope with all 10 children. He found it difficult sharing a room with his six brothers, in three double beds. There was always food on the table, but they ran riot. One by one, nine of the children were taken into care. Wally hated it so much that he was first kicked out of school, then flung out of the residential care home and allowed to return home.

He had no qualifications, there was no work, and he quickly got into trouble with the police. "Theft of motor vehicles, robbery, drink-driving – daft little things, but it sticks with you," he says. Hesitantly he sees a connection with the closures of the shipyards and the steelworks. "I wouldn't have gone off the rails if there had been an apprenticeship to go to."

Work has never formed part of his life. He recalls a few weeks he had back in 2000 when he was employed, at the jobcentre's pleading, as a night-time safety official at the nearby ICI plant. He was sacked after three weeks because he missed a shift. Later, he did some graffiti removal for the council. This represents the sum total of his working career.

Instead, in a way, he has focused on his family. He has had nine children by two women, Jean and Dawn, and been around for them, more available than working parents might have been. Despite this, he doesn't view his own children's prospects with much optimism. "I hope they find work, but there's nothing here for them. If you want work, then you have to move out," he says. "One of my daughters was a carer at a nursing home. She got paid off after 12 months."

The way Wally constructs his sentences is tersely bleak, one short and hopeless statement followed by another, equally bald and gloomy.

"I don't worry about it [not working] so much now, but I used to, when the children were growing up. I can't see any chance of finding a job now, with the cutbacks and everything the government is doing. The government should come here before they close these plants down. They should come around here and see how we live. They are just cutting the poorer off. Most people here aren't working. If you haven't got it, you learn to live with it. We don't have a car. That would be a luxury."

Wally has little time for the employment preparation classes he is obliged to attend in order to receive his welfare payments. "The courses are a waste of government money. We're just sent into a classroom, talking to each other. It is all stupidity. Maybe one in 10 people gets something out of it. The rest – they're still just stuck where they are. You can't get something that isn't about. I've been every place: scrapyards, wasteyards, recycling yards. I've been to all of them. They all say we'll keep you on file. There are no jobs."

Aside from its industrial past, South Bank's one claim to fame is that it is where magician Paul Daniels was born. When Channel 4's Location, Location, Location described Middlesbrough as the worst place to live in Britain (a claim that triggered an Ofcom investigation), it broadcast footage of firebombed houses in South Bank to illustrate the claim. But older residents are passionately loyal to the estate, which used to be known (with real affection) as "Slaggy Island" in honour of the slag heaps that once surrounded it. Online, a South Bank Nostalgia Society mournfully charts the area's slow demolition, with pictures of people standing in front of their childhood front doors as the buildings are "readied for oblivion".

Two retired sisters working as volunteers in a nearby church remember their childhood, when the atmosphere here was different. "Our parents moved here because of the work. We lived with every colour of smoke you could think of. We never thought of it as dirty; it's only now we realise how dirty it was," the older sister says. "I worked in the boom time. If you left your job on a Friday, you could start another one on the Monday morning. It was a very happy, thriving area. At that time, if your father worked in the shipyards or the steelworks, you would be sure to get an apprenticeship. I worry for the children coming out of school now. They're leaving with nowhere to go to. They go for further education but there's still nothing for them here. It's not the norm for school-leavers to get a job."

Keeping his mother company, half-watching an auctioneer value antiques on television, Mark also expresses worries for the next generation. Although he left school with no qualifications, he managed to find work by travelling to London to jobs on building sites. But he thinks it is harder to get work now without any qualifications, and besides, he thinks there has been a dwindling of motivation; the teenagers who live on the estate now have no "hup and go", he observes.

"I feel sorry for the youngsters. I wouldn't like to be 21 and living back here. There is nothing for them around here. I'd move out of South Bank like this." He clicks his fingers. He can't leave now because he doesn't want to abandon his mother.

"You try to tell them. You say, go to college, do something. They say, why? They've got no qualifications, no interests. I think most of them have gone beyond the stage where they want to work. In the 80s at least I was looking for work. These ones, they don't even think about it. They're just drinking and messing about in gangs. They see all the other people in the area and they say, 'Well, they haven't got to work'," he says. "There are no role models for them here. The most successful people – the drug dealers and the moneylenders – they're the sort of people who are making money round here."

Around the corner, Natalie's 15-month-old son, Ashley, is sleeping next to her on the chair, his breath a heavy, soothing rattle. She's finished feeding him a bottle and is waiting for the day to end, looking through the window to the street, where the drizzle is making the England flags hang limp.

She worries about what her brother will do when he gets back from prison. "He's always had a temper on him," she says. Ben, who was sentenced on his 17th birthday, will be welcomed home by his young son and ex-girlfriend, and by another woman who is about to give birth to his daughter. "He was 15 when he had his son. Everyone has babies young here," Natalie says. "Probably because there's not much to do."

None of her friends' parents ever had any work, and she can name only one school friend who has a job now. "There is a girl around the corner. She had a job in a shop in Middlesbrough. Now she's working for Corus as a cleaner."

She hopes her own son will do better than she has. "I hope for him that he goes to school and gets his qualifications and he does what he wants."

For herself, she'd like to get a job, so she could afford to take a family holiday. Eventually, that might involve leaving South Bank. The couple have thought about moving to a place where there are more jobs (a strategy favoured by the Conservatives) but are anxious about giving up their council house without having somewhere else to move into. "You'd have to go on to another council house waiting list and there'd be people better off than you higher up the list," she says.

She has been sent on courses to improve her employability, courses that advised her on how to dress for a job interview – advice that is academic, she points out, since she has never been called for an interview and cannot find anything she is qualified to do. Her partner, also called Ashley, used to do some work as a scaffolder, but since being given an asbo has found it hard to get work.

Natalie has never been to the docks or the disused steelworks where her grandparents and great-grandparents worked, and would not point to their closure as the start of her family's problems, but she has a dim sense that life in South Bank used to be better. "The way people describe this place... It used to be a very good place to live. People talk about how everybody used to get on and there was hardly any fighting. Now there's fighting nearly every weekend, with sticks and knuckledusters. That's just how people are," she says. "It is more of a depressing place than a nice place, but it is the place where I have lived all my life so I'll stay here." Still, she knows the place has a deadening effect.

"It is boring."

2 NOVEMBER 2010

'This sort of prolonged frivolity ... I haven't had that in years'

DECCA AITKENHEAD

I last met Ann Widdecombe when I interviewed her 13 years ago. Although already out of government, she was still in her Doris Karloff phase – practically boasting about being "short and fat and ugly", and stridently anti-image, anti-celebrity, anti-vanity. But my suspicions were aroused when she got her office to call three times in the following week, to enquire about when the piece would appear. Hmm, I remember thinking. Not quite without vanity after all, then.

So I wasn't entirely surprised when the MP went blond, lost two and a half stone and became, of all things, a reality TV star. She appeared on Celebrity Fit Club not once but twice, hosted Have I Got News For You, starred as a fiercely intolerant agony aunt in Ann Widdecombe to the Rescue, and was dispatched to tick off hoodies and girl gangs and other miscreants in a series called Ann Widdecombe Versus...

So I *was* right, I thought to myself, rather unkindly. What a fraud! For all Widdecombe's protestations of indifference to celebrity, she really was a whopping show-off after all.

Joining the cast of Strictly Come Dancing seemed, therefore, to make perfect sense. Widdecombe, 63, has become highly adept at colluding in her own caricature, and what better arena in which to do so than Strictly, a camp comedy of sequins and slightly surreal sexuality?

Every Saturday night, as you would expect, Widdecombe plays the comic role of dissident to perfection – "galumphing like an elephant", as she puts it, giving as good as she gets to the judges, and giving every impression of delighting in her own famous sexlessness. So the last thing I'm expecting to find when we meet is someone so deeply affecting that when I think about her afterwards, I'm moved almost to tears.

Of course, she still presents herself with the vintage no-nonsense Widdecombe front – brusque, impatient, bossy. We meet at a gym in Bath where she is training with her dance partner Anton du Beke, and she bustles the three of us straight off to lunch – "Come on! We haven't any time to waste! This way!" She cuts an extraordinary figure – short, slim, but almost capsized by a colossal bosom that she refers to as "my upper circumference" – and her voice is practically operatic, her every word enunciated with military precision.

Widdecombe's instincts are robustly combative; when drawing up her contract with Strictly, "I wanted it in writing that I wouldn't wear anything that I considered too revealing. And then I said I wouldn't carry out any moves that I considered immodest or suggestive." I ask if, nevertheless, she has something of the exhibitionist in her, and she retorts: "It would be nonsense to try to suggest that somebody who tried to rouse 2,000 people to their feet – which is what I used to do at conference – doesn't have any element of exhibitionism about them. I mean, *what* sort of statement would *that* be?"

She keeps having to explain to people, she says, that she is taking part in Strictly to have fun. "I'm having *fun*. Nobody understands that I'm having fun. Nobody understands fun. I'm retired, remember? Retired? And I'm having *huge* fun." Her attachment to this exotic new sensation is hilariously literal-minded: she can't imagine why most contestants usually cry at some point during Strictly – "silly asses" – and looks genuinely confused. "Why cry? I'm having fun. You don't cry when you're having fun, do you?"

I ask when she last had this much fun, and her reply is so precisely calibrated it's as if she considers the concept to be some sort of legal classification. "Well, I spent 23 years in politics, and bits of that were fun. But even when you're having fun, there's a hugely serious side to it, because everything you do in politics, from the way you handle a piece of casework to the way you vote in the House of Commons to the policies you approve as a minister, every single thing you do affects somebody, for better or for worse. It really matters. Dancing? Doesn't matter at all. So if you define fun simply as enjoying yourself, well, I enjoyed many aspects of politics. But if you define fun as frivolity, and nothing depends on it, then I don't know when I last had that. But this sort of *pro-longed friv-o-lity*, which is all I can describe Strictly as..." Du Beke interrupts, pretending to take offence: "What are you saying? It's serious art!" She dismisses him with a playful toss of the hand: "Yeah, I know you may think so, but I don't. No, this sort of *pro-longed* frivolity is something I haven't had since, I don't know, Oxford days, I suppose." With a politician's vigilance, she throws me a sharp look and adds quickly, "Don't say I haven't *enjoyed* myself since Oxford."

When Widdecombe entered parliament in 1987 it had never occurred to her that she would become a figure of fun, mocked for her frumpy appearance, her celibacy, her lack of femininity. Convent-educated, from an MoD family, she was a serious woman with an Oxford PPE degree and a career at Unilever and the University of London behind her. Yet over time even her virginity was to become part of her public identity. "When I first went into public life," she reflects, "that sort of thing wasn't talked about at all." But every single article I've read about her mentions that she once threatened to sue a reporter for doubting it. Is that true?

"I can tell you exactly what happened," she says wearily. "The reporter said to me, 'Well, you've had one sexual experience [referring to Widdecombe's one romance, with a fellow student at Oxford].' And I said, 'Do be careful, that's the way to get yourself sued.' I didn't say to her, 'I'm going to sue you.' And yet it's gone down in the apocrypha of Widdecombe." But if I were to write "Ann Widdecombe is not a virgin"? "You probably would be sued," she laughs. "I suggest you avoid that."

How painful has the personal ridicule been, I ask? "Well, I've always said that if I'd had all of that mockery and personal criticism on my second day in parliament I would have been devastated by it," she says briskly. "But it comes slowly. You get inured by degrees, and now it's water off a duck's back."

The more she talks, the more one can see quite how far she has had to shut down, to protect herself and her dignity. She retired from parliament at the general election in May this year, and when I ask if she ever had a wobble, or thought about staying for one more term, her answer is heartbreakingly odd.

"No, I knew I'd got it *exactly* right when I went into the House of Commons a couple of months after I'd left, and it was as if I'd never been there. I have ex-colleagues who say they feel a twinge when they go in. But to me there wasn't even a sense of relief that I wasn't there. I'd just never been there. I'd never been there. There was no emotion at all."

She tells the anecdote with unmistakable pride, apparently oblivious to how alienated it makes her sound. How did she interpret her numbness, I ask? "That I'd got the point of retirement dead right."

For a moment I consider asking if it ever occurred to her that she might be emotionally cut off. But before I can decide to risk it, Du Beke intervenes with a flirtatious, teasing little laugh. "Ann, that's the first time you've got timing right since I met you."

To watch Du Beke flirt with Widdecombe as the day wears on is one of the most unexpectedly touching spectacles I have witnessed. Immaculately groomed, flawlessly gentlemanly, the ballroom dancer is a paragon of decorum, and as he courts her with old-fashioned chivalry she comes alive and positively flowers. Her usual defences don't exactly melt away altogether, but beneath the "Oh what rot!" and "Ye Gods!" it is possible to glimpse an entirely unfamiliar version of her, flushed and girlish to the point of coquettish.

Fun really is a revelation to Widdecombe. I can't imagine she came across many men like this in politics, but I wish she had, for I bet this is the sort of charm she once dreamed of a long time ago. Instead, in the cruel world of Westminster she turned herself into the version we know, abnegating her own femininity for fear of being made to look a fool, for so long that it is all but gone. As Du Beke steers her round the dance studio, I'm startled by how tender I find myself feeling towards her, and how sad it seems that this revelation should have come so late.

Needless to say, Widdecombe would reject this as utter stuff and nonsense – or even worse, psychobabble. "Everybody who talks about Strictly talks psychobabble," she says scornfully. "They say they're going on a journey, or trying to build their confidence, or getting over a divorce or something. People say there must be a deep reason to do these things. But there isn't! I'm just having fun."

She will concede a certain sadness at how the career she chose, and for which she sacrificed so much, has lost much of its grandeur and dignity in her eyes. "Parliament was an institution of enormous standing when I was aspiring to go in. It isn't now. When I first went in we had very significant people there. I mean, in our intake there was a brain surgeon on the Labour side, a consultant gynaecologist on our side, we were taking in quite a high level, not a whole load of career politicians. And you look at parliament now and you cannot see the top lawyers, the top medical men, the top businessmen. They are not there. And a part of it is the intrusion into not just your own private life – that's fair – but your family's life." She fixes me with a characteristic stare. "So your profession – journalism – has got to look at itself, for the part it has played in that."

If she were a young woman today, would she look at parliamentary politics and think it was the career for her? "Good question. Don't know. I don't know if I would still have the same sense of awe and ambition that I had then, I don't know. I suspect I might not, but it's only a very faint might not. When I went in, if I'd stayed a backbencher I wouldn't have minded because being part of the institution itself would have been worth it. Of course, I'd have wanted to be prime minister, but what I'm saying to you is that if that had never happened, I would still have been proud to be a member of that institution. I don't think you could say that now."

Reality television programmes such as Ann Widdecombe Versus... Girl Gangs, or Ann Widdecombe Versus... Prostitution are a poor substitute for political action, she admits. "They were quite good at highlighting issues," she suggests, but agrees that they probably didn't achieve much in terms of actually persuading their participants to stop taking drugs or beating people up. That doesn't stop her telling her fellow contestants on Strictly to put more clothes on – "I say to the girls, 'Aren't you cold in that?'" – or appear to have altered her basic approach to political life, which essentially consists of telling people what they should be doing.

I wonder why she thinks this approach works, when on Celebrity Fit Club she herself flew into a rage when a motivational speaker was drafted in to try to talk her into losing weight. "Oh, silly ass! Silly ass," she exclaims. But wasn't that just what she's been doing for all these years – telling the nation to buck up and pull its socks up? "Well, no," she disagrees, "with Ann Widdecombe to the Rescue I didn't just go marching in there. The people had asked for help." But on Celebrity Fit Club she had asked for help to lose weight, hadn't she?

"But I don't need psychobabble!" she erupts. "What I needed was exercise. I don't want rubbish. No, rot! Rot! It's like Strictly, it's all psychobabble! No, go away, go away!" She starts flapping her arms, shooing away the invisible psychobabble as if warding off evil spirits. "Have fun! Dance! It's not a world war! And I think it is a result of what I said earlier: if you've spent 23 years affecting people's lives almost every time you breathe – when you've gone from that to Strictly, I cannot understand why people think it's so major."

"Don't say it in such a derisory tone," jokes Du Beke, feigning wounded feelings, and Widdecombe laughs and relaxes again.

Last Saturday's paso doble – a truly jaw-dropping spectacle performed to a soundtrack of Wild Thing by the Troggs – was likened to a car crash by the judges, but a John Sergeant-esque momentum of public support is building behind her. Having begun the contest as the bookies' favourite to be first to leave, Widdecombe is now 10-1 to win. In the event of these odds narrowing further, she has no intention whatsoever of bowing out, as Sergeant did, to protect the integrity of the show as a serious dance contest. Would it be fair to say she is quite a competitive person, I ask. "Yes," she flashes back, unabashed. "I would say that would be perfectly fair."

Two weeks ago, she performed a tango that involved being suspended with wires in a harness and lowered on to the dance-floor. Talking about it, she can barely contain her excitement, trilling, "Dry ice, smoke, everything!" She had hinted at "something spectacular for next week" on the previous show, which I'd thought rather shrewd, but she explains, "Everyone thinks it was a political strategy to try to tease the audience, but really it was to put pressure on myself." In fact, she confides, she is terrified of heights, and so had feared she might get cold feet and pull out of the stunt unless she committed herself to it publicly.

"Wooo-ooh!" exclaims Du Beke triumphantly. "I like it. And you say there's no psychobabble, Ann. You see, it *is* all about the journey!" He lets out a great whoop of laughter, and spins a twirl. "Ann conquering her fears, conquering her fear of heights. It's the narrative arc – quite literally!"

"Oh, rot," she huffs, looking as if she might actually swoon with delight.

11 NOVEMBER 2010

The ancient British roar of 'Tory scum' echoes once again across Westminster

MICHAEL WHITE

Right on cue, exactly six months into David Cameron's premiership, the ancient British roar of "Tory scum" echoed across central

London again. In honour of the coalition's deal on higher tuition fees, student protesters spliced their message with cheerful abuse of Nick Clegg. After almost 100 years of apathy Lib Dems can hold their heads high – hated at last.

It is a cosy cliche of demonstrations that get out of hand that the kind of "unrepresentative minority" which attacked the Millbank Tower and its squat neighbour, 30 Millbank, had spoiled an otherwise good-tempered protest. Yesterday this was true.

Nobody riots in the rain, so the weather must share some blame. As hundreds of student buses converged on central London the sun shone provocatively from a blue sky. Streams of students poured into the Strand, the LSE contingent louder, as usual, than those from nearby UCL. "Banks don't cure disease", declared one gentle placard; "Science is more useful than duck islands" and "Ancient Norse is not a luxury", said others.

The aggressive note struck by the inevitable Socialist Workers party's "F**k the Fees" poster was a hint of things to come, although the SWP asterisks hinted at tactical restraint in a way that the chant "Nick Clegg / We Know You / You're A Fucking Tory Too" did not.

Shoppers, bemused tourists and non-graduate building workers in hard hats showed little hostility. David, a graphic designer from Devon, who has been "paying more than my fair share of tax" since graduating in 1966, was disdainful: "There is no such thing as free education. It is paid for by our taxes."

In Trafalgar Square an irate bus driver confessed: "I was sympathetic until they blocked my bus. Where are the police?" Good question. Parliament itself, key Whitehall ministries and Lib Dem HQ in Cowley Street were well protected, but this was a decidedly under-policed demo – until it was too late.

The first and more violent Grosvenor Square demo against the Vietnam war in 1968 attracted a reported 60,000, the poll tax riots of 1990 three times as many, the Chartist demo in 1848 even more. Yesterday's estimates ranged from 30,000 to 50,000, angry but polite. Diane Wheeler, a sixth-form teacher from Milton Keynes, carried a banner on behalf of her students. "Mrs Wheeler says No to higher tuition fees", it read.

The students of 2010 seem much better dressed than the *soixante-huitards*. Old ideological certainties have also faded, but the crowd reflected the multicultural face of modern Britain. There were brand-new Oxbridge scarves ("only six of us from St Anne's: I'm afraid everyone's too busy working"), six busloads from Canterbury's assorted campuses and four teenagers from Manchester sporting neat hijabs and a "Don't Crush My Dreams" poster.

Creative arts students seemed especially fearful that their courses might be axed. Public school students ("my father's a diplomat, so I can afford the extra fees") declared solidarity with talented but poorer colleagues who might be squeezed out. "Cut fees – or we'll cut off your balls", declared the poster held by a young woman in pink trainers.

The idea was that, after lobbying MPs – Cheltenham's Martin Horwood was the only Lib Dem MP to risk venturing outside – the throng would arrive outside Tate Britain for stirring speeches from the NUS leadership, many of whom will be MPs too in due course.

But the unrepresentative minority had heard that the Millbank complex (in an earlier building the birthplace of Tony Benn) housed the Tory party HQ. Bare-chested, masked and armed with staves, they set about smashing windows. Why? "Tory HQ, property of the capitalist state, mate," explained one. Anarchists, street gangs, Trots or undercover police provocateurs – plenty of theories about the assailants' identity bounced around the crowd.

Few took part, but many cheered. Inevitably they broke into both buildings. Eggs were thrown along with looted flowers.

"Some twats have just decided to spoil it for the rest of us," cried Dan Hamilton, a mature student from Leicester. Only when the vanguard had reached the roof and started throwing things ("that's a fire extinguisher, completely out of order") did the Met's tactical support group appear in sufficient numbers to get a grip.

Outside the Tate a female police officer nursed a badly bleeding head, a colleague a sharp blow to her face. Seven protesters were hurt too.

Leaving their banners outside, some opted to duck out of the ruck and into the Tate's tranquillity for soup of the day (£3.85) and this month's special exhibition: the 18th-century Romantics – another group of frustrated young people breaking free of their elders. It seemed appropriate.

15 NOVEMBER 2010

The words you read next will be your last. Because I'm going to strangle every single one of you

CHARLIE BROOKER

The moment I've finished typing this, I'm going to walk out the door and set about strangling every single person on the planet. Starting with you, dear reader. I'm sorry, but it has to be done, for reasons that will become clear in a moment.

And for the sake of transparency, in case the powers-that-be are reading: this is categorically not a joke. I am 100% serious. Even though I don't know who you are or where you live, I am going to strangle you, your family, your pets, your friends, your imaginary friends, and any lifelike human dummies with haunted stares and wipe-clean vinyl orifices you've got knocking around, perhaps in a secret compartment under the stairs. The only people who might escape my wrath are the staff and passengers at Sheffield's Robin Hood airport, because they've been granted immunity by the state.

Last week 27-year-old accountant Paul Chambers lost an appeal against his conviction for comments he made back in January via the social networking hoojamaflip Twitter, venting his frustration when heavy snow closed the airport, leaving him unable to visit his girlfriend.

"Crap!" he wrote. "Robin Hood airport is closed. You've got a week and a bit to get your shit together otherwise I'm blowing the airport sky high!!"

Anti-terror experts intercepted this message and spent hours deciphering it, eventually uncovering a stark coded warning within, cunningly disguised as a series of flippant words.

Chambers' use of multiple exclamation marks is particularly chilling. He almost seems to find the whole thing rather funny. The violent destruction of an entire airport – hundreds of passengers and staff being blasted to shrieking ribbons by tonnes of explosive, all because one man's dirty weekend has been postponed – yet all this senseless carnage is little more than an absurdist joke in the warped mind of Paul Chambers.

Funny is it, Mr Chambers? A big old laugh? Tell that to the theoretical victims of your hypothetical atrocity. Go on. Dig them out of the imaginary rubble. Listen to their anguished, notional screams. Ask how loudly they laughed as you hit the make-believe detonator. Go on. Ask them.

If you dare.

At least when Osama bin Laden broadcasts a warning to the west, his intentions form part of an extremist ideology informed by decades of resentment. Chambers issues blood-curdling threats at the drop of a snowflake. This makes him the very worst kind of terrorist there is – the kind prepared to slaughter thousands in the name of inclement weather conditions.

Mercifully, in this case, before any innocent blood could be shed, Chambers was arrested, held in a police cell, and convicted of sending a "menacing electronic communication". His appeal was rejected last week by Judge Jacqueline Davies, who described his original tweet as "menacing in its content and obviously so. It could not be more clear. Any ordinary person reading this would see it in that way and be alarmed."

Quite right too. In fact, throughout this case, the authorities have behaved impeccably – which is why it's such a crying shame I'm going to have to strangle all of them too. But strangle them I must.

Why? Because many of his fellow tweeters, outraged by Judge Davies' ruling, have retweeted Chambers' original message in a misguided show of solidarity. Thousands of people, all threatening to blow Robin Hood airport "sky high". Clearly they have to be stopped – but infuriatingly, many of them hide behind anonymous usernames. The only way to ensure they all taste justice is to punish everyone equally, just to be sure. Hence the strangling, which doesn't feel like too much of an overreaction under the circumstances. I'm just following the authorities' lead. They ought to give me a medal. From beyond the grave. After I've strangled them.

Still, loth as I am to strangle every man, woman and child on the planet, it won't be an entirely thankless task. Clearly I will feel no remorse while strangling Chambers. He is a dangerous madman, and I look forward to sliding my hands around his neck and slowly choking the life out of him.

I also relish the prospect of strangling another tweeter-in-crime: Gareth Compton, the Tory councillor who ran afoul of the authorities last week for tweeting the words "can someone please stone Yasmin Alibhai-Brown to death? I shan't tell Amnesty if you don't. It would be a blessing, really."

He later apologised for what he claimed – outlandishly – was "an ill-conceived attempt at humour", even though I'm sure Judge Jacqueline Davies would agree that it was menacing in its content and obviously so, and in fact could not be more clear, and that any ordinary person reading it would see it in that way and be alarmed.

Reassuringly, the bloodthirsty maniac Compton was arrested hours later, presumably after being cornered in his lair by a Swat team. I'd like to shake every member of that team by the hand, which sadly won't be possible while I'm strangling them.

Anyway, I'm writing this on Friday, so by the time you read this on Monday my strangling rampage will have begun – unless the authorities have intercepted these words and arrested me in the interim, in which case I'd like to make it absolutely clear that I intend to strangle everyone in the prison before turning my hands on myself. Attention home secretary: you've got three days and a bit to get your shit together. Otherwise I'm strangling this planet sky-high.

26 NOVEMBER 2011

Five days inside a Taliban jail

GHAITH ABDUL-AHAD

After the battle with US special forces, helicopter gunships and Afghan government troops, two Talibs were dead and several more injured.

We had been asleep in a guest room belonging to a man from east London who was a mullah and a fighter when the attack happened. But the timing of the firefight made the Taliban suspicious and Bilal, one of the senior commanders in this district of Baghlan province, told us politely that we would have to answer some questions. Our phones, bags and cameras were confiscated.

They detained us first in a madrasa – a religious school – a compound-style building flanked on one side by a mosque and on the other by a government school. In the courtyard there were pools of congealed blood where some of the casualties had been brought that morning. We were led into a room where Amanulah, a bespectacled teacher in his 30s, sat with his students, who ranged from seven-year-olds to fuzzy-bearded teenagers with turbans and guns.

Amanulah's handsome face was dwarfed by his oversized turban and his eyes were red from lack of sleep. He and his older students had spent the night fighting with the rest of the district chief Lal Muhammad's Taliban. One madrasa teacher had been hurt in the fighting. His son had lost his eye.

Amanulah sat beneath the school emblem, a black curtain embroidered with Qur'anic verses in golden and white threads and covered with the emblems of the Taliban fighter: a Kalashnikov assault rifle with a shining bayonet, RPG launchers, grenades and knives of different shapes and sizes. Among the embroidered words were: "By the name of God the most gracious the most merciful."

"I learned English for 12 years in Pakistan," Amanulah said in correct but extremely slow English. "But here I haven't used English for a long time." He had come to the school three years ago because it had a good reputation. "There are very few good schools now in Afghanistan," he said. "We had many during the Taliban rule but they are closed now or under government control.

"I didn't want to be a Talib," he said in a softer voice. "I was just a student. I came here to study. But all my brothers in the school, the teachers and students, were already fighting [with Lal Muhammad's Taliban] and they asked me if I wanted to join and I said yes."

In the thousand-year-old madrasa system, men like Amanulah are both students and teachers. While he studies the texts needed for him to become a mullah he teaches the younger children the essentials of the Taliban's particular brand of Islam.

"You join at the age of six or seven, depending on your family. You are taught the basics of belief, religious rituals and grammar. Later you study Persian language and poetry, then you go into basic Islamic law and all along you study and memorise the Qur'an and Arabic grammar."

Around 8am the smaller children left the room to prepare breakfast. Two of them picked up a blackened teapot while two others went outside to collect food donations.

They spread the breakfast out on a cloth on the floor: tea, a cold flat loaf of bread, some smaller bits of stale bread and one warm piece of bread cooked in butter. The younger students didn't touch the hot buttery loaf but politely munched on the old bread.

When breakfast was tidied away, Amanulah picked up his books and went to study with one of his teachers. One of the small boys started sweeping the yard while the rest moved into another room of the madrasa.

The second room resembled the type of classroom I have seen all over the developing world. Its walls were mottled with patches of paint and chipped plaster, the floor covered with torn bits of carpet. There was a soiled mattress, a very low desk and a bookshelf lined neatly with copies of the Qur'an covered in green embroidered fabrics.

Students came in and out of the classroom, picking up books to kiss them, read, then talk and joke. One eight-year-old boy crouched in front of the desk reading a book about fasting and prayers. Then he picked up a Kalashnikov that was laid against the wall and rested it on the desk. He started fiddling with it, trying to cock it and lift it, but the gun was too heavy, so he rested it on the desk, closed an eye and whispered tatatatatata at an imaginary enemy on the wall. I asked some of the students why they were here in the madrasa. They answered that they were fighting the holy war.

We spent most of the day in that room. From time to time we were questioned and told that we would be released once the military Komissyon – the Taliban council – had finished its investigation.

Bilal came in the late afternoon to tell us our release was imminent, but two hours later we were told the area was not safe because of drone activity. That evening, they moved us to the jail.

We were given a change of clothes and allowed to keep a book, a pack of cigarettes and some worry beads, then we were blindfolded and handcuffed and put in a car which followed a winding, climbing road. After an hour the car came to a halt and, with our eyes still covered and our hands tied, we were led up a steep slope.

After some time thick fingers untied my blindfold, and in the light of the moon a majestic view unfolded of a wide path framed by two dark mountains which appeared like giant gateposts.

"Walk!" hissed one of the shadows behind us. I heard the metallic click of the safety catch being released and the clank of a bullet being pulled into the chamber. I waited for the shot to come, but it never did.

Led by two men in thick military jackets, we climbed the ragged mountain path for nine hours, our hands still tied behind our backs. Shortly before daybreak we reached a barn on top of a mountain. This was where we would be incarcerated for the following days.

The word prison usually implies a thick-walled building with gates, padlocks and guards. But in the Taliban concept of a jail, the gate doesn't exist. The jailer was the gate, the prison cell, the executioner and sometimes, if you were lucky, your friend.

The jailer in Dhani Ghorri was a short man with bent legs, a chest-long beard and vicious eyes. Taliban commanders from different groups and factions in the area handed him their captives and he would keep them, interrogate them and execute them if the orders were given.

Wherever he was, the cell went with him. It could be a cave or a room in a farmer's house. In our case it was a barn somewhere between Baghlan and Kunduz. It measured two metres by four, with no windows and a very low ceiling. Inside it was dark most of the time. The dirt floor was covered with goat and sheep droppings.

The prisoners and the guards lived in the same room, divided by an invisible line. Both groups slept on flimsy mattresses covered with an almost black layer of shining grime.

For the first night we were blindfolded with chequered Afghan scarves that reeked of grease and which served as our towels and prayer mats. After that night, we were only blindfolded when we were led into the adjacent barn to wash and relieve ourselves. The floor of this barn was covered with droppings of goats and humans.

Our feet were held by a thick cast-iron chain and padlocks.

We ate three times a day: green tea and dark bread for breakfast and dinner. Lunch was the notorious Afghan shorba, bread soaked in meat broth.

Many people had passed through this cell in the past few months, the jailer said. There was a truck driver whose crime was to transport goods for Nato from the northern border of Afghanistan to Kabul. His truck was burned along with several others when the Taliban ambushed the convoy on the road. "We released him after 10 days, but he paid a big fine." Then there was an Afghan National Army officer who was also released after his tribesmen pledged that he wouldn't go back to the army.

But not all of the prisoners were let go. "We don't beat the prisoners unless we get orders to question them," he said solemnly. "Then we beat them to get them to tell us the truth.

"Before the truck driver we had a spy who stayed here for two months. We beat him every day until he confessed and finally he was executed. I hanged him myself."

Hanging has become the Taliban's favoured method of execution after Mullah Omar, the Taliban's spiritual leader, issued orders banning beheading, which had generated bad coverage in the media.

The jailer sometimes came into the cell with gifts. One day he brought us a small plastic bag of sweets, another day it would be an old toothbrush or even a bar of soap.

Apart from the jailer, I counted seven guards in all, from frail teenagers to big, tough fighters. They lived in conditions that were not much better than the prisoners'. They were not allowed to leave or carry mobile phones and had to spend the night in the cell with the prisoners, often with their feet tied to those of their prisoners. They were fed the same meagre food.

Most of them were the lowest-ranking Taliban fighters, all poor and illiterate. The only privilege they had was their authority over their captives. They sometimes relished that petty power, moving prisoners away from the light, unnecessarily blindfolding their captives, or just being rough.

The jailer himself was no stranger to prisons. Two years before, he had been detained in Pakistan while visiting some Taliban commanders. "They beat me only on the first day and for three months after that they kept me chained and blindfolded in a dark cell," he said. "My brother is still there."

We were in the jail-cum-barn for five days before our credentials were verified by Taliban leaders in Quetta and local commanders.

Word came that we were to be released and we walked the long path down the mountain.

Lal Muhammad and the rest of his command council had gathered in the madrasa at Dhani Ghorri. They apologised to us and returned our equipment.

As we were about to leave, Lal Muhammad produced a thick bundle of dollar bills and tried to give us a hundred each. "This for your trouble," he said.

We refused, and began the long journey back to Kabul.

29 NOVEMBER 2010

Why do we hate modern classical music?

ALEX ROSS

A full century after Arnold Schoenberg and his students Alban Berg and Anton Webern unleashed their harsh chords on the world, modern classical music remains an unattractive proposition for many concertgoers. Last season at the New York Philharmonic, several dozen people walked out of a performance of Berg's Three Pieces for Orchestra; about the same number exited Carnegie Hall before the Vienna Philharmonic struck up Schoenberg's Variations for Orchestra.

The mildest 20th-century fare can cause audible gnashing of teeth. Benjamin Britten's Serenade for Tenor, Horn and Strings is a more or less fully tonal score, yet in 2009 at Lincoln Centre, it failed to please a gentleman sitting behind me. When someone let out a "Bravo!" elsewhere in the hall, he growled: "I bet that was a plant." I resisted the temptation to swat him with my pocket score.

Some of this behaviour can be blamed on the notorious bad manners of certain New York patrons, but the problem is widespread, as any music administrator with a yen for 20th-century repertory will tell you. Some Prommers are still traumatised by the shock of encountering Harrison Birtwistle's ultraviolent piece Panic at the 1995 Last Night of the Proms. For decades, critics, historians and even neuroscientists have been pondering the question of why so-called modern music seems to perplex the average listener. After all, adventurous artists in other fields have met with a very different reception. The highest-priced painting in history is Jackson Pollock's swirlingly abstract No 5, 1948, which sold in 2006 for $140m. Tycoons and emirs covet avant garde architects. James Joyce's Ulysses inspires worldwide drinking parties every 16 June.

Once, these cultural untouchables were dismissed as charlatans – merchants of the "emperor's new clothes", to employ a phrase that remains commonplace among unappreciative concertgoers. A New York Times editorial threw a "new clothes" insult at Marcel Duchamp's Nude Descending a Staircase when it showed in 1913. The same conceit was trotted out in 1946 by a commentator who perceived no difference between a Picasso and a child's drawing. TS Eliot's The Love Song of J Alfred Prufrock was cited for its "incoherent banalities". These days, you would draw puzzled stares if you announced at a dinner party that Pollock is a crock. But if you said the same of John Cage, you might get no argument.

Explanations for the abiding resistance to musical modernism have proliferated, their multiplicity suggesting that none quite holds the key. One theory holds that a preference for simple tonality is wired into the human brain. Attempts to test this proposition have produced ambiguous results. For example, a couple of studies suggest that infants prefer consonant to dissonant intervals. Yet infants hear tonal music almost from the moment of birth, and so have been conditioned to accept it as "natural". Moreover, visual arts research demonstrates that children prefer representational images to abstract ones. The 327,000 people who came to see bleak late Mark Rothko works at Tate Modern in 2008 and 2009 overcame that inclination; the same can happen with music.

There's also a sociological explanation: because concert audiences are essentially trapped in their seats for a set period, they tend to reject unfamiliar work more readily than do gallery visitors, who can move about freely, confronting strange images at their own pace. Yet if the style of presentation conditioned the response, one would expect that dance, theatre and movie audiences would show the same revulsion toward novel ideas.

The relative popularity of George Balanchine, Samuel Beckett or Jean-Luc Godard suggests otherwise. Indeed, it's striking that film-makers have made lavish use of the same dissonances that concertgoers have found so alienating. Stanley Kubrick's 2001: A Space Odyssey, with its hallucinatory György Ligeti soundtrack, mesmerised millions in the late 1960s. Martin Scorsese's Shutter Island, which deploys music by Cage, Morton Feldman, Giacinto Scelsi, and Ligeti again, was a recent box-office hit. Michael Giacchino's score for the TV series Lost is an encyclopedia of avant garde techniques. If the human ear were instinctively hostile to dissonance, these and 1,000 other Hollywood productions would have failed.

The core problem is, I suspect, neither physiological nor sociological. Rather, modern composers have fallen victim to a long-smouldering indifference that is intimately linked to classical music's idolatrous relationship with the past. Even before 1900, people were attending concerts in the expectation that they would be massaged by the lovely sounds of bygone days. ("New works do not succeed in Leipzig," a critic said of the premiere of Brahms's First Piano Concerto in 1859.)

The music profession became focused on the manic polishing of a display of masterpieces. By the time Schoenberg, Stravinsky and company introduced a new vocabulary of chords and rhythms, the game was fixed against them. Even composers who bent over backwards to accommodate a taste for Romantic tonality encountered scepticism; they could not overcome, except by drastic measures, the disadvantage of being alive.

Museums and galleries took a markedly different approach. In America, the Museum of Modern Art, the Art Institute of Chicago, and other leading institutions propagandised for modern art. Wealthy patrons embraced some of the most radical new work; dealers whipped up publicity; critics romanticised Pollock and company as go-it-alone heroes. The idea took hold that museums could be sites of intellectual adventure. On a recent trip to MoMA, I was struck by a poster at the entrance: "Belong to something brilliant, electrifying, radical, curious, sharp, moving ... unruly, visionary, dramatic, current, provocative, bold..."

At present, no major orchestra is able or willing to describe itself in the same terms. But a few organisations are moving in that direction. Beginning in 1992, Esa-Pekka Salonen gave the Los Angeles Philharmonic a bolder profile, and he is now applying the same model to the Philharmonia in London. Youngish crowds of 1,000 or more show up for the Chicago Symphony's MusicNOW series, which cannily offers a supplement of free pizza and beer.

London's Southbank Centre and the Barbican have drawn eager throngs to evenings of Edgard Varèse, Iannis Xenakis, Luigi Nono and Karlheinz Stockhausen. Even in New York, the situation isn't entirely hopeless. Alan Gilbert, who took over as the New York Philharmonic's music director last season, has had startling successes with such rowdy fare as Ligeti's Le Grand Macabre, Varèse's Amériques, and, at the beginning of this season, Magnus Lindberg's Kraft. Veteran observers were agog at the sight of Philharmonic subscribers cheering Lindberg's piece, which contains hardly a trace of tonality and requires the use of discarded car parts as percussion. What made the difference was Gilbert's gift for talking audiences through unfamiliar territory: in a mini-lecture, he mapped out the structure of the piece, demonstrated a few highlights, made jokes at his own expense, and generally gave people the idea that if they left early they'd be missing out.

All music is an acquired taste; no music is everywhere beloved. A couple of months ago, the blogger Proper Discord noticed that the top-selling album in America that week – Katy Perry's precision-tuned pop medley Teenage Dream – had been purchased by only one in 1,600 citizens. Certainly, some genres are more popular than others, but individual tastes change dramatically. When I was young, I loved the 18th- and 19th-century repertory to the exclusion of 20th-century music, both classical and pop. Then, once I acknowledged the force of dissonance, I went from Schoenberg to Messiaen to Xenakis, and, following the path of noise, moved on to the post-punk sound of Sonic Youth. Some of my contemporaries found classical music by proceeding in the opposite direction: they began not with Mozart but with Steve Reich or Arvo Pärt. To build the audience of the future, classical institutions should make more of unexpected bridges between genres.

What must fall away is the notion of classical music as a reliable conduit for consoling beauty – a kind of spa treatment for tired souls. Such an attitude undercuts not only 20th-century composers but also the classics it purports to cherish. Imagine Beethoven's rage if he had been told that one day his music would be piped into railway stations to calm commuters and drive away delinquents. Listeners who become accustomed to Berg and Ligeti will find new dimensions in Mozart and Beethoven. So, too, will performers. For too long, we have placed the classical masters in a gilded cage. It is time to let them out.

15 DECEMBER 2010

From prison van to stately home: Assange offered rural bail haven

LUKE HARDING AND SAM JONES

His supporters include teenage hackers, freedom of speech activists and a motley group of celebrities. But it was the maverick British establishment that rode to the rescue of Julian Assange, offering to whisk him from dull confinement in Wandsworth jail to a large and comfy manor house on the Norfolk-Suffolk borders.

For once, Assange was not the star at the afternoon bail hearing at Westminster magistrates' court. Dressed in a white shirt and blue suit, he watched the proceedings impassively. Instead the hero was Vaughan Smith, a former army officer, journalist adventurer and rightwing libertarian. For much of the past five months, until his arrest last week, Assange has been living at Smith's Frontline Club in Paddington, west London.

Standing to address district judge Howard Riddle, Geoffrey Robertson QC announced that "Captain Smith" was now ready to put Assange up at his rambling country home in Norfolk, Ellingham Hall, which sits near the town of Bungay in Suffolk – that is, should he be granted bail. The WikiLeaks saga has so far been short of jokes. But Robertson had one ready-made.

It would not be so much "house arrest as manor arrest", he quipped. Not only that, but it was inconceivable Assange would attempt to escape "since darkness descends rather early in that part of Britain". Additionally, Assange was willing to give up his Australian passport and wear an electronic tag. Finally, he wasn't likely to get very far given that "media exposure" had made him "well-known around the world", Robertson said with understatement.

Last week Assange was refused bail after he unwisely gave an Australian postal address as his place of residence. This time his legal team would allow no such mistake.

Robertson, Assange's new barrister, asked Smith to give his own assessment of WikiLeaks' controversial founder, in the light of Sweden's attempts to have him extradited on sex allegations.

"He is a very honourable person, hugely clever, self-deprecatory and warm. Not the kind of things you read about," Smith said loyally. But the clincher came when Robertson asked Smith to explain what precisely Assange's new rustic home would look like. After establishing that Smith was a former Guards officer and one-time captain of the British army's shooting team, the QC asked for details of Smith's family home and organic farm. "It has 10 bedrooms and 600 acres," Smith replied. Better still, there was even a police station. "It's a short distance on a bicycle. I can cycle it in about 15 minutes," Smith explained. "It's about a mile. Perhaps a little bit more." Smith added helpfully: "It's an environment where he would be surrounded. We have members of staff. My parents live in proximity as well. My father was a Queen's Messenger and a colonel in the Grenadier Guards."

On the second floor of the court several celebrity supporters had gathered outside next to the coffee machine and green metal benches – John Pilger, Jemima Khan, Ken Loach, Bianca Jagger, and others. But it turned out they weren't really needed – though their money was. Outside on the pavement, a polyglot scrum of journalists waited impatiently for news.

Judging from his appearance, Assange appeared to be surviving his ordeal in Wandsworth prison pretty well. From inside a glass box for the defendant, he confirmed his identity and address. He also gave a cheery thumbs-up to his team.

Robertson, however, made clear that Assange was having a miserable time of it. His conditions inside Wandsworth were nothing short of living hell, he suggested. "He can't read any newspapers other than the Daily Express. This is the kind of Victorian situation he finds himself in," Robertson lamented. He went on: "Time magazine sent him a magazine with his picture on the cover but all the person would allow him to have was the envelope!"

To no one's great surprise, the judge announced that "bail was going to be granted under certain conditions". These turned out to be not overly onerous: an electronic tag, an afternoon and night curfew and a requirement to report to Bungay police station between 6pm and 8pm every evening. Oh, and £200,000 in cash.

Assange's lawyers asked if it might be possible to hand cheques in to the court instead. The magistrate was unimpressed, insisting in these financially troubled times it had to be money upfront.

Outside, the tweeted news of Assange's bail brought a loud cheer from the 150 or so people who had gathered opposite the court to cheer on their hero and share their banners and placards with the world.

One read: "Sex crimes! My arse!" Another, "That's just what we need – another innocent man in jail", and a third: "Sweden:

muppets of the US." Despite the indignant slogans, the judge's verdict plainly delighted the protesters. Three young activists were so thrilled, in fact, that they broke into an impromptu chorus of We Wish You a Merry Christmas.

Soon afterwards, however, there was confusion as news filtered through that the Swedish prosecutor was to appeal against the bail decision, meaning that Assange has to remain for the time being in jail. But his lawyers appear confident he will be out in time for Christmas.

Pheasant dinners, port and brisk walks around the estate may be only a matter of days away.

16 DECEMBER 2011

Top NoW editor linked to Sienna Miller phone hacking

Winter

Heroic masters of the Ashes

MIKE SELVEY

They came in their thousands to form an English corner of a foreign field for the climax, a day of days in the history of the England team and another one of abject misery for a once-proud Australian team fallen on hard times. Not even the snap showers washing in to interrupt play, and a flatness to the team on the field, could deny them a third overwhelming victory which came, by an innings and 83 runs, at 11.56, four minutes before the Shipping Forecast, and just as Billy the Barmy Trumpeter was playing a poignant Last Post for the demise of Australian cricket.

To Chris Tremlett went the honour, the debutant tailender Michael Beer chopping on to his stumps to spark the celebrations that would go on long into the night. But it took the second new ball to finish the job, as Steve Smith, who remained unbeaten on 54, and Peter Siddle, who had denied England when they had hoped to finish things on the fourth evening, took their eighth wicket stand to 86 before Siddle (43) hit Graeme Swann precisely to Jimmy Anderson at deep midwicket.

Anderson then found the edge of Ben Hilfenhaus's bat for Matt Prior to take his 23rd catch, an England record for a five-match Ashes series. It took Anderson – the fellow too soft to bowl to Australians, remember, according to Justin Langer – to 24 wickets for the series, more than any England pace bowler in Australia since Frank Tyson terrorised them in 1954-55. Australia have now been beaten by an innings three times in the series, unprecedented for them.

It was set up on the fourth day by Anderson, not just Good but Brilliant Jimmy, indisputably the bowler of the series with daylight second, who plunged the knife into what life was left in the twitching carcass of the Australian cricket team. The old ball reversed, as it always seems to do for England – the same England, said the sages here in the pre-series propaganda war, that would not know how to use a secondhand Kookaburra – and not for Australia.

But Anderson did not just use it, he had it talking, gabbling away, a ball with verbal diarrhoea. With it, he produced one of the best cameo spells of the series, and knocked the heart out of the middle of the Australian innings: the left-hander Usman Khawaja, tyro and promising but given a strong lesson in this match that there is a giant step up to the top level, seduced outside off stump as the ball wafted away from him; the right-handed skipper Michael Clarke, destined perhaps to try and pick this side from the basement and not a great player in sight, put through the wringer, utter torture, before he found no answer to an away swinger and mercifully also edged to Prior.

This was an Australian side in distress. The first innings in Brisbane and the third Test in Perth were their peaks in a series of otherwise total England domination. The stuffing had long been knocked out of them by the England batsmen, but there was a sorry capitulation where fight was needed. Shane Watson flamed briefly but ran himself out for once rather than his partner, and Tim Bresnan took advantage of Phil Hughes's laboured endeavours to become an opening batsman of substance by sliding one across him and watching as the bat nibbled out like a fish taking the bait. It was all too easy.

Throughout the bulk of the series, Australia have been offered little respite by the England attack. Wave of attack had followed wave. Key to this has been the reverse, and England are masters at it, their ability to get a ball into a condition to go after no more than 20 overs a skill that in part involves bowling it with a cross seam so that it first scuffs on the surface (such a delivery accounted for Hughes) and is then polished on one side only. But then comes the further skill in using it, for anyone might have a lock pick but not everyone can pick a lock. Each of the three seamers is a practitioner and each benefited. When Anderson gave way to Bresnan after his mesmeric spell, the Yorkshireman responded by getting Mike Hussey caught in the gully, just as Hussey had opened the series by catching Andrew Strauss there with the third ball. And when, at the Randwick end, Graeme Swann conceded the crease to Chris Tremlett, the giant thundered in to rip out Brad Haddin and Mitchell Johnson with successive deliveries, a brutal bouncer followed by a wicked inswinger. When he had the bit between his teeth and the crowd roaring behind him, he looked a very serious proposition.

The thing that truly disheartened Australia though, that to which there was no response, was another monumental innings from England. In the second innings at Brisbane they made 517 for one to give notice of their potential; in Adelaide it was 620 for five; and Melbourne 513. Killer innings all. But here they made 644 before the final wicket fell, by which time Australia had taken a third new ball and sent down almost 178 overs.

To place it in context, it is the seventh highest total England have ever made and their highest in Australia. It meant that England's runs per wicket for the series stood at 51.14. There were more records, for surely this has been a record series for records. The century that Prior scored, the fourth and most robust of his Test career, came from 109 balls, the fastest for England since Ian Botham's flogathon at Old Trafford in 1981, with nine fours, a six and a lot of scampering. Having added 107 for the seventh wicket with Ian Bell, Prior then helped Bresnan put on 102 for the eighth, before Swann added insult to Johnson's bowling injury. No side in the history of Test cricket has managed century stands for sixth, seventh and eighth wickets in the same innings.

11 JANUARY 2011

My father's murder must not silence the voices of reason

SHEHRBANO TASEER

I can't help but roll my eyes when I'm informed I must keep a guard with me at all times now. After my father, Salmaan Taseer, was assassinated by his own security guard on 4 January – my brother Shehryar's 25th birthday – does it even matter? If the governor of Pakistan's largest province can be shot dead by a policeman assigned to protect him in broad daylight in a market in the federal capital, Islamabad, is anyone really safe?

It was after lunch that I started receiving one message after another from friends inquiring about my father. I rang him. No answer. I called his chauffeur in Islamabad. He was wailing and incoherent. I told him to calm down and tell me everything. The governor had been about to step into the car after lunch at his favourite local cafe, he said. He had been shot in the back. There was a lot of blood, he said. I told him everything would be fine: my father was a fighter and he would make it.

According to the postmortem report I read, they recovered 27 bullets from his body, which means the gunman actually reloaded his weapon so nothing would be left to chance. Each one of my father's vital organs was punctured by the hail of bullets, except his heart and larynx – his mighty, compassionate heart and his husky, sensible voice.

The assassin, Mumtaz Qadri, had reportedly asked others in the governor's temporary security detail to take him alive. Almost a dozen, including security personnel, are now under arrest. Speaking to camera crews the same day from jail, 26-year-old Qadri said he had killed my father because he had criticised the country's draconian and often misused blasphemy laws. It seems that Qadri was also inspired by the rally against my father on 31 December, at which rabid protesters demanded his blood. Yet no arrests were made over this brazen incitement to murder.

The blasphemy laws were foisted on Pakistan by Islamist dictator General Zia-ul-Haq in the 1980s. As an intellectual firebrand of the Pakistan People's Party, my father endured jail and torture during that dictatorship. We had thought the nightmare and brutality of the Zia regime was over when the general's aircraft fell out of the skies in 1988. We were so wrong.

Some 200 lawyers – men of the law – garlanded Qadri and showered him with pink rose petals on both his days in court. The president of the lawyers' wing of the opposition party Pakistan Muslim League-Nawaz was reportedly among them. The smiling assassin has become the poster boy for the unholy ambitions of the self-deluded. Lawyers who fought for an independent judiciary are standing in support of a self-confessed murderer. This is not the Pakistan for which my grandfather, MD Taseer, fought alongside founding father Mohammad Ali Jinnah.

The inability of the state to prosecute terrorists successfully is proving fatal for Pakistan. The country's anti-terrorism courts, where Qadri was presented, have a sorry record on convictions, and have been clogged by non-terrorism cases. The state is unable to gather evidence properly, make a cohesive case and ensure the safety of those who provide evidence against the militants. It is a different matter when it comes to trying poor, underprivileged Pakistanis – Muslims and non-Muslims alike – accused of blasphemy. Under pressure from the mobs outside, Pakistan's lower-level courts convict quickly, but these convictions are almost always overturned by the higher judiciary, although the accused (and in some cases the judges) are then killed by vigilantes.

My father was buried in Lahore on 5 January under high security. Cleric after cleric refused to lead his funeral prayers – as they had those of the Sufi saint Bulleh Shah – and militants warned mourners to attend at their own peril. But thousands came to Governor House on that bitterly cold morning to pay their respects. Thousands more led candle-lit vigils across the country. But the battle is not going to be over any time soon.

In Pakistan, the voices calling for reason and tolerance are in danger of being wiped out. The fear is palpable. The militants have issued a warning against further vigils for my father. Yesterday, a rally in support of the blasphemy laws was held in Karachi, at which mullahs incited violence against former information minister Sherry Rehman – my mother's close friend, and the brave woman I was named after – who tabled a bill in the National Assembly in November proposing blasphemy-law amendments. The politician and former cricketer Imran Khan, and former prime minister Chaudhry Shujaat Hussain – both conservatives – have also come out in support of my father's position: amending the blasphemy laws to prevent their misuse. The ruling party – my father's party – continues to equivocate.

My father's assassination was a hate crime fuelled by jihadist fervour, abetted by some irresponsible sections of the media and sanctified by some political actors. All that is necessary for the triumph of evil is that good people do nothing. The loss of one good man must not deter others. Pakistan's very future depends on it.

18 JANUARY 2011

News Corp's claims unravel in hacking case

Investigator was directed by News of the World executive, high court told

22 JANUARY 2011

Coulson quits as hacking scandal rocks Downing St

27 JANUARY 2011

Bloody and bruised in the back of a truck, destination unknown

JACK SHENKER

In the streets around Abdel Munim Riyad square the atmosphere had changed. The air which had held a carnival-like vibe was now thick with teargas. Thousands of people were running out of nearby Tahrir Square and towards me. Several hundred regrouped; a few dozen protesters set about attacking an abandoned police truck, eventually tipping it over and setting it ablaze. Through the smoke, lines of riot police could be seen charging towards us from the south.

Along with nearby protesters I fled down the street before stopping at what appeared to be a safe distance. A few ordinarily dressed young men were running in my direction. Two came towards me and threw out punches, sending me to the ground. I was hauled back up by the scruff of the neck and dragged towards the advancing police lines.

My captors were burly and wore leather jackets – up close I could see they were *amin dowla*, plainclothes officers from Egypt's notorious state security service. All attempts I made to tell them in Arabic and English that I was an international journalist were met with more punches and slaps; around me I could make out other isolated protesters receiving the same brutal treatment and choking from the teargas.

We were hustled towards a security office on the edge of the square. As I approached the doorway of the building other plainclothes security officers milling around took flying kicks and punches at me, pushing me to the floor on several occasions only to drag me back up and hit me again. I spotted a high-ranking uniformed officer, and shouted at him that I was a British journalist. He responded by walking over and punching me twice. "Fuck you and fuck Britain," he yelled in Arabic.

One by one we were thrown through the doorway, where a gauntlet of officers with sticks and clubs awaited us. We queued up to run through the blows and into a dank, narrow corridor where we were pushed up against the wall. Our mobiles and wallets were removed. Officers stalked up and down, barking at us to keep staring at the wall. Terrified of incurring more beatings, most of my fellow detainees – almost exclusively young men in their 20s and 30s, some still clutching dishevelled Egyptian flags from the protest – remained silent, though some muttered Qur'anic verses and others were shaking with sobs.

We were ordered to sit down. Later a senior officer began dragging people to their feet again, sending them back out through the gauntlet and into the night, where we were immediately jumped on by more police officers – this time with riot shields – and shepherded into a waiting green truck belonging to Egypt's central security forces. A policeman pushed my head against the doorframe as I entered.

Inside dozens were already crammed in and crouching in the darkness. Some had heard the officers count us as we boarded; our number stood at 44, all packed into a space barely any bigger than the back of a Transit van. A heavy metal door swung shut behind us.

As the truck began to move, brief flashes of orange streetlight streamed through the thick metal grates on each side. With no windows, it was our only source of illumination. Each glimmer revealed bruised and bloodied faces; sandwiched in so tightly the temperature soared, and people fainted. Fragments of conversation drifted through the truck.

"The police attacked us to get us out of the square; they didn't care who you were, they just attacked everybody," a lawyer standing next to me, Ahmed Mamdouh, said breathlessly. "They ... hit our heads and hurt some people. There are some people bleeding, we don't know where they're taking us. I want to send a message to my wife; I'm not afraid but she will be so scared, this is my first protest and she told me not to come here today."

Despite the conditions, the protesters held together; those who collapsed were helped to their feet, messages of support were whispered and then yelled from one end of our metallic jail to another, and the few mobiles that had been hidden from police were passed around so that loved ones could be called.

"As I was being dragged in, a police general said to me: 'Do you think you can change the world? You can't! Do you think you are a hero? You are not'," confided Mamdouh.

"What you see here – this brutality and torture – this is why we were protesting today," added another voice close by in the gloom.

Speculation was rife about where we were heading. The truck veered wildly round corners, sending us flying to one side, and regularly came to an emergency stop, throwing everyone forwards. "They treat us like we're not Egyptians, like we are their enemy, just because we are fighting for jobs," said Mamdouh. I asked him what it felt like to be considered an enemy by your own government. "I feel like they are my enemies too," he replied.

At several points the truck roared to a stop and the single door opened, revealing armed policemen on the other side. They called out the name of one of the protesters, "Nour", the son of Ayman Nour, a prominent political dissident who challenged Hosni Mubarak for the presidency in 2005 and was thrown in jail for his troubles.

Nour became a cause celebre among international politicians and pressure groups; since his release from prison security forces have tried to avoid attacking him or his family directly, conscious of the negative publicity that would inevitably follow.

His son, a respected political activist in his own right, had been caught in the police sweep and was in the back of the truck with us – now the policemen were demanding he come forward, as they had orders for his release.

"No, I'm staying," said Nour simply, over and over again and to applause from the rest of the inmates. I made my way through the throng and asked him why he wasn't taking the chance to get out. "Because either I leave with everyone else or I stay with everyone else; it would be cowardice to do anything else," he responded. "That's just the way I was raised."

After several meandering circles which seemed to take us out further and further into the desert fringes of the city, the truck finally came to a halt. We had been trapped inside for so long that the heat was unbearable; more people had fainted, and one man had collapsed on the floor, struggling for breath.

By the light of the few mobile phones, protesters tore his shirt open and tried to steady his breathing; one demonstrator had medical experience and warned that the man was entering a diabetic coma. A huge cry went up in the truck as protesters thumped the sides and bellowed through the grates: "Help, a man is dying." There was no response.

After some time a commotion could be heard outside; fighting appeared to be breaking out between police and others, whom we couldn't make out.

At one point the truck began to rock alarmingly from side to side while someone began banging the metal exterior, sending out huge metallic clangs. We could make out that a struggle was taking place over the opening of the door; none of the protesters had any idea what lay on the other side, but all resolved to charge at it when the door swung open. Eventually it did, to reveal a police officer who began to grab inmates and haul them out, beating them as they went. A cry went up and we surged forward, sending the policeman flying; the diabetic man was then carried out carefully before the rest of us spilled on to the streets.

Later it emerged that we had won our freedom through the efforts of Nour's parents, Ayman and his former wife Gamila Ismail. The father, who was also on the demonstration, had got wind of his son's arrest and apparently followed his captors and fought with officers for our release. Shorn of money and phones and stranded several miles into the desert, the protesters began a long trudge back towards Cairo, hailing down cars on the way.

The diabetic patient was swiftly put in a vehicle and taken to hospital; I have been unable to find out his condition.

2 FEBRUARY 2011

'For everyone here, there's no turning back'

AHDAF SOUEIF

A great cry goes up from the square: "*Ir*hal! *Ir*hal!" (Leave! Leave!) Everybody is looking in the same direction. You follow their gaze to see a long banner unfurling, falling gracefully from the sixth-floor balcony of an art deco building. We read: "Do us a favour: leave!" Holding it from the balcony is a young woman with big hair. She is jumping up and down and holding up her hand in a victory salute. The crowd salute back: "*Ir*hal! *Ir*hal!"

Four generations, more than a million people (according to the army count at 2pm) are here. They are all doing what they have not been able to do for decades; each and every one is having their say in their own way and insisting on being counted. Their dominant demand, of course, is for Mubarak to step down.

In the regime's response to this people's revolution they have displayed the same brutality, dullness, dishonesty and predictability that have characterised their 30-year rule. They have shot and gassed their citizens, lied to them and about them, threatened them with F16s, tried to foist a "new" cabinet on them – everything except the decent thing: go.

Meanwhile the citizens on the ground have come into their own. Tahrir is about dignity and image as much as it is about the economy and corruption. People are acutely aware of how much their government has messed with their heads, worked to divide them, maligned them to the world. "She says we only care about a slice of bread," a young labourer says, "We care about bread. But we also care about pride." A bearded man with a wife in a niqab says: "We're all Egyptian. Was I born with a beard?" He grins: "When Mubarak leaves I'll be able to afford a razor!"

Together, in the square, over the last four days, people have rediscovered how much they like themselves and each other and, corny as it may sound, how "good" they are. They offer each other water, dates, biscuits. Young men are constantly collecting the litter. I sneeze and someone passes me a tissue. And all the time the chant continues, the demands are articulated, options for the future are discussed.

It is not possible to say what will happen next. Everything is up in the air, our communications are still cut (but you can still follow us online). Mubarak has said he will leave but more than two million of us are occupying the main squares of Cairo and a further two to three million are occupying other Egyptian cities. For every person in this revolution there is no turning back.

Tanks surround Tahrir Square but the army has declared it will never attack the people. Young Egyptians surround the tanks, chatting with the soldiers. Last night there was a football game – "the people versus the army" – with a tank as the prize. The people won. They did not get the tank. But then one of the most popular chants in Tahrir today is: "The people, the army as one hand".

I would not have thought a scenario possible where we welcome military intervention but the Egyptian army is very much part of the fabric of Egyptian society. And in both 1977 and

1985 it refused direct orders to fire on Egyptian demonstrators. An oath taken by every soldier is that he will not shoot Egyptians. So at the moment the army is securing for us this space in our country where we are carrying out our peaceful, democratic, young, inclusive, open-source, grassroots revolution.

I write this sitting on the grass under a variety of banners. A bank of loudspeakers has gone up at one end of the square and we are waiting for a concert by the popular band Eskenderella. We are all happy and we are proud to be here.

10 FEBRUARY 2011

Letter: Silent but deadly

RAYMOND LEVY

The Malawi ban on farting has attracted great attention in the British press (Editorial, 9 February). One thing that is not clear is which type of farting is forbidden. Until recently, I thought that Arabic was the only language with two words for fart. "Zarta" for the loud one and "fassia" for the silent but deadly type. I am now informed that Turkish slang also has two words: "murad" and "yousef", respectively. I wonder how widespread this linguistic richness is.

Emeritus Professor Raymond Levy
London

19 FEBRUARY 2011

Egyptian dignity in the face of death

NAWARA NAJEM

I am from a generation that has known no Egyptian leader besides the ousted president, Hosni Mubarak. When Anwar Sadat was killed, I was seven. I do not remember much about him other than he had a habit of screaming during speeches that lasted for hours. I also remember the regular periodic detention of both my mother and father for undisclosed reasons.

Mubarak began his rule by releasing all Sadat's political prisoners, and replacing them with his own. He assured the public that he would not stay in office for more than two terms, and then stayed for over 30 years because, he said, only he could ensure "the safeguard of security and stability". This translated into permanent governance through emergency laws renewed every two years. Usually, just before the laws came up for renewal, a terrorist bombing would occur – by pure chance! – which would "compel" the People's Assembly to vote for renewal of the laws.

For the sake of this security and stability, systematic torture became widespread. Some of the methods used were devised by the police, others were imported from the United States.

Every citizen ought to carry the responsibility for security and stability along with the leader, as the country is going through "a critical stage"; "a bottleneck"; "a difficult period". "Egypt is under threat"; "it is in imminent danger"; "compliance is necessary" and "fear is the route to safety". Every individual should be aware of the dangers of democracy. Democracy is a foreign plan to undermine the foundations of Egypt. Democracy is the key to occupation, "can you not see what happened to Iraq"...

Because Egypt has a large population, the residential areas were divided into quarters to make controlling people easier. A large group were created, who were so crushed by poverty that they came to think of election season – parliamentary, local and presidential – as a celebration when everyone gets a blanket, a meal and perhaps a woollen jacket, all in return for a simple task: to enter the electoral tent and put a mark in the green circle for "yes". As for the middle classes, they had to work day and night to make counterfeit gains that in reality belong to the bank.

Egypt has received large amounts of US aid – given in return for Egypt's neutralisation as a player in the Arab-Israeli conflict, and conditional on following World Bank "good policies". These include privatisation, whereby the Egyptian regime undertakes to dismantle factories, public-sector enterprises and infrastructure, and sell them at the lowest possible prices to "investors" who in turn lay off workers, cut wages or sell on to foreign investors. The president and his retinue received a cut of every sale.

The Tunisian revolution has had a great impact. Egyptians and Tunisians have a long history of feuds over football matches; a fact the tyrants exploited to exert control. The surprise was that these rival groups of football fans were one of the key elements in both the Tunisian and Egyptian revolutions. The call to demonstrate on 25 January was not the first. Other calls to protest against price hikes, torture, emergency law and Mubarak, and to demand a minimum wage, were issued daily on Facebook. I took up the 25 January call just as I took up every previous one, convinced that the demonstration would be attended by 500 people at best.

That day's demonstration did indeed begin with about 500 people; but then it was joined by crowds of passersby until the numbers in Tahrir Square reached 50,000. The masses had broken through the fear barrier; by the following day, their numbers had doubled. They began to plan how to outmanoeuvre the security forces; experiences of football crowds which have long faced off against the security forces were helpful here. Then people began to fear that the matter would end at this point and their unprecedented achievement would be aborted, and so on the third day their numbers doubled again.

Then the regime chose to use the full extent of its repressive force to end the situation once and for all. However, the masses that confronted security forces were not the Facebook youth and neither were they the internet activists. Rather, they were segments of Egyptian society whose anger had been ignited by seeing the dead bodies, and so suddenly and unexpectedly they decided that they would risk being shot. Repressive forces want to kill hundreds in order to terrorise the millions, and the only way to foil such a plan is for millions to make the collective decision that they do not fear death. This was the key to both the Egyptian and Tunisian revolutions.

Why did the people not fear death? No one knows. It was not only religion, because some of those who died were not believers. It was not only poverty, because many of those who faced death were from the comfortable classes. It was not only despair, as the millions who came out on to the streets were full of hope for change. Perhaps the answer is human dignity. No force, no matter how tyrannous, is able to deprive human beings of this. People broke through the fear barrier, and Christians discovered that Muslims are not terrorists while Muslims discovered that Christians are not agents of the occupation. The poor discovered that they have rights and the middle classes discovered that freedom from counterfeit gains releases the soul. And discovered that they do not need either a leader or a commander. Indeed, they don't even need security forces to maintain "security and stability". This revolution is a people's revolution. Whoever claims leadership of it is a liar and whoever claims to be its instigator is a vagabond. Leadership was and remains the property of the masses.

The Egyptian revolution is not yet over. The people have toppled the head of the regime and still they strive to cleanse the pockets of corruption. Let the dictatorships, international forces and beneficiaries clamour. No one can exert control over the will of nations once they have flared up.

23 FEBRUARY 2011

Police dined with NoW during hacking scandal

26 FEBRUARY 2011

Two cars, two deaths

KIRA COCHRANE

This is the story of two cars, moving at the same speed, that killed two people. The first death was my older brother, Gleave, who was eight at the time. It was a few weeks before Christmas, 1983, and while my mother, her boyfriend, my younger brother and I stayed

8 JULY 2011

Andy Coulson, former editor of the News of the World, leaves Lewisham police station after being arrested and bailed as part of the Met's phone-hacking inquiries. SEAN SMITH

21 JULY 2010

Julian Assange of WikiLeaks. LINDA NYLIND

A bride in profile: Kate Middleton. GRAHAM TURNER

11 MARCH 2011

With an oil refinery burning in the background, rebel fighters man an anti-aircraft gun outside Ras Lanuf, Libya. SEAN SMITH

home, hanging baubles on the tree, Gleave rode his BMX round the corner to spend the afternoon with his best friend, Robert. They were lively, funny boys; both had that distinct lack of fear that allows people to do wheelies or fling themselves down hills on rollerskates.

As it grew dark, and my mother's boyfriend left for the night, there was a phone call, a jumble of swallowed breaths and sylla-bles, and a bundling of my younger brother and me into a car. Gleave had been standing by the side of the road with his bike, and a driver had sped past and hit him. My mother drove us to Robert's house, dropped us off, then went straight on to the hospital in the ambulance.

The evening took on a strange, glassy sharpness. Robert had just been bought a toy pellet gun, and so we spent minutes, maybe hours, chasing around the house, shooting pieces of carrot and potato at one another. I was six, Robert was eight and his older sister Caroline was in her mid-teens, which seemed impossibly mature and glamorous. She kept saying Gleave had probably just broken an arm or a leg, but every time her mouth opened her lower lip would plummet suspiciously at one corner, and start twitching fast.

Fish and chips were delivered, and we sat chomping deliber-ately, hopefully, as if routine could keep bad news at bay. Then my mother arrived from hospital. Gleave was dead. I was sent upstairs to share Caroline's double bed, and as I lay curled up in my underwear, breathing hard into the duvet, I wondered at the noises coming through the wall. I had never heard a person howl like that. It wasn't a human sound. Years later, my mother would tell me that losing my brother had been like having a limb ripped out.

The man who had hit Gleave had been driving at just over 40mph along a road at dusk, a child of his own in the back seat.

When he collided with my brother, when he broke his neck, he thought he had hit a dog. Gleave's death led to an inquest that recognised the driver was 10mph over the speed limit, but didn't bring any penalties against him. He could still drive; there was no fine. There was the possibility of my mother pursuing him for compensation, but this would have meant months or years spent chasing a few thousand pounds, money that couldn't possibly bear the weight of a death. What amount could?

My mother had other problems to deal with. My father had died of a heart attack four years previously, while she was pregnant with my younger brother, Frazer, and, perhaps as a result, he had been born with serious learning disabilities. She had moved us all to this small, stifling, ultra-conservative retirement town on the Essex coast – a place where there was no pub, where one of the few places to drink was the hotel where my mother worked as a barmaid – in the hope that her parents, who lived a few streets along, might be of some support.

But by the time Gleave died, she and her parents were locked in a feud that would last until their deaths. My mother had been born while her father was away in the second world war, and this might be why they never bonded; why she always felt her parents were set against her. Their relationship was in one of its more positive phases when we moved nearby, but as soon as my mother started seeing her boyfriend, as soon as her father felt he was losing some control over her, the situation quickly deteriorated.

My grandparents started making vicious insinuations, sending social workers to our house, telling our schoolteachers to check us for bruises, making silent phone calls to my mother punctuated with mocking laughter. There was vague talk of them trying to get custody of me and my younger brother. Leaving town became a matter of urgency. My mother's relationship with her boyfriend had fizzled out by the time he fell off a roof, breaking his wrists, his head crashing on the ground, leaving him hospital-ised. If I tell you he was a roofer, would this latest turn of events seem less strange?

My mother, my brother and I moved to another part of Essex, and over the years I tried to work out how I felt about my broth-er's death. So much had happened before I turned seven that it was difficult to address each incident individually. One random, irrevocable event followed another, so all you could do was fan them out like a pack of cards and hold them to the light one by one. And all this proved was that there wasn't a winning card, that all of it was ugly, shitty, completely unchangeable.

I would think about Gleave while listening to a crackling mix tape he had recorded from a radio show before he died – Billy Joel singing Uptown Girl, Culture Club singing Victims – and I would think about the man who had killed him. I knew very little about this man because he had never contacted us, never apologised, never sent a letter; and if I'm honest, I hated him for that.

All that reached us was the rumour that he had found it difficult to drive after Gleave's death, that the experience had spooked him. It didn't seem enough. Why had he not given up driving altogether? Why had he not curled up in a corner and cried for months? The dearth of communication was a wicked, vexed lacuna. The victims and perpetrators in an accident are two parts of a whole: if one side doesn't admit to grief or meaning, where do you find the heart of it all?

When my younger brother was six or seven, he was also hit by a car, this time not fatally. It had been snowing that day, and a boy in his late teens had been driving up and down the road, to the bottom of the hill where we lived, trying to impress one of our neighbours. My brother and I were out playing and, with the line between the pavement and the road erased by snow, Frazer wandered into the path of a car that arrived silently, speedily, from nowhere, knocked him into a clumsy somersault, his flight only broken by the ground. It was the full cinematic collision, a moment plucked from a novel, but after a night in hospital he was fine.

I was shocked by the way the driver ran to my mother's door and began apologising and justifying himself, words skidding from noble to weasel-like, back and forth, but with the distinct advantage of being words, some expression of apology, terror, shock. It was proof that this moment meant something to this boy, this poor girl's Nick Kamen, that it was an experience that would stay with him, that would make his stomach shake. I was grateful then, for that.

It's another snow-covered day when I visit the writer Darin Strauss in New York. Strauss has just published the memoir Half a Life, which tells of the second road death in this story, an accident that took place in 1988, when he was an 18-year-old high school student on Long Island. Strauss was heading out with friends for the day when Celine Zilke, a 16-year-old schoolmate, rode by on her bike and turned directly in front of his car. There was nothing he could do to avoid her; he was moving at 40mph when she hit his windscreen. She died soon afterwards. And though he was absolved of responsibility for the crash – he was not over the speed limit, he had not been drinking, his driving was not neglectful, he did not hit and run – there began years of trying to make sense of this moment, trying to draw meaning and relief from the smash and full stop.

Strauss's book shows how similar the experience of those on either side of a fatal accident can be: the survivor's guilt, the sudden antipathy to risk, the shrill, grey hours spent imagining other outcomes. In writing about his immediate reactions, he also captures the strange, disconnected quality of thoughts during and after a catastrophe, how feelings and behaviour can be a long way from the heaving shoulders, the emotional carwash, that TV and films lead us to expect.

He describes a moment directly after the crash, still standing in the road, when a couple of girls from his school approached and asked whether he was involved. He acknowledged that he was, "and sensing the girls were still watching, I dropped to my knees and covered my head with my hands – fingers between the ears and temples, like a man who has just won the US Open. This plagiarised 'emotional' reaction, acted out for girls I'd never see again, is one more stomach-turning fact of that afternoon."

The day after Gleave's death, I remember a similarly stomach-turning reaction. I wondered vaguely, almost hopefully, whether this latest tragedy would be mentioned on the radio. Had our family finally reached a newsworthy level of horror?

I am unusually raw-nerved when I go to meet Strauss, thoughts swimming, racing, urgent. I knew as soon as I heard about his book that I wanted to interview him, that it felt somehow necessary, but I didn't tell him about my own experiences in the emails before we met. To be honest, I worried he would refuse the interview. But then, as the time approaches, I worry he'll feel set up. I know I have to tell him early on – it would be gratingly misleading to sit there nodding silently – but what if he reacts angrily? What if he ends the interview? And what if he doesn't? How, in all candour, do you sit down, the two of you, two sides of two accidents, and talk about these things?

Strauss is friendly, quiet and thoughtful when we meet in the small office where he works, teaching creative writing, and when I tell him briefly about Gleave, 10 minutes in, he is kind, interested, apologetic. The perfect reaction. I'm relieved, but the conversation is still awkward; too personal, wincing, as if sunlight's being poured in my eyes. Every few minutes we hurtle off topic, down rabbit holes of jagged, bad jokes.

In the book, Strauss wonders whether his actions immediately after Celine's death were right – he attended her funeral, he visited her parents – and I tell him I think they were, that there's something to be said for just showing up. "I'm still not sure," he says. "It's hard enough for them anyway, without having to face me."

He would find out in his first year of college that there was reason to suspect Celine had veered in front of his car on purpose. Just before her death, she had written in her diary words to the effect of "Today I realised that I am going to die", words that Strauss clung to for years as evidence of a suicide, before accepting they weren't conclusive, and what difference would it make anyway? All it would mean was that a 16-year-old had been sad enough to kill herself.

When I started reading, I wanted Strauss to feel bad. I needed him to feel bad. I was surprised by his shocked reaction in the book to the question a date once asked, "How can you even go on living?" After all, if you've killed someone, albeit accidentally, what other question would you ask yourself? I ask him why he reacted so strongly, and he says it was the result of two deep fears. "One was that maybe I shouldn't be living with myself – maybe I'm a bad person because I can. And the other was, maybe these feelings will get worse and I won't be able to deal with them."

But as I carried on reading, I wished Strauss felt better. I wished he hadn't had to have stomach surgery as a result of his guilt; I wished he hadn't contemplated suicide himself; I understood what he meant when he asked that accusatory date of his: "How much thinking about it would be enough?" Trying to find meaning in a death is like trying to find meaning in a canyon; you can keep going down, further and further, and it's still enormous, and it's still just a hole. He says in the book that he used to think if he and Celine had had their roles reversed he would like her not to have remembered him, but over the years he changed his mind because "if she'd been too comfortable with my dying, she wouldn't have remained a fully live person herself".

That's true. If you walked away from a car accident in which you had killed someone without feeling terrible, you wouldn't be human. If you responded to the death of a sibling with a shrug, you wouldn't be human either. The problem is that a surfeit of grief and guilt doesn't make you more human. Your pot doesn't fill up with goodness; your sadness doesn't alter what happened a whit. As Strauss writes: "Regret doesn't budge things; it seems crazy that the force of all that human want can't amend a moment, can't even stir a pebble."

I tell him how angry I was that the person who killed Gleave never contacted us, never even wrote a letter. "But, you know, it definitely did affect him," Strauss says gently. "One of the people I heard from after writing about this said his best friend in high school had hit a cyclist, and the cyclist died, and the friend seemed totally unaffected, and that almost ruined their friendship. Then, when he was 30, this friend committed suicide. So you never know what a person's dealing with. Maybe he didn't write to you, not because he was callous, but because he couldn't."

11 MARCH 2011

Drugs, murder and redemption

RORY CARROLL

It started one humid afternoon when a seven-year-old boy flicked something out of a school-bus window at a teenager on García de

Sena street. Some say it was a piece of popcorn, others a rolled up piece of paper. Whatever it was, the older boy took umbrage. He strode to the window and slapped the child, sending him home crying to El Cementerio, a few blocks up the hill.

The mother, aunts and sisters stomped down the hill and confronted the teenager, jabbed him, prompting his own female relatives to jab back. Insults flew. That night, shots were fired into El Cementerio. The neighbourhood did not see who was shooting but returned fire. And so began another war.

Eight months and multiple ambushes later, seven youths from El Cementerio are dead, as are an uncertain number of their rivals down the hill. Richard Nuñez, the soft-spoken leader of the Cementerio youths, lifts his T-shirt to show fresh scars on his belly, back and right arm. "They got me when I was riding past the police station, shot me right up." He survived, but wonders if he will be as lucky the next time. "Things are pretty hot. This isn't over."

Over. A hopeful word. As if the violence has a destination, an end point. This is Venezuela, where more than 14,000 people were murdered last year, according to human rights groups. That is about three times bloodier than Iraq, which has a similar population. The government does not publish full statistics but says the official murder rate is 48 per 100,000 people, more than double South America's average. Some estimate the rate in Caracas to be as high as 140 per 100,000, making it one of the world's deadliest capitals. Hospital emergency wards overflow, especially at weekends, with bleeding, punctured casualties. Corpses stack up in morgues while grief-stricken relatives gather outside, noses cupped against the smell.

What makes this corner of South America, once best known for oil and beauty queens, a Hobbesian lottery? The short answer is gangs. Young men with guns drop bodies as they battle over turf and drugs in winding, rubbish-strewn streets. The catch-all description for them is *malandros*, supposedly feral thugs and ne'er-do-wells perpetually at war with themselves and the rest of society. They inhabit, Venezuelans tell you, the land "up there": hillside barrios. *Malandros* flit across television screens and newspapers as cadavers or hooded suspects paraded by police. Either way, they are anonymous ciphers who do not speak, leaving their motivations, their world, incomprehensible to outsiders. A war over a piece of popcorn?

This is the story of one gang. Of its rise and fall and resurrection in a dusty, sun-baked slum, and of the reasons it does what it does. Some of the plots and characters make US crime dramas seem tame. There is the hitman who became a minister's bodyguard. The straight-A student suspected of black magic because no one can kill him. The mugger who found love while dodging police. The prison cannibal who found God. And the aristocratic rum merchant who proved an unlikely saviour. The narrative tilts between decay and hope, corruption and redemption.

Fifty years ago El Consejo was a sleepy farming village of 2,000 people ringed by sugar cane plantations. Today it is home to 50,000 people, none of whom farm, and whose brick-and-tin homes cling to steep slopes. It is a community marooned without jobs and proper housing by dysfunctional oil booms that stunted industry and agriculture.

Caracas is 60km east, at the end of a potholed motorway, but El Consejo feels like a ramshackle extension of it. Tucked into its concrete mazes, unmarked on most maps, is the two-block neighbourhood of El Cementerio, so named because it abuts a graveyard. Here, says Jimin Perez, a former police officer, is where you don't want to stop and ask directions. "The kids stick a gun in your face and steal your things. Then the adults dismantle your car for parts. If you make it out and go back with the police, no one has seen anything."

This is the fiefdom of the Cemetery gang: two narrow roads lined with bleached houses from which eyes appraise all who enter and leave. Everybody knows each other, and many are related. Most men are gone – absconded, dead, jailed – leaving wives and widows as matriarchs to raise broods alone. The nearest school, Manuel Cipriano Perez, is so overcrowded its 1,117 students are rotated in two shifts. Often there is no electricity or air conditioning, so pupils slump in the tropical heat. The computer room is locked and empty. "Children don't have many recreation options," says Damaris Costa, the director. "They throw stones at their own school."

A five-minute walk down the hill from El Cementerio brings you to identical-looking streets, but this is the territory of *Los Pelucos* (The Wigs), the other gang in the "popcorn war". Walk 10 minutes west and you are in the territory of the *5 de Julio* (Fifth of July) gang. It too is at war with El Cementerio but over a motorbike stolen in 2008. Bubbling under these disputes is competition to sell drugs, mostly cannabis and cocaine, to outsiders.

Wedged in by bigger rivals, El Cementerio has responded with tough leaders, none more so than Darwin Ospino, aka *Pata Piche*, or Rotten Foot. The nickname is ironic. Fastidious about deodorant and aftershave, Ospino is the neighbourhood's closest thing to a metrosexual. His fame, however, rests on reputedly having killed 26 people, a number that happens to match his current age. His first gun was a 765 revolver. "It felt like a trophy," he says, perched on his bed, freshly showered. "The first time I used it? A party. A gang showed up, made some trouble..." Ospino's voice trails off. He does not care to dwell on the details.

Alberto Vollmer, who owns a rum company that rehabilitates local gangsters, is more open. "Darwin was the hitman. He started at 16 and is still a legend around here. He's respected even by his enemies." Some stories are particularly chilling – dragging people from homes and families and shooting them in the face, killing a woman's husband, then killing her second husband after she remarried – but Ospino's manner is courteous and quiet, even diffident. "My papa abandoned us when I was small," he says, when prompted. Ambitions for the future? "Stay alive and be a good father." He has two young children but is separated from the mother.

Ospino apparently stopped killing in 2003 when, en masse, the Cementerio gang, exhausted from ever-present danger and stress, joined the rehab programme run by Vollmer's Santa Teresa rum company. Ospino, who inspired such fear that victims' relatives never pressed charges, was hired as a bodyguard by a government minister, Jesse Chacón. All went well for five years until he was accused of another killing, which he denies. Until the case is heard, a court has confined Ospino to the Santa Teresa hacienda, which he patrols on a motorbike. "If he goes to prison he's a dead man, he's got too many enemies," says Vollmer.

Venezuela has no capital punishment but prison is often a death sentence. On average more than 420 inmates die violently each year, according to the Prison Observatory, a watchdog group. A system designed for 14,000 holds 38,000, most of them on remand. Guards control, at most, the perimeter, leaving inmates to fend for themselves. A September riot in Tocoron jail, which serves El Consejo, officially left 16 dead but families say the true figure is higher. Images recorded on mobile phones show bodies, some decapitated and dismembered, being piled on to a pickup truck.

Outsiders are denied access, but in a phone interview one Tocoron inmate, Luis Viña, related atrocities from his 16 years at different prisons. Speaking machine-gun fast between gulps of air, exhilarated by contact with the outside world, the convicted rapist and murderer's litany of horrors included beheading a rival and eating his brains: "He was making problems for me." Viña is not insane: it was an effective message to others not to mess with the cannibal. He has been forsaken by his family but not Jesus, he says. "With God's help I have recovered my values."

When Ospino led about three dozen foot soldiers in 2003 into the rehab programme, which is called Alcatraz, the Cementerio gang briefly disappeared. Instead of robbing and getting high, members went camping, took training courses and grappled with rugby – an idea of Vollmer's to make them equal through learning an alien sport. After graduating, many found jobs as security guards, bottlers and cooks on the hacienda. "You could see their faces physically change," says Vollmer, a Venezuelan anglophile of German descent. "At first the muscles were really tense, and gradually they relaxed."

Alcatraz is a success story: local murder rates fell, attracting interest from the government and Harvard academics. Graduates such as Juan Silva, 30, a former drug addict, turned their lives around. Watching him at home playing with his three young children, dog and cats while his wife makes lunch, it is difficult to imagine him killing. But he did. "When I think back to that bus driver, it hurts. I think of him as a father and a husband, a human being. I cut his throat with a bottle. It was almost an obligation in the gang to show you were hard, to earn respect. I was 15, maybe 16."

One day, aged 19, Silva mugged a bus passenger for her jewellery. He fled on foot and caught another bus, conscious of a police patrol ahead. Seated behind him was a pretty girl. "I wanted to say something cute to her but the only thing I could think of was: 'Will you hide my revolver?'" he recalls. The girl smiled and hid it in her purse. Love was born. The couple dated, married and Yainna, now 27, laughs at the memory. "What can I say? I liked him." Evangelical Christians, they pray every day. When not bottling at the rum factory, Silva coaches football and at night studies mechanics.

You hear a similar story from Williams Duran, 30, a wiry, cheerful bundle of energy. "I was a drug addict and thief for so long I robbed everything. But now I'm straight, have a job as a cook, a wife, two kids. I've even got furniture and a bank account."

It would be nice to end the story there but the Cemetery gang, along with other groups that entered rehab, has revived. Shops and houses have barred windows and fresh bullet holes, and kidnappings plague the area. Luis Yuraima, the 20-year-old son of a shopkeeper, has just been rescued after four days in the hands of the *Pelucos*, who demanded an $83,000 (£52,000) ransom. How was he treated? Without a word he pulls off his T-shirt: purple slashes and puncture wounds cover his back. Johnny Brito, owner of the La Estación cafe, is downbeat about the future. "Some guys get rehabilitated, great, but there's always a new generation behind them," he says.

When Ospino and others entered the hacienda, the vacuum in El Cementerio did not last long. A new leader, José Daniel Nuñez, aka Kibiri, emerged. It was not out of choice but necessity, says his brother, Richard. "Others were coming into our neighbourhood, threatening people. We had to defend ourselves." Kibiri, by common consent, is exceptionally bright. Top of his class, articulate, wily, he is also, depending how you look at it, incredibly lucky or unlucky. Seven years ago, aged 15, he was ambushed and shot 14 times. He survived and hobbled out of hospital, one-eyed, ostensibly reborn. He entered the rehab programme and befriended those who had shot him. Then he killed them. "One at a time," says Richard.

Kibiri was expelled by Alcatraz, caught by police and jailed. Inside, somebody stabbed him 13 times. Again, he survived. "People think he's made a pact with the devil, that he's immortal," says Jimin Perez, the former police officer who now runs the Alcatraz project. Belief in *santería*, a voodoo-tinged African-Caribbean import, is widespread, especially among gangsters who pray to *santos malandros*, holy thugs, for success and survival.

Who else, after all, can they turn to? According to the police many of the gangsters' mothers deal drugs. The head of the neighbourhood association allegedly is the main supplier, with a sideline renting revolvers. The state is largely absent save for the police, and their reputation for brutality and corruption rivals that of the gangs. "We learned that the police are more criminal than the criminals," says the ever-blunt Vollmer. "They outsource crimes to the gangs."

Asked about cops, a group of El Cementerio teenagers stop kicking a deflated football to volunteer anecdotes. They sell you 50 bullets for 400 bolivares ($48), says Carlos Noguera, a topless, chubby 15-year-old. He knows about bullets: more than 30 mangled the features of his older brother, a casualty of the popcorn war. If police catch you with drugs or guns they let you go for 100 bolivares, says Juan Carlos Nuñez, also 15. If you're clean they plant stuff so you still have to pay, says his older brother, Richard. Police accidentally shot dead the Nuñez boys' grandmother while chasing a suspect through their home.

Perez, the grizzled former cop, does not deny any of it and has his own stories, including that of two officers who raped a woman in a park. A request to interview the police chief for Aragua state, which includes El Consejo, was declined on the grounds he did not know the Guardian's "political leanings". Even the likes of Inspector Enrique Aray, a dedicated, honest cop who patrols slums in east Caracas, admits ignorance about gangs. "We don't have good information," he says, peering from his Jeep at shadowy figures who flit across his headlights on a rainy, gloomy night. Later, when two shots crack in the distance, he smiles apologetically. "A .38. It's normal here."

With Darwin Ospino confined to the rum hacienda, and Kibiri in jail awaiting trial for murder, the Cementerio gang's fate hangs in the balance. The popcorn war's origins are petty, but if the gang does not prevail, or at least keep fighting, it will forfeit clout, and with it drug sales, to rivals. Kibiri's natural successor is Richard. Smart like his brother, and physically similar, the 18-year-old must decide between taking the crown or breaking with family tradition and pursuing a legitimate career. "He is softer, more gentle," says his mother, Yelitza. A tough matriarch, it's not clear she means it as a compliment.

"I've been in shoot-outs but haven't killed anyone," says Richard, seated in a barely furnished living room. On top of a closet, peeking from folded jeans, is a revolver. He acknowledges it, shrugs. "I won't kill. That's not me." He sighs and rubs the bullet scar on his belly. "This life, always afraid, looking around the corner, over your shoulder ... it's not good."

Richard has a fantasy that one day the father he has not seen in two years will drop by, share an empanada and take him out to a movie. "We'd just sit there, watching it, with a Coke." His thousand-watt smile lights at the thought. He knows it won't happen. His father lives just one hour away but rival gangs would spot him entering and leaving and assume he was delivering bullets or drugs. "They'd kill him."

Against the odds, Richard has stayed in school and is on the verge of graduating. He is thinking, he says, of becoming a mechanic. A crumbling home on a dusty hill in Venezuela, and a young life that must choose between two paths. One filled with danger, good money, prestige and the chance to "defend" the community. The other filled with long hours, a minimum wage and a lesser but still real chance of getting killed just because some kid flicked a possible piece of popcorn. Which would you choose?

18 MARCH 2011

A day at the races

JULIAN GLOVER

Cheltenham is a town of peeling stucco, imperial avenues and festivals. There are famous events for jazz and books, science and classical music – and then this week, and for me the best of all, the annual four-day jump race meeting.

Highbrow to lowbrow, some might sneer: 50,000 inebriates all cheering a field of small men on large horses. But the Cheltenham Festival, which ends today with the Gold Cup, is more than that because, unlike so much modern sport, it hasn't been drained of life by commerce, with the spectator reduced to an item in a business transaction and the thrills distilled and predictable.

You don't watch the festival. You really do take part as well: you cheer, stamp, shout, sing, bet and drink. You can cross the course and stare up the famous final hill whose punishing incline is disguised by television – a freedom that will hopefully survive the idiotic protester who ran on to the course during a race yesterday. You can almost touch the horses as they walk on to the course from the parade ring; and look up at jockeys who take huge risks but get few of the rewards loaded on the mollycoddled football superstars.

Without its crowd, Cheltenham would be nothing. I doubt there is any more joyous or energising experience on the planet this week than standing, as I did, in the happy company of others, screaming support as the winners and losers come home. This is an event largely without malevolence: not tribal, or angry. Everyone is more or less on the same side, which is why despite the crowds (a quarter of a million people over four days) there isn't much need for security or control. It can be a bit shambolic, mournful even as the drunks roll home poorer after the last race of the day, but there is a strong sense of collective human experience.

Escapism is often used as a derogatory term, but this grim spring we should value events that allow us to run away for a time from the world's troubles.

Millions of people are now queueing up online with their credit cards to buy seats for the Olympics in London. "The greatest tickets on earth", organisers claim – but I doubt this slick multibillion-pound event will match the raw joy to be found at a shabby racecourse by a gridlocked road outside a town in the west of England.

Britain, I suspect, can be broken into two parts: one that has never heard of the Cheltenham Festival and one that adores it. Ireland – which, as everyone always says, is part of what gives the festival its spirit – is different. There everyone knows about Cheltenham. But to the British it is a secret world: a club that draws out the sort of people for whom metropolitan fashions matter little. It is classless, in that it mixes classes with none of the pretension attached to the great fixtures of summer flat racing, events as horribly flashy as gold and crystal on a designer Swiss watch.

Cheltenham is more about mud than money. Yes, huge amounts are bet, the best horses are expensive, and only millionaires can afford to train them. But jump racing isn't a rich industry or even a financially viable one – especially after the Irish financial crisis – and the connection between the amateur sport and the best is strong. From time to time, the National Velvet tale of the home-bred nag who steals victory from the favourite comes true.

Of course there are risks, to the horses – some, happily not many, are injured or killed – and to the jockeys, whose bodies are battered and whose every bone looks in danger of being broken.

It can't be denied that the risk is part of the thrill: if jump racing were safe it would be dressage.

But I don't think the attraction is the cruelty; rather the sense that mundane rules that apply to so much else about life are lifted for a time. In that sense Cheltenham is liberated, a place that really doesn't have too much to do with officialdom. It is everything the smart middle classes claim for the Glastonbury Festival, a step out of usual life – except that I think Glastonbury's claim to anarchy is contrived. If you really want to tune in, turn on and drop out, come to Cheltenham.

19 MARCH 2011

Safe in their hands?

MARGARET DRABBLE

The threatened NHS has been much in all our minds this week, and, pestered by online petitions and appeals for support, I've been going over my long relationship with it. Our experiences of the NHS are woven deeply into the fabric of our lives, and most of mine have been good. All my children were born and cared for on the NHS, and have been well served by it. And for those nearing the end of life, my GP used to bake and ice a cake for each of his patients who reached the age of 100.

It has been a recurrent theme in my fiction, as it has been an integral part of my life. The narrator of The Millstone (1966), a young unmarried mother, in a central confrontational scene, actually delivers herself of the line "I love the National Health Service", while insisting on access to her sick baby in Great

Ormond Street hospital. How things have changed since then, and sometimes for the better. When I went to visit my granddaughter a few years ago, as she recovered from minor surgery, the atmosphere was festive. Our generation of mothers had complained, we had made ourselves heard, and life on the wards had improved. That's how it worked, and should work. It is for us, it is ours, and the professionals do listen.

And now we seem to be on the brink of losing all of this. It isn't wholly unexpected. I predicted creeping privatisation in my 1996 satirical condition-of-England novel, The Witch of Exmoor, written at the somewhat ridiculous and squalid end of the failing Major government. We had already become wary about the selling off of public assets and services into private hands – gas, water, prisons, railways. One of the novel's more sympathetic characters, an advertising man, works for a firm which is given the task of updating "the corporate image of the National Health Service".

"Update is the word that is used: alter is what is meant. It has become clearer, as we approach the end of the 20th century, that we cannot afford a National Health Service for everybody, all the time. Some may have kidney transplants and some may not. Some may have their varicose veins tended, and some may not. Some may live to be 90, and some may not. So we must alter the perceptions of the people. We must adjust their expectations. We must encourage private health insurance ... We must reassure the rich that they have a right to what they want provided that they pay so much for it that the surgeons, the anaesthetists, the insurance brokers, the insurance companies and the shareholders all get what they want too. And they want a lot ... This makes healthcare very expensive indeed, and ever more inaccessible. There is no justice, no equity in this situation. Nobody would choose this if their eyes were veiled by ignorance, for each of us knows that we may pull the short straw. We can't all imagine being poor, but we can all imagine being disastrously, expensively, prohibitively ill."

The reference in this passage to John Rawls's classic concept of the "veil of ignorance" – which encourages us all to imagine in what kind of society, under what kind of healthcare regime we would choose to live if we knew we had to choose a personal outcome blindfold – haunted me much at that time, and still does. We know we wouldn't choose the pre-Obama US system, with its ludicrous insurance premiums and its neglected multitudes. I think we would all cling to the NHS, that brilliant and beautiful construction that has meant so much to my generation. You could call it an irrational devotion – I was struck by the reference, in Julia Langdon's recent fine obituary of Susan Crosland, to the way she had bought her husband Tony Crosland's politics "like someone buys a watch as a work of art because the mechanism is so beautifully constructed, and not because it tells the time particularly well". Yes, maybe we were emotional, irrational in our devotion. But in our time, the NHS did serve us well, and we long for it to continue to do so.

Some of us old lefties were tempted to believe David Cameron when he said the NHS was safe in his hands, its funding ring-fenced. We weren't persuaded to vote for him, but when the coalition came to power we hoped for the best. Cameron had shown himself human and vulnerable through his son's illness and need for years of care, he seemed to know there were some things money can't buy, and he had said all the right things about doctors and nurses. He looked eager, young, well-meaning. The Lib Dems also ought to have been reliably NHS-friendly – had not the Liberal party been at the forefront of its creation in the 1940s? Neither party had put anything about radical NHS reform in their manifestos – quite the reverse. Yet today we find this friendly summer coalition combining to present us with a package of proposals that is causing alarm throughout the electorate and the medical profession – except, perhaps, in the bosoms of those super-doctor-banker GPs who are looking forward to the £300,000-a-year salary predicted in a Guardian report earlier this week.

We know that demands on the NHS have increased enormously in the four decades since The Millstone was written. Expectations are higher, patients are less patient, more and more miraculous interventions have been discovered. We concede that mounting claims on the NHS compel constant reviews of funding and assessment of what is value for money. Triage is necessary (the heroine of one of my late novels, The Red Queen (2004) is writing a book on "Triage in the NHS", a clear sign that the problem had been preoccupying me for some time), NICE guidelines are necessary, some new drugs are extraordinarily costly, we cannot have everything for free. This is not a new problem. In the 1990s, I interviewed various people in the healthcare business, and was persuaded that we ought to take more seriously the notion of compulsory health insurance, as required by some successful European health services. This wouldn't be a private Bupa-style scheme, a speculative, competitive, for-profit scheme, but a basic insurance to top up the national insurance we'd all been paying for years anyway.

Some of the private insurance people I met while researching my fiction were amazing. They were like those timeshare salesmen in the Canaries who try to tie you into contracts that make you go on paying for nothing long after you are dead, while persuading you it is all in your own best interests and an amazing bargain at that. Nobody can have failed to notice the recent rash of pale-blue Bupa adverts in newspapers, magazines and on hoardings, where smiling, carefully posed and chosen models assure you that all will be well if you sign up now. Join Bupa and you will never die. If most of us belonged to private health schemes, in that pale blue but slightly menacing world, the insurance companies would be a lot richer, and the NHS could concentrate on the unprotected and the indigent. Is that the plan?

Of course, those who can afford it may feel safer with private health insurance. (I've never had any and never will, unless everybody else has to by law, in which case I would pay my share willingly, as I pay my taxes.) Some in regular employment get a package that includes insurance as a taxable benefit. But what will happen to the rest of us, if the NHS fails us, if we get increasingly – as we will – a two-tier service, for the rich and the poor, for the insured and the uninsured?

I am not clever enough to be able to read the government's real agenda, and I am sure the government hopes that most of us are even more stupid than me. But I have been tipped off to look out for affordability expert Paul Kirby, new head of policy development at No 10, and author of a paper called Payment for Success. Mr Kirby believes in promoting the "disciplined freedoms enjoyed by the private and voluntary sectors in real markets, where organisations are financially disciplined by the need to earn their living from paying customers by beating the competition". His argument seems to imply that contracts will be awarded to "any willing provider" on a cost basis, surely a dangerous notion – we wouldn't hire a builder to fix our roof on that basis, let alone a doctor to fix our heart disease, or a nurse to tend our dying mother.

The spirit of commercial competition and the motives of financial gain are not appropriate to a health service, and phrases like "beating the competition" have no place in it. The true spirit of the NHS was a treasure beyond price, beyond valuation, and it has been one of the glories of our time, one of those great ennobling concepts that changed the way we live and feel about ourselves and our country.

The NHS cannot be perfect. We all know true stories of patients who feel forced to go private because of inadequate diagnoses, or who seek specialist interventions not readily available. We know of elderly people who would rather die than be put back in hospital. Susan Crosland herself, like me an emotional believer, contracted the superbug MRSA in a London NHS hospital. Her faith had not inoculated her. But it is my conviction, as a committed "consumer" of NHS healthcare, that during my lifetime the NHS has improved. I would like to think that The Millstone played its small part in improving the way parents and children are treated. We cannot throw all this away in favour of an American system where you can't cross the threshold until they've swiped your credit card.

19 MARCH 2011

Stories from across the tsunami zone as survivors count the cost

JONATHAN WATTS

A week after the deadliest disaster in modern Japanese history, Shigeki Matsumoto has moved from terror and tragedy to a determined search for closure.

Last Friday, a massive earthquake shook his world, then a tsunami took his mother. Since then, he has travelled across the mountains every day in a search for her remains in the wasteland of Ryoishi – a narrow coastal valley in Iwate prefecture that was once their family home.

"The body could be anywhere. But even if I could find her clothes or shoes, I'd be satisfied," the factory worker says, choking back a sob. "The rescue workers here have told me to stop looking, but I'll come back again tomorrow and the day after."

Similar stories can be heard across the disaster zone, where nearly half a million refugees are struggling to accept the devastating loss of homes, hopes and loved ones.

After marking the first week with a minute's silence on Friday, the central government wants the country to look forward in a more positive spirit.

"We do not have room to be pessimistic or discouraged. We are going to create Japan once again from scratch," the prime minister, Naoto Kan, said in a televised speech.

But while bulldozers and earthmovers have started to clear the charred carcasses of buildings so that roads, railways and shops can reopen, it is proving more difficult to sweep away terrifying memories and the enormous loss of life, which has still to be properly calculated and processed.

Take the burned-out husk of Otsuchi. Despite a devastated landscape that resembles the aftermath of carpet bombing, the official death toll here is 274 out of a population of 15,000 people.

This is based only on the bodies that have been found so far and does not include victims who may have been buried or washed out to sea.

Kozoh Hirano, the deputy chief of the city's disaster relief headquarters, admits this may prove far short of the final figure.

"We just don't know how many people died here," says the city official, who narrowly escaped with his own life. "If I estimate, it's frightening. There might be 1,000 or more. "

It is a similar story nationwide. The official death toll, according to the National Police Agency, is 6,900 confirmed dead and thousands more reported missing.

This is already Japan's worst disaster in more than 60 years, but it is almost certainly a major underestimate, given the damage.

Bodies are still being found in the rubble and washing up on the shores of Iwate and Miyagi prefectures. Identification is not always easy, which can add to the confusion and trauma of bereavement.

Matsumoto believes his mother is dead. He was at work in a nearby city when the tsunami struck. "As soon as I saw it, I called home. It rang and rang, but there was no answer. I wanted to tell my mother to run. But it was too late."

After spending that first night shivering in his car with his wife, he walked across the hills to the family home, where survivors described how his mother was unable to reach safety on high ground.

His search for her remains has taken him to several temporary morgues in school gymnasiums. At one, police said a quarter of the 100-plus bodies had still to be identified. They remain wrapped in tarpaulin. Most of the rest are in white coffins. Loved ones come to burn incense and place flowers, sake and favourite food on the coffins.

They too, though, must wait for the customary closure. Normally, once a body is identified, the family take it away and prepare for cremation.

But this is impossible for the many people who have lost their homes. The huge number of bodies and the shortage of fuel has also overwhelmed the capacity of the local crematorium, which takes two hours to burn each body.

Officials are now considering whether to use crematoriums in neighbouring cities, including those in Morioka – more than 100km away. A decision must be made soon. The bodies have kept in reasonable condition thanks to the freezing weather, but the issue of how to deal with corpses is becoming an increasingly urgent concern.

"The bodies are very important, though the priority is the living," said Daiji Matsui, head of the press office in Kamaishi city. "We need to consider the living standards of the evacuees."

Temporary shelters in the city now house 9,883 people – almost a quarter of the population. Their conditions remain dire, although medicine and food shortages have eased and most people can now eat two meals a day instead of the single rice ball they had up to a few days ago.

At the Kamaishi No 1 middle school, hundreds of people snuggle under blankets in the gymnasium and huddle around a handful of kerosene heaters as the temperature plunges below zero. The main electricity supply has been cut off since the earthquake. A small generator provides enough power for a few small lamps, but when night falls, a gloom descends on the refuge.

"It's very cold, especially when it snows outside," said Chikano Fujima, an 85-year-old geisha, who had to leave her kimonos behind when she was carried to safety just moments before the tsunami tore through her home. The professional musician and former courtesan is now bundled in thick clothes and blankets, which make her initially reluctant to pose for a photograph. Her appearance, however, is the least of her worries.

Her loss is economic and cultural. Fujima sensei – as she is known locally – is the last geisha in the city. She performs at city festivals, teaches young people the arts of dancing and shamisen playing, and lends out expensive kimonos. They are all lost, along with twenty obi belts worth 1m yen each and a shamisen instrument, also worth 1m yen. Of greater concern to her is the loss of her legacy. An apprentice, whom Fujima was grooming to inherit her role, died in the tsunami.

"I have no insurance. It's the end. My life is over," she said. "And I'm the last who could teach these skills."

The stress has taken its toll, particularly during the five days she had to manage without her medication. Her blood pressure surged from 130 to 224 until Thursday, when doctors arrived with the necessary tablets. She was fortunate. Other refuges have reported several deaths of elderly evacuees who survived the tsunami only to succumb to the cold and hunger of the shelters.

Many believe the long-term impact of the tsunami will be on their health and mental wellbeing as well as their wallets. Mitsuko Hanaishi, a former nurse, saw 200,000 yen get washed away that she had just withdrawn to pay for a ceremony for her late husband. Her home is destroyed and she has no insurance. "I'd move to the city to work, but I am too old," said the 68-year-old. "My health is declining. I've never had high blood pressure before, but it has gone up since the disaster. "

She is still traumatised by the recollection of the tsunami. "It was like a monster that got nearer and nearer," she said. "It's frightening. I've had to get medicine because I cannot sleep." Many of the survivors said the drills and sea walls that had been put in place to prepare for a tsunami proved totally inadequate because the earthquake and water surge that followed were far in excess of all forecasts.

Public signs indicate which areas are supposed to be safe and which dangerous. But they too were swamped and are now surrounded on all sides by devastation.

Officials say the rebuilding plans will inevitably include stronger sea defences, though this alone is unlikely to reassure residents, many of whom want to move out after the horrifying experience of natural disaster followed by a shortage of necessities.

"We are not used to food queues and having to cope with only two meals a day," said Matsumoto. "Only the generation who lived through the war have such an experience."

But that physical hardship is easier to endure than the emotional trauma of losing a mother and not being able to find her remains.

"I have not been sleeping well. My eyes open at 3am and then I can't get back to sleep," says Matsumoto, although he had his first partial success during that day's search.

"Today, I found a photo of my aunt that we had on our family shrine. I'm very pleased. I might be able to sleep tonight."

21 MARCH 2011

War rains down on Libya

CHRIS MCGREAL

The dozen or so men clustered behind the last smouldering tank looked as if they had died while they slept.

Their blankets bore no burn marks so perhaps it was the force of blasts – powerful enough to rip the turrets off the Russian-made tanks and toss them 20 metres or more across the open field near Benghazi – that killed Muammar Gaddafi's soldiers.

The air attack came at 4am yesterday, after the tanks pulled back from a day-long assault on the rebel stronghold of Benghazi. The crews chose to rest in a field about 10 miles from the de facto capital of the anti-Gaddafi revolutionaries.

It must have seemed safe to the soldiers. The rebels were far away and the tank crews would have seen any threat approaching by road. They gathered to eat and sleep behind the tank furthest into the field.

But it was no protection from the threat in the sky. The tanks and their operators were sitting ducks in the open and probably never heard the planes. The French pilots did not even have to be concerned about the risk of harming civilians.

Within moments, three of the four tanks in the field were shells.

What was not immediately incinerated was mangled, thrown into the sky and dumped in bits on the earth. Machine guns twisted into grotesque shapes, broken engine parts and flattened shells lay among the wreckage.

Four hours later, two of the tanks were still smouldering. A flatbed lorry used to haul them to the edge of Benghazi was on fire. A handful of pickup trucks, one carrying tins of food for the troops, had been burned out. Scavengers were picking over the corpses of Gaddafi's dead soldiers.

Wreckage was strewn in similar scenes along nearly 15 miles of road beyond Benghazi, the result of air strikes on targets across the country that turned the struggle between Gaddafi and Libya's revolutionaries on its head in a moment.

The barrage of attacks led by France, Britain and the US on Libya's army, airbases and other military targets drew threats of a prolonged war from Gaddafi himself. But on the ground many of his forces were in disarray and fleeing in fear of further attacks from a new and unseen enemy.

The air assault halted and then reversed the advances by Gaddafi's army on Benghazi and other rebel-held towns. But yesterday the revolutionary leadership wanted more. It appealed for an intensification of the air assault to destroy the Libyan ruler's forces and open the way for the rebels to drive him from power.

The first of the decapitated tanks sat just three miles outside Benghazi, but perhaps its crew was luckier than others. There were no bodies to be found and from the boxes of dates and long-life milk lying on the ground a short walk across the field, it appears they may have been far enough away to survive the blast and flee.

Another seven miles farther on lay a larger tank graveyard, at al-Wafia, and beyond that many more miles of destruction on the road toward Ajdabiya. Eight tanks, brought up to Benghazi to continue the terrifying assault on the city that began on Saturday, were destroyed altogether. More than a dozen other armoured vehicles were wrecked, their remnants scattered on the scorched tarmac.

A couple of multiple rocket launchers sat at the roadside. One appeared to have no damage at all. Perhaps it broke down, or maybe its driver decided to get away from it fast – part of the intended effect of the air strikes to break the will of Gaddafi's army to fight.

Young rebels, known as *shabab*, danced on the armoured carcasses. They fired guns and chanted: "Here come the shabab. Gaddafi is finished."

Western powers leading the air assault said again that the attacks are about protecting civilians from Gaddafi, not regime change. But many of the revolutionaries see the coalition forces as fighting on their behalf.

The air bombardment is regarded among rebel military commanders as creating a more level battlefield by removing Gaddafi's advantage of heavy armour.

"There must be more attacks, to destroy his forces and heavy weapons," said Kamal Mustafa Mahmoud, a rebel soldier on the edge of Benghazi. "Then they can leave Gaddafi to us. We know how to fight him but we are afraid of his heavy weapons. I want them to destroy the ground forces of Gaddafi."

A rebel commander in Benghazi, Ahmed al-Diwani, said that the air strikes open the way for the rebels to retake the towns they have lost in recent fighting and then continue their campaign toward Tripoli. But he acknowledged that it would be wrong to assume that the government's army is a spent force because of the air strikes.

"Gaddafi's advantage was tanks and rockets. That was what was defeating us. When we did not face them we were winning. Now we can go forward again. We will still have to fight, but when they see that they cannot win, it will be over," he said.

As Gaddafi's soldiers fled from around Benghazi after the air assault, the rebels seized the advantage to move back toward Ajdabiya, a town the two sides have battled over for nearly a week. Late yesterday, people in the town said Gaddafi's forces could no longer be seen.

The revolution's political leadership shares the fighters' view that the air assault is about regime change.

Salwa el-Deghali, of the national transitional council, said: "I'm happy the air strikes have started, but at the same time I'm worried that the international community will not keep up the attacks long enough to remove Gaddafi. There must be more attacks on Gaddafi's forces, and fast. We need these attacks until he is crushed."

Asked if she thought the goal of the air attacks was regime change, she replied: "Yes, it's to push him from power."

Deghali said that the revolutionary leadership is counting on the air assault to destroy Gaddafi's army, either by killing its soldiers or encouraging them to desert. She said that when the threat of violent repression is removed, the council plans to call on Libyans to rise up in cities across the country.

"When Gaddafi's forces are destroyed, he will have no power. It will be easy to press forward," she said.

Essam Gheriani, a spokesman for the national council, said that with the air strikes destabilising Gaddafi, the revolutionaries would organise fresh popular uprisings in cities still under the Libyan leader's control, in the belief that it will be difficult for him to find the forces to put them down.

However, beyond the broad plans to blend popular uprisings with armed resistance, the revolutionary council does not appear as yet to have decided how to take advantage of the shift in the military situation.

Some of its members fled Benghazi during the government's assault on Saturday. Others remain trapped in Gaddafi-controlled areas.

For all the revolutionaries' appeals for foreign help, there are limits. Deghali reiterated the condition laid down since the beginning of the uprising: the air assault is welcomed, but foreign troops will not be accepted on Libyan soil. The country's history of occupation by the Italians and strong views about the invasion of Iraq have created a deep-seated suspicion of foreign armies.

"We don't want what happened in Iraq with international intervention," she said. "Foreign troops on the ground, no. Just the air strikes."

22 MARCH 2011

Why Fukushima made me stop worrying and love nuclear power

GEORGE MONBIOT

You will not be surprised to hear that the events in Japan have changed my view of nuclear power. You will be surprised to hear how they have changed it. As a result of the disaster at Fukushima, I am no longer nuclear-neutral. I now support the technology.

A crappy old plant with inadequate safety features was hit by a monster earthquake and a vast tsunami. The electricity supply failed, knocking out the cooling system. The reactors began to explode and melt down. The disaster exposed a familiar legacy of poor design and corner-cutting. Yet, as far as we know, no one has yet received a lethal dose of radiation.

Some greens have wildly exaggerated the dangers of radioactive pollution. For a clearer view, look at the graphic published by xkcd.com. It shows that the average total dose from the Three Mile Island disaster for someone living within 10 miles of the plant was one 625th of the maximum yearly amount permitted for US radiation workers. This, in turn, is half of the lowest one-year dose clearly linked to an increased cancer risk, which, in its turn, is one 80th of an invariably fatal exposure. I'm not proposing complacency here. I am proposing perspective.

If other forms of energy production caused no damage, these impacts would weigh more heavily. But energy is like medicine: if there are no side-effects, the chances are that it doesn't work.

Like most greens, I favour a major expansion of renewables. I can also sympathise with the complaints of their opponents. It's not just the onshore windfarms that bother people, but also the new grid connections (pylons and power lines). As the proportion of renewable electricity on the grid rises, more pumped storage will be needed to keep the lights on. That means reservoirs on mountains: they aren't popular, either.

The impacts and costs of renewables rise with the proportion of power they supply, as the need for storage and redundancy increases. It may well be the case (I have yet to see a comparative study) that up to a certain grid penetration – 50% or 70%, perhaps? – renewables have smaller carbon impacts than nuclear, while beyond that point, nuclear has smaller impacts than renewables.

Like others, I have called for renewable power to be used both to replace the electricity produced by fossil fuel and to expand the total supply, displacing the oil used for transport and the gas used for heating fuel. Are we also to demand that it replaces current nuclear capacity? The more work we expect renewables to do, the greater the impact on the landscape will be, and the tougher the task of public persuasion.

But expanding the grid to connect people and industry to rich, distant sources of ambient energy is also rejected by most of the greens who complained about the blog post I wrote last week in which I argued that nuclear remains safer than coal. What they want, they tell me, is something quite different: we should power down and produce our energy locally. Some have even called for the abandonment of the grid. Their bucolic vision sounds lovely, until you read the small print.

At high latitudes like ours, most small-scale ambient power production is a dead loss. Generating solar power in the UK involves a spectacular waste of scarce resources. It's hopelessly inefficient and poorly matched to the pattern of demand. Wind power in populated areas is largely worthless. This is partly because we have built our settlements in sheltered places; partly because turbulence caused by the buildings interferes with the airflow and chews up the mechanism. Micro-hydropower might work for a farmhouse in Wales, but it's not much use in Birmingham.

And how do we drive our textile mills, brick kilns, blast furnaces and electric railways – not to mention advanced industrial processes? Rooftop solar panels? The moment you consider the demands of the whole economy is the moment at which you fall out of love with local energy production. A national (or, better still, international) grid is the essential prerequisite for a largely renewable energy supply.

Some greens go even further: why waste renewable resources by turning them into electricity? Why not use them to provide energy directly? To answer this question, look at what happened in Britain before the industrial revolution.

The damming and weiring of British rivers for watermills was small-scale, renewable, picturesque and devastating. By blocking the rivers and silting up the spawning beds, they helped bring to an end the gigantic runs of migratory fish that were once among our great natural spectacles and which fed much of Britain – wiping out sturgeon, lampreys and shad, as well as most sea trout and salmon.

Traction was intimately linked with starvation. The more land that was set aside for feeding draught animals for industry and transport, the less was available for feeding humans. It was the 17th-century equivalent of today's biofuels crisis. The same applied to heating fuel. As EA Wrigley points out in his book Energy and the English Industrial Revolution, the 11m tonnes of coal mined in England in 1800 produced as much energy as 11m acres of woodland (one third of the land surface) would have generated.

Before coal became widely available, wood was used not just for heating homes but also for industrial processes: if half the land surface of Britain had been covered with woodland, Wrigley shows, we could have made 1.25m tonnes of bar iron a year (a fraction of current consumption) and nothing else. Even with a much lower population than today's, manufactured goods in the land-based economy were the preserve of the elite. Deep green energy production – decentralised, based on the products of the land – is far more damaging to humanity than nuclear meltdown.

But the energy source to which most economies will revert if they shut down their nuclear plants is not wood, water, wind or sun, but fossil fuel. On every measure (climate change, mining impact, local pollution, industrial injury and death, even radio-active discharges), coal is 100 times worse than nuclear power. Thanks to the expansion of shale gas production, the impacts of natural gas are catching up fast.

Yes, I still loathe the liars who run the nuclear industry. Yes, I would prefer to see the entire sector shut down, if there were harmless alternatives. But there are no ideal solutions. Every energy technology carries a cost; so does the absence of energy technologies. Atomic energy has just been subjected to one of the harshest possible tests, and the impact on people and the planet has been small. The crisis at Fukushima has converted me to the cause of nuclear power.

22 MARCH 2011

Digested read: Wonders of the Universe by Professor Brian Cox

JOHN CRACE

The universe is amazing. You are amazing. I am amazing. For we are all one. Everything we are, everything that's ever been and everything that will ever be was all forged in the same moment of creation 13.7bn years ago from an unimaginably hot and dense volume of matter less than the size of an atom. And that is amazing. What happened before then in the Planck epoch is a matter of conjecture; we lack a theory of quantum gravity, though some believe the universe was formed from a collision of two pieces of space and time floating for ever in an infinite space, but I feel I'm losing you at this point, which isn't so amazing.

So let's go to the Temple of Karnak at Luxor to watch the sunrise. Because in the beginning was the same light that now reflects the deep hazel of my eyes as I stare into the middle distance. By following this light we have mapped our place among the hundreds of billions of stars in the Milky Way and we have looked backward in time almost to the dawn of creation.

Light is amazing. It is both particles and waves, oscillating electric and magnetic fields propelling each other through space at a finite speed of 299,792,458 metres per second. It's hard for us to comprehend just how fast this is, so here I am in a jet fighter travelling at the speed of sound, which is a lot slower but still very fast. And now I'm at Victoria Falls, looking at the rainbow arcing across the sky. Try to imagine the colours of the spectrum as a way into redshift and the invisible light of the cosmic micro-wave background. I did say try.

High up in the Himalayas we find the circle of life. Every atom of carbon, calcium and oxygen in my body is the same as the carbon, calcium and oxygen everywhere else in the universe, though mine have been arranged rather more photogenically than most. To understand this we have to go to Chile, where I can blow bubbles to show how, from quarks and anti-quarks, the first hydrogen and helium atoms were formed 400,000 years after the big bang, how they coalesced to form galaxies and stars that in turn burned out into death stars, which created all the elements in the universe today. To imagine the collapse of a star, just watch me blow up an old prison in Rio and then think of something a lot bigger and more powerful. Amazing.

Gravity is the great organisational force of the cosmos; without it we would float around like I am in this Vomit Comet. Everything we know, from the Fish River Canyon here in Namibia, carved over millions of years by droplets of water bound by the equation $U=mgh$, to my shiny hair that cascades soulfully over my eyes, is subject to the effects of gravity first observed by the Chinese in 1054 as they looked up towards the Crab Nebula from Chaco Canyon, where I now am. But what is gravity? Isaac Newton stated that the gravitational force between two objects is the product of their masses, but we now know his theory of universal gravita-tion is not correct; rather it is what Einstein called the curvature of spacetime. I've lost you again. But as I stand on the top of a Norwegian mountain with a helicopter hovering overhead, we can only wonder at the gravitational meaning of the black hole. In the budget.

Time feels human, but we are only part of Cosmic Time and we can only ever measure its passing. As I stand in front of the great glacier that towers over Lake Argentino, time seems to almost stand still, yet as I explain the effects of entropy in the Namibian desert as sandcastles crumble around me, you can see that the transition from order to chaos can happen almost in the blink of an eye. One day, perhaps in 6bn years, our universe will stop expanding, the sun will cool and die, as all stars must, and everything will collapse in on itself, back into a black hole singularity. I leave you with this last thought: that we, too, will only really die when the universe dies, for everything within it is intrinsically the same. And that if you take this book to bed you are, to all intents and purposes, sleeping with me. Now that is amazing.

Digested read, digested: Wonders of Mr Universe.

23 MARCH 2011

How the home of Mini Rolls and Smash was gobbled up

JOHN HARRIS

Among the thousands of people who join the big anti-cuts march this Saturday will be a coachload from Wirral. Though where they live has been suffering from the public-sector axe since 2009, their cause is less about austerity than a story that extends from the looming closure of a 60-year-old biscuit factory into the byzantine workings of the modern business. Given that the demonstration – organised by the TUC – is titled the "March for the alternative", they surely have something crucial to contribute: an argument not just against cuts, but the kind of flimsy, imbalanced economy that makes millions of people even more vulnerable to them.

The Burton's Foods factory has been in the pinched suburb of Moreton since 1953. For the first 30 years of its life, with a workforce peaking at nearly 5,000, the factory was part of the confectionery empire run by Cadbury's, with an enlightened labour relations model and an array of fondly loved brands that tumbled from its production lines: Mini Rolls, Chocolate Fingers, Smash instant mash.

But in 1986, there was a management buyout, and its troubled second act began. Since then, the company that renamed itself Burton's Foods has switched owners at least five times, and a recent private equity buyout saddled the firm with very serious debts. Now the biggest shareholders are the Canadian Imperial Bank of Commerce, and a multinational finance outfit called Apollo Global Management. Burton's biscuit production turns a profit, and life for its board seems very nice indeed. Last year, directors' pay rose by an average of 97.5%, and the most handsome package went up by 119.9%.

There are no such glad tidings in Moreton. After serially cutting production here, the company now plans to close the factory with the loss of 342 jobs. Worse still, Wirral borough council is set on shedding more than a thousand people – a sixth of its payroll – by the summer, and for every local job vacancy there are currently 17 applicants. When George Osborne delivers today's budget, he will doubtless point to supposed sunlit uplands of recovery, and perhaps underline his belief that, as he hacks back the public sector, private firms will fill the gap. Not here.

I came to Wirral after we appealed on Comment is free for word from the frontline of British trade unionism. On the thread that followed, hostile voices ("unions need to be crushed") took issue with more supportive contributors ("people have a fundamental right to collectively improve their lot"), and a few people mentioned the dreamy idea of European-style social partnership, whereby British labour relations might lose their traditionally adversarial charge.

In Moreton, on the union's side at least, that has happened. For four of the last 10 years the workforce has agreed to a pay freeze. Since 2001 they have delivered £12.7m of cost savings, while the success of the lines they produce has often skyrocketed. In 2007, when closure was first suggested and the Unite union led a successful campaign – without a strike – to save the factory, at the cost of 500 jobs, the firm promised to turn one production line into "a centre of excellence", and not to attempt any more big changes before May 2012. To quote the local MP, the shadow Treasury minister Angela Eagle: "None of the workforce could have done any better – and what is their reward? The sack."

Listening to people who fear being left at the mercy of a non-existent job market, I was struck by one thought: as far as mainstream politics is concerned, talking about the root of this place's predicament is clearly off limits. Yet ideas are out there: Unite talks about working at an EU level to give deals struck with employees legal force, so the shadowy financial interests that control increasing parts of the economy cannot always devastate communities on a whim. More generally, there is the kind of enlightened business approach urged last weekend by Andrew

Witty, the chief executive of GlaxoSmithKline, who bemoaned not only corporate tax avoidance, but the entire economic culture in which bottom lines are relentlessly pushed downwards, and the social costs are always someone else's concern.

Witty summed up the great misstep of business over the last 20 years: "They've allowed it to be perceived that it's all about money. It shouldn't be about that ... We want to make a return, yes – we're not a charity. We want to make a good return for our shareholders. But we're going to do it by being in step with society."

Somewhere in those words, even if he himself may not know it, there is not just a pithy diagnosis of what has gone wrong, but a tantalising hint of how things could be different. Not the standard free-market cartoon of a world returned to the 1970s, but corporate social responsibility pushed beyond the odd bit of charity, and politicians on the left realising that if they think seriously – and internationally – about all this, some business people might not be quite as hostile as they think.

To echo the title of the big march, there is an alternative. But on a grey day in Moreton, it seems light years away: distant, theoretical, and no compensation for the blows to come.

Spring

Spring

The life, the looks, the movies, the smarts, the talent. And age could not wither her

HADLEY FREEMAN

The Cleopatra costume will, surely, dominate the news reports but with all respect to the Egyptian queen, Liz was bigger than that.

Elizabeth Taylor evokes more images than the number of husbands she had. She was the breathtakingly beautiful child who – unlike her near contemporary, Judy Garland – seemed to slip into adulthood unscarred by her precocious professional success; the sultry dramatic actress; the compulsive bride, who went through husbands like fashion trends; the scarlet woman who broke up America's sweethearts, Eddie Fisher and Debbie Reynolds; the female half of what can very legitimately be described as the greatest love affair of the 20th century; the most beautiful woman in the world; front-page stalwart of the National Enquirer; star of some of the best movies of her era; star of some of the worst celebrity perfume adverts; the gay rights campaigner; the defender of Michael Jackson. Next to Taylor, Marilyn Monroe looks monochrome and monotone.

Even towards the end of her life, Taylor, despite near incapacitation, still not only understood the increasingly ridiculous celebrity world, but proved that – to paraphrase a quote from her most photographed role – age could not wither her. Her Twitter feed was so Tayloresque as to be nigh-on parodic, mixing passionate defences of Jackson with shout-outs to reality TV android Kim

Kardashian and the occasional – necessary – denials that she had re-re-re-re-re-re-re-re-remarried ("Jason is my dearest friend!" she tweeted last year, at the age of 78, with an understandable giggle).

Those born in the 40s will probably remember her as the wife of Richard Burton and the actor who radiated sex without ever being as coarsely upfront with her assets as, say, Monroe or Jane Russell. Those born in the 70s will have the slightly less erotic image of Taylor as the wife of the unforgettably named Larry Fortensky, sporting makeup, jewellery and hair that makes Russell Brand today look a bit low-key. Yet she was equally famous to those born in either decade, and this is not just because of her ever fluid image but her fearlessness at breaking social mores.

Her close friendships with gay actors – most notably Rock Hudson and Montgomery Clift – showed her to be more open-minded than most in an age when homosexuality was career-threatening. Taylor did more than pretty much anyone in her era by helping to remove the stigma of both homosexuality and, tragically, Aids by her loyalty to Hudson when he was dying from the disease.

Just as scandalous in its way was Taylor's relationship with Burton. Both were married when they met and neither made any attempt to hide not just their love for one another but their lust. Now divorce is as common among actors as undeserved Oscars but Taylor and Burton still look red-blooded next to today's anaemic Hello! wedding spreads. The publication last year of Furious Love: Elizabeth Taylor, Richard Burton and the Marriage of the Century, by Sam Kashner and Nancy Schoenberger, truly puts to shame today's pretenders, not least with its inclusion of Burton's love letters to Taylor. But there was one letter even Taylor, the consummate celebrity, couldn't share with the public: the last one Burton wrote to her just before his death in 1984, saying he wanted to come home, and Taylor was home. That letter remained in her dressing table drawer, next to her bed.

Carrie Fisher compares her mother, Debbie Reynolds, and her father, Eddie Fisher, to Brad Pitt and Jennifer Aniston, with Taylor – who made Fisher her husband number four – playing the Angelina Jolie role. It is a smart riff, neatly evoking the media hysteria that accompanied Fisher and Taylor's affair while he was still with Reynolds and the ensuing marriage (and, inevitably, divorce – there was no way little Fisher could ever compete with the mountain of machismo that was Richard Burton).

But the real joke is the comparison between Jolie and Taylor. Jolie's fame rests entirely on her personal life, which can be summed up as "married Rachel from Friends' husband, fond of adopting". As Jolie has amply proved, one doesn't need to be a good actor, or even appear in any good films, to be an A-list celebrity these days: one just needs to be thin and have a fondness for being photographed. Taylor had the life, the looks, the movies, the smarts and the talent, and she – unlike Jolie – looked as if she not only enjoyed the occasional plate of pasta but my God, to watch her eat it would have been an experience in itself. As they say in Hollywood, it's the pictures that got small.

26 MARCH 2011

Confessions of an undercover cop

SIMON HATTENSTONE

There are two distinct images of Mark Kennedy that have emerged in the press. The first is a long-haired, unshaven, multi-earringed rebel – that is Kennedy the undercover cop in his role as eco-activist

"Mark Stone". The second is a man with short hair, swept to the side, clean-shaven, so spruce you can almost smell the soap – the "real" Mark Kennedy, returned from life undercover.

Today, it takes me a while to recognise him. He could be a composite – the hair is longer and unkempt, the face unshaven, tattoos are on display under his rolled-up sleeve. He seems to be morphing back into the eco-activist before my eyes.

Kennedy was an undercover police officer who spent seven years infiltrating a group of environmental activists under the alias Mark Stone. In 2009, as protesters planned to occupy and temporarily shut down one of Britain's biggest coal-fired power stations at Ratcliffe-on-Soar in Nottinghamshire, Kennedy passed on the information to his handlers. Nottinghamshire police subsequently arrested 114 people in a late-night swoop. Among them was "Stone" himself, who faced a prison sentence for conspiracy to commit aggravated trespass. Kennedy was trapped – if he was not charged, it would blow his cover, yet he couldn't appear in court as somebody who did not actually exist. In the end, the case collapsed, leaving a trail of collateral damage – up to £1m lost on the trial, hundreds of thousands wasted on his surveillance work, a community torn apart, lives shattered.

The story led to four ongoing inquiries about the nature of undercover policing and questions in parliament: did the environmental protesters need to be monitored so closely? Wasn't it a waste of police time and taxpayers' money? Were police acting as agents provocateurs? Did they have any right to inveigle their way into people's lives in such a manner? The story caught the popular imagination, not least because it emerged that for many of his years undercover, Kennedy – who was married with children – was involved in a serious relationship with one of the activists.

What kind of man could do that: nurture, befriend and ultimately love a group of people, then betray them? Kennedy, 41, wants to tell his side of the story. But at times he no longer seems sure what that story is.

He grew up in Orpington, Kent. His mother was a housewife, his father a traffic police officer. At 19, Kennedy also joined the police. He considered himself a modern cop with modern attitudes – he had no time for the old racist views, was sympathetic to protesters in the environmental movement, and believed the job of the police was to enable society to operate fairly and democratically. He worked initially in uniform, then undercover in south London, buying drugs and weapons from dealers and passing information back to Scotland Yard. He was good at the job and was headhunted by the National Public Order Intelligence Unit, a secret body that runs an intelligence database of political activists. They asked him to help expose race-hate crimes – more undercover work. This was just the kind of thing he had joined the police to do. Again, he was successful. It was then suggested that he hook up with a group of environmental activists in Nottinghamshire. Yes, it was infiltration and, yes, it involved spying on people he regarded largely as good guys, but he convinced himself he was on the side of the angels – if he could tip the wink to his handlers about extremists and demonstrations, they could be policed efficiently and he would be working as a good officer while assisting a movement to which he was sympathetic. Of course, if his fellow activists had known this at the time, they would have regarded it all very differently.

"My role was to gather intelligence so appropriate policing could take place," Kennedy says. "It wasn't to prevent people from demonstrating. I met loads of great people who would go out every weekend and show their concern and demonstrate. Then there were other people who would want to take things further and maybe want to break into somewhere or destroy things, and then you start infringing on the rights of other people to go about their lawful business."

Kennedy still talks like an officer. His sentences are punctuated with words such as "tasked", "gatherings" and "proportionate policing". We meet at the offices of the publicist Max Clifford, whose help Kennedy sought when he reached a nadir. He had lost everything – his old friends, his family, his activist friends. I had expected a cool, confident man – a James Bond or Jason Bourne – but Kennedy is fidgety and diffident. His neck reddens as he talks and only one eye focuses because of a childhood accident (at two, he climbed inside a cardboard box and a loose staple ripped an ocular muscle). After a few minutes he starts to stammer – a schoolboy affliction that has only recently returned.

It was not easy to immerse himself among the activists, he says. They were a group of close-knit friends, many of whom had known each other since school. He went to meetings and marches, and gradually became accepted. The more involved he became, the more he changed physically. His hair grew long enough to wear in a ponytail, he got more piercings and tattoos. Gradually, he proved himself an indispensable comrade – he could drive (many activists couldn't or wouldn't), he had money (made, he said, by drug dealing in Pakistan – he told the activists he now wanted to turn his life around), he was a skilled climber and, perhaps most importantly, he was popular.

Somehow, he successfully managed both lives. While Stone had a thrilling time visiting 22 countries on a false passport, demonstrating against the building of a dam in Iceland, touring Spain with eco-activists, picketing arms fairs in London and penetrating anarchist networks in Germany and Italy, Kennedy quietly slipped information back to the police, even managing occasionally to get back to visit his wife, Edel, and two young children in Ireland. The couple were estranged, but maintained they were together for the sake of the children (four and two when he went undercover in 2002). If they asked, he would tell the activists that he was working away for a few days as an industrial climber.

Did he have to be an incredibly good liar to do this job? "Yes." Was he always a good liar? "Not in that sense. I was lying because it was my job to lie. I'm not a dishonest person. I had to tell lies about who Mark Stone was and where he was from for it to be real." He pauses. "To be fair, a lot of the things you do, say and talk about are very much based upon who you are as a person and the places you've been to and the things you've done, because five years later somebody will go, 'Ah, Mark, didn't you say you went here?' and you have to remember that. So a lot of the things I would talk about were pretty true."

Such deceit was on a different level from what he'd practised on the streets, buying drugs and guns. "If I'm going to buy a kilo of coke, the dealer doesn't really want to know me that well; it's all about the commodity. But this is different. People don't actually want anything from you – all they want is to know you and be your friend."

Is it possible to do the job without becoming paranoid? "I'd use a different phrase. I never became complacent." That's a very different phrase, I say. He ums and ahs and stutters his way to a conclusion. "I never... I always liked to... I suppose I was a little bit paranoid." Can you do the job without it mentally unbalancing you? "I don't know." Where does Kennedy end and Stone begin? "Well... there is no line. You just can't say." He finally reaches a conclusion of sorts: "I always have understood and had a concern for the issues I was infiltrating. I don't think you could do this work if you didn't care about the climate."

Perhaps that is what ultimately made life impossible for Kennedy: he wanted to honour both sides – be the honest cop and the genuine activist. But in the end he was caught in the middle, despised as a Judas by both sides.

Kennedy experienced heavy-handed policing first-hand. In 2006 he was beaten up by officers on the perimeter fence of the Drax power station. He says he was trying to protect a woman being hit on the legs with a baton when he was jumped by five uniformed officers – they were there only because he had tipped off his handlers. "They kicked and beat me. They had batons and pummelled my head. One officer repeatedly stamped on my back. I had my finger broken, a big cut on my head and a prolapsed disc." There were plenty of other incidents, he says. "I experienced a lot of unjust policing. At times, I was appalled at being a police officer."

But he says that some of the best things in his life also happened as Mark Stone – and not just the dramatic stuff. "There are some amazing social centres that are all voluntary-based. Take the Sumac Centre in Nottingham, a community garden that provides free food. If you had a social centre like that in every city, it would be great. And I was fortunate enough to be involved in that and see how it works."

And this became his community? "Yes. So many people I knew, or Mark Stone knew, became really good friends. It wasn't just about being an activist all the time."

I ask if he ever wanted to be Stone, and he gives a surprising answer. No, he says, because it was so frustrating failing to achieve what he had set out to do. "There was a lot of commitment and effort and tears put into things that didn't change anything." The activists were too conservative? "Yeah, I would say, and just very small in numbers." Actually, he says, they were a bit useless at the most basic things – an effective group of protesters needs a number of competent climbers, to scale fences and gain access to buildings and power plants, and there were hardly any. Recently, it was announced there wouldn't be a climate camp this year, and that horrifies him. What better time to discuss the environment and policing and all the issues that have come about with his case?

It's bewildering listening to Kennedy make the case for a more radical and committed group of ecowarriors. The bottom line is that he went in to betray them and did just that. Does he feel guilty? "It's something I find very hard to think about. When you're on the frontline in a riot situation, the people around you are your buddies. Everybody looks out for each other, and I experienced that on numerous occasions. There were people who, if they had only a couple of quid left, would buy you a pint. So, yes, there are some great people who didn't need to be reported on. They believed I was something else, and that hurts a lot."

And then there are the women. Those in the environment movement claim Kennedy had many sexual relationships through the years, and some believe it was a systematic means of gaining trust and gathering intelligence. One woman with whom he had a relationship overseas said she felt "violated" when he was outed as a police officer. Kennedy maintains there were only two relationships, one of which was serious.

Look, I say, it's easy to talk about the trauma of betraying a guy who buys you a pint, but when it's a lover, surely that's on a different level? Silence.

"For me, that whole kind of incident..." He starts again. "That's not the right word. I felt in some ways that I was really alone, that I was the only person as an undercover officer who had ever done that; subsequently, I discovered everyone was doing it. The person I had the relationship with is an amazing person, a really amazing person. The love I shared with her and the companionship we shared was the realest thing I ever did." More real than his marriage? "Yeah, there were no lies about that at all," he says without irony.

How did he feel when he was in bed at night? Was there not part of him desperate to confess? "Yes, all the time. All the time. Yes." But how could he continue in a relationship with someone who might be the love of his life and know it's all based on a lie? "It's one for the psychologists," he says quietly. "It's just how it was. I don't know." Did he never think of coming clean, begging forgiveness and leaving the police? "No, no. I'm not saying it didn't cross my mind, it just wasn't a realistic proposition. It would never have worked." Because he'd have ended up rejected by both sides? "Absolutely." He looks at me. "You know, our relationship was remarked upon in the activist community as being a great relationship."

Things reached a head in April 2009, when the activists planned to break into the Ratcliffe-on-Soar power plant. It was initially suggested that "Stone" climb the power plant, but he refused. This was Kennedy the good policeman – if he led the protesters, any subsequent case could collapse because he would be regarded as an agent provocateur. He says he told his handlers that he had passed on all the necessary information and didn't want to be part of the protest, but they told him they wanted him there. He eventually agreed to drive a lorry. He recorded two meetings held at Iona school on 12 and 13 April, where protesters discussed shutting down the plant, and passed on the recordings. At one point activists heard there had been a leak and that security had gathered at the power station. According to activists, it was Kennedy who went to recce the station and reported back that all was clear.

On 14 April, the day before the planned takeover, the police arrested 114 activists. While the other 113 shared one law firm, Bindmans, Kennedy's handlers said he did not need one because he was a police officer. "I said, look, everybody else has got a solicitor, Mark Stone hasn't – it looks really odd. They said, don't worry about it, and I said, well, I have to worry about it because I'm now on bail to go back to be re-interviewed." The Nottinghamshire detectives had no idea that an undercover officer was involved. "As far as they were concerned, they were interviewing Mark Stone, a thorn in their side for the past seven years – he's a catch, let's make sure we push charges."

Every day for three months, Kennedy phoned his handlers to ask what was happening, and heard nothing. Eventually, a week before the day on which he and 26 others had been told they would be charged, the case against him was dropped. He had suggested that if he was released without charge, the other drivers should be, too, to avoid suspicion, but he was ignored and all the remaining 26 activists were charged. It left him in an impossible situation. "It totally exposed me. To sit in a pub with everyone else and for them to say, 'How did you get off?' What could I say? I didn't say anything. That was hugely stressful. Certainly it raised a lot of questions among people."

Soon after the case was dropped, he received a message from his handlers: the surveillance operation was being dropped and he was to tell the activists that he was leaving to visit family in America for an indefinite period.

When he returned to the Met in October 2009, he discovered two alarming things – one, his time undercover had left him out of touch; and two, he was now a pariah in police circles. "Over seven years, there was no training or keeping me up to speed with what was going on in the police. So when I went back, I probably wasn't even qualified to drive a Panda, didn't know how to use a radio. I didn't know how any of the systems worked. I went for an interview with the personnel department and they didn't even have my file." When they asked Kennedy what he wanted to do now, he told them, "I need a role that keeps me off the streets, reasonably covert, some kind of detective job." That was all very well, they said, but he'd have to apply like anyone else. "They said, 'We can't give you a job on merit of having done a good job before. You're not really qualified to do anything.'

"I was not looked after at all. I didn't think there was anything left for me in the police, so I left." Kennedy does not believe he is alone. He says he has talked to other former undercover officers who feel they were cast aside on their return to mainstream policing and later left the service suffering from post-traumatic stress.

In early 2010, he returned as Mark Stone to his friends in Nottingham. Perhaps he didn't know where else to go. He wanted to try to make things work with his girlfriend – or at the very least provide a more satisfactory ending to their relationship and his years among the protesters. (He had done a course on servicing wind turbines, and told his old friends he was going to travel the world doing that.) But when they were on holiday last July, his girlfriend came across a passport belonging to Mark Kennedy in the glove compartment of his van. Again, he lied and told her he had many passports from his drug smuggling days.

She might have given him the benefit of the doubt, but when she told the other activists, they did not. They demanded a meeting in which he was quizzed for four hours. "I was absolutely shitting myself. They sat in a semicircle around me. It was hugely menacing. I told them nothing to start with. They just kept saying they knew I was a cop, that I was married with kids. They knew my mum. They knew my home address." Eventually he broke down, and that was when they brought in his girlfriend. "The look of devastation on her face destroyed me."

He was asked to make a statement confessing everything. He said he would think about it, then ran away. Was it a relief that he was forced to come clean? He nods. "Yeah, a huge relief." He stops to correct himself. "Later it became a relief, after the initial shock."

He hoped to manage his own public outing, but was overtaken by events. Last December, 20 of the charged activists were convicted of trespass offences. Then, in January, the case of the remaining six collapsed. There were a number of stories circulating as to why – and Kennedy was at the centre of them all. One suggested that he had gone native – in one recorded phone conversation, he suggested he could give evidence for the defence and said the police tactics with which he was involved were like using "a hammer to crack a nut". Another version of events suggested that by taking such an active role in the protest, he had become an agent provocateur. But, ultimately, the case seems to have collapsed for less noble reasons – it is thought the CPS realised that the evidence Kennedy had recorded at the school actually helped the activists, showing that most were still making up their minds about whether and how to participate. If that was the case, the prosecution could not win – if they used the evidence, they undermined their own case; if they didn't use it, the defence would accuse them of non-disclosure.

Kennedy found himself front-page news. There was a rush of stories about him and, appropriately enough, it was impossible to distinguish fact from fiction. It was suggested that he had set up his own companies after leaving the police (true – he says he planned to start a business abseiling down skyscrapers to clean their windows) and that he had worked in private security spying on the activists after he had left the police (false, he insists – he was asked to advise a company on trends in activism, but says he declined).

According to Kennedy, the police did their utmost to distance themselves from him, telling reporters in off-the-record briefings that he was "a bad apple" and wholly unrepresentative of undercover officers. But a week after he was exposed in the national press, a number of similar stories emerged, including that of undercover officer Jim Boyling, who had married an activist he met while infiltrating Reclaim the Streets.

By now Kennedy had nowhere left to run. Every bridge was burned – he had not seen his children for three months, and neither the police nor the protesters wanted anything to do with him. He wasn't sleeping, barely eating, and was terrified. He was hiding in America, convinced his former police bosses were looking for him and that activists wanted revenge. A group of German anarchists said they hoped Kennedy "spends the rest of his life looking over his shoulder. That is the minimum price he should have to pay." In the US he told a psychiatrist that he was suicidal.

Kennedy returned to England in a desperate state but, having no fixed address, he could not sign up to a GP. While undercover, he should have received an assessment from a police psychologist every three months, but claims he went two whole years without even one. He also says he received no counselling from the police when he was removed from undercover work. When asked if they were remiss in their pastoral care, both the Metropolitan police and National Public Order Intelligence Unit declined to comment in light of ongoing inquiries.

"I felt hugely alone," Kennedy says. He looks away. "Still do. It was a really dark time. I had two choices: I was either going to top myself or try to get some help."

All the time we've been talking, I've wondered one thing: how would he have felt if his girlfriend had ended up in prison because of his actions? For the first time he seems shocked by a question. "She was nothing to do with anything." Why not? "She was doing something else." By chance, she was not involved in that particular protest. And if she had been? "It didn't occur to me."

As for the future, he hasn't a clue what it holds. There is a documentary being made about him, talk of a movie, even, but he knows that's not going to see him through the rest of his working life. He says he'd like to use his experience to show people that police officers and activists don't always fit a neat stereotype, but he's not sure how. For now, though, he says, he has plenty of work to do on himself. This week he is visiting his family to try to make a fresh start with the children. He says they were distraught to see him in the newspapers, and admits that his daughter is "quite frosty" with him.

Does he think people will ever trust him again? "Do you mean people I used to associate with? No, never. Never. I shattered that trust, I accept that."

Does he think he will ever be able to trust himself again? "In what way?" he asks. Well, I say, is he confident that he knows who he is now?

"No, not at all. Deep down, I know I have these core values, but it's going to be a long process to find out who I am."

28 MARCH 2011

The American right is trapped in a hyperbolic and dysfunctional world

GARY YOUNGE

Polls suggest there are between one in three and one in four Americans who would believe anything. More than a third thought President George Bush did a good job during Hurricane Katrina; half of those thought he was excellent.

Throughout most of 2008, as the economy careered into depression, just over one in four believed Bush was handling the economy well. As Bush prepared to leave office in January 2009, bequeathing bank bailouts, rampant unemployment, and Iraq and Afghanistan in tatters, a quarter of the country approved of his presidency.

These are national polls that span the political spectrum. So you can imagine how concentrated the distortions become when filtered through the tainted lens of the right. A poll earlier this month revealed that a quarter of Republicans believe a community rights organisation called Acorn will try to steal the election for Barack Obama next year, while 31% aren't sure whether it will or not. It won't. Because Acorn does not exist. It was defunded and disbanded after a successful sting operation by conservatives a couple of years ago.

Meanwhile, a poll last month showed that a majority of Republicans likely to vote in the primaries still believe Obama was not born in the United States. He was. But no number of verified birth certificates will convince them.

Such is the nature of the electorate that will select Obama's principal opponent for the 2012 election. And such is the reason why a viable Republican contender has yet to emerge despite trough-loads of money and the Republican successes of the midterms. Among Republicans the latest polls suggest a crowded, splintered field of possibles with Mike Huckabee leading on 19%, followed by Mitt Romney on 15%, Sarah Palin on 12% and Newt Gingrich on 10%.

And if Republicans are unconvinced, Democrats are untroubled. When Obama is pitted against any of them in six states he took from Republicans in 2008, polls suggest he would win all but one – he would lose to Huckabee in North Carolina by 1%. He fares best against Palin, trouncing her by double figures everywhere but Ohio. Despite his favourability ratings suggesting the nation is evenly divided on his job performance, a national Pew poll suggests 47% would back Obama's re-election against 37% who would prefer a Republican and 16% who did not know.

The challenge for the primaries is neither new nor unique to the right. The tension between appealing to the base and to moderates is the perennial test of any successful candidate in national United States politics. To win the party nomination you must appeal to your motivated base. To take the country as a whole you generally must engage the wavering centre.

What is relatively new, however, is the level of logical dysfunction and hyperbole within the American right, trapped in a fetid media ecosystem where all the Kool-Aid has been spiked. In short, what you need to say and do to be credible within the Republican party essentially deprives you of credibility outside it. The Republicans seem to realise this but, like an obese glutton at an all-you-can-eat buffet, they just can't seem to help themselves.

When asked which of their possible contenders they believe to be qualified for the job, they can think of one, Mitt Romney, and even then barely 50% believe so. The person they say they like the most, Sarah Palin, is also the one they believe is least qualified: only 29% believe she can actually do the job.

This was evident in Iowa, the state that holds the first caucuses in the primary process next year, where many of the possible candidates converged over the weekend. On Friday, at a forum for Iowa pastors called "Rediscovering God in America", Mississippi governor Haley Barbour, an outsider, vowed to do "everything that we can to stop abortion". The next day at the Conservative Principles Conference, where Barbour spoke, abortion didn't come up. "It is absolutely critical that we elect a new president," he said. "I think the best way, perhaps the only way, is for us to make sure the 2012 campaign is focused on policy." He added: "The American people agree with us on policy."

When it comes to Libya, Newt Gingrich has vacillated from "Exercise a no-fly zone this evening", on Fox News 12 days before bombing started, to "I would not have intervened" four days afterwards. Meanwhile, congresswoman Michele Bachmann, who once called for an investigation of "anti-American" lawmakers, told the conference: "It can't just be a Republican. Do you hear me? It can't just be a Republican." She urged Iowa conservatives to set the tone for the nation, saying: "We need to have people who have guts, who you won't see melt like wax when they get there."

Some feared that Iowa, which holds such a crucial role in the nomination process, could be too extreme to pick a competitive candidate. "We look like Camp Christian out here," Doug Gross, a Republican activist and former nominee for governor, told the New York Times. "If Iowa becomes some extraneous rightwing outpost, you have to question whether it is going to be a good place to vet your presidential candidates."

Strategically the division between social and fiscal conservatism has largely been settled. With just a few exceptions only social conservatives (anti-abortion, anti-gay marriage, pro-gun) can get elected within the Republican party, so it has ceased to be much of an issue in primaries. Once nominated, candidates stress only fiscal conservatism for fear of scaring away centrists. Once elected they emphasise both, evidenced by the growing efforts to restrict access to abortion by legislators who barely raised the issue of abortion on the stump.

When I saw Rand Paul speak before 35 people in Leitchfield, Kentucky, just over a year ago, he never mentioned abortion, and nor did anyone else. "I'm not running for preacher," he told me. "I'm running for office." Now he's a senator who supports slashing aid to planned parenthood. Meanwhile, the Kentucky legislature has recently passed a bill requiring a woman to view an ultrasound before she has an abortion.

But the strategic question of where and how to strike a balance between principle and pragmatism, or even whether such a balance is desirable, still eludes them. So too does any consensus on the kind of facts – Obama's religion and place of birth being just the two most obvious – that would enable others to take them seriously.

With little more than 18 months to go before the election, there is still time for a candidate to emerge who can fudge the difference and straddle the divide. An event like the Arizona shootings might also force a reckoning between the right and reality. But generally speaking, incumbent presidents lose elections; challengers don't win them. Obama is vulnerable on many fronts. With unemployment still high, poverty and home repossessions growing, Guantánamo still open, two old wars not yet over and a new one just begun, he deserves more than token opposition. There is just over a third of the country who think that Republicans are providing it. But then they believe anything.

30 MARCH 2011

Yates defiant in face of further phone-hacking allegations

2 APRIL 2011

Mysterious homage to Picasso that sums up the spirit of Catalonia

COLM TÓIBÍN

The street they named for Picasso is one of the least glamorous streets in Barcelona. It is on the edge of the Parc de la Ciutadella; it is a busy, dusty street, full of trucks and commercial traffic.

There is a grittiness and brutality about it which the old master might have savoured. It was the area of the city he knew best, close to the apartments where his family lived, the art school where his father taught and where he studied, the studios he had as a young painter and the bars he drank in.

It is here also that the monument to him made by the Catalan artist Antoni Tàpies stands, a piece of work filled with a fierce sort of mystery. There is nothing to explain what it is or what it means. There is no sign even saying who it is by.

For me it is one of the most beautiful objects in the city, and it carries with it something uncompromising, complex and exalting which I associate with the Catalan spirit.

It is a large glass box in a pool of water. Inside the box it seems that some vast accident has taken place in a domestic interior, like a scene after a bomb or an explosion. There is some old wooden furniture – a dresser and some chairs – with ropes, and there are iron girders running crossways through the furniture, ramming it.

Old sheets are thrown around and there are words written on those sheets, a quick message to whoever would discover the

catastrophe which has occurred. I have never been able to deci-
pher what is written on the sheets, and I imagine this is part of
the intention.

As I walk around it I am never sure that I am reading it correctly.
It is not as though it is simply ambiguous, or even surreal.

It is rather that the monument represents the imagination
itself and the image as something single and fierce and untamed,
the artist working at the deep splashing edge of the unconscious,
the world of unwaking dream.

This monument to Picasso will do anything to resist meaning,
or easy interpretation. If it represents anything, I take it to represent the mind in its search for freedom, for imagery that comes
unbidden and unresolved; but the monument is also contained,
deliberate, almost stately and austere, as though it came naturally
to Tàpies who dreamed it up and then made it and put it here.

It is an exciting piece of public sculpture. The fact that the
glass is often broken and the water often does not flow around
it as it is meant to do almost adds to the strength of its appeal,
helped too by dead leaves in the water and the odd daub of pigeon
shit on the glass.

The lives of Picasso and Tàpies in Barcelona tell us a great deal
about a century in the city, and help us to understand the ironies
and complexities of life in Barcelona and Catalonia now.

Picasso's family came to Barcelona in 1895 when he was not
yet 14. His family lived first in Carrer de la Reina Cristina and
then around the corner in the Carrer Llauder; both streets gave
on to the port.

Soon they moved to Carrer de la Mercè, one street back from
the waterfront, to a second-floor apartment in a building which
has now been demolished. From his earliest time in the city,
Picasso made drawings and sketches, filling notebook after notebook, many of which are in the Picasso Museum in Barcelona.

His early studios were also in the old city, in streets such as Carrer de la Plata, Carrer dels Escudellers Blancs and Carrer Nou de la Rambla. His early associates were young Catalan painters; like most citizens of Barcelona, he spent time in the Catalan countryside, in places such as Horta de Sant Joan in the province of Tarragona and Gósol in the province of Lleida.

Even though he was an outsider, Picasso's career until he was in his early 20s was the same as any Catalan painter of his generation, many of whom were also from lower middle class families.

Like the others, he became acquainted with the two senior painters in the city, Ramon Casas and Santiago Rusiñol, in the bar Els Quatre Gats. Like his contemporaries, Picasso looked to Paris as his headquarters rather than Madrid.

His first months in Paris were spent almost exclusively among Catalans. There were great similarities between his early career and that of the Barcelona painter Isidre Nonell, for example; they both painted the poor of the city; they both exhibited in Els Quatre Gats; they both went to Paris when they could, where they shared an address at rue Gabrielle, as they shared a landing at No 28 Carrer del Comerç in Barcelona.

In the early years of the century, they both painted women in states of solitude and desolation. Indeed, for the rest of his life Nonell continued to paint such portraits, including many paintings of Gypsies; while Picasso went through many phases, Nonell's style did not change.

The paintings of Tàpies, who was born in Barcelona in 1923, are often abstract in tone and philosophical in origin. Despite the fact that his art has a deeply private aura, in the 1960s and 70s he was involved as a public figure in the campaign for democracy in Spain and autonomy in Catalonia.

"There was a time when the Franco regime was at its height," he has said, "when I believed that certain clearer political messages could contribute to a general revulsion for the regime."

But such a time came to an end after the dictator's death in 1975. As democracy came, politics freed him from having to paint about politics.

"His response to mysticism, the esoteric and the magical has been explained through his Catalan identity," one critic has written of his work.

"Many motifs appearing in his work have been recognised as references to his Catalan roots, but his Catalan identity has also been explained on a deeper technical and formal level.

"The significance of craftsmanship in his work, especially his profound knowledge of the material he employs, has been associated with Catalonia's traditional craftsmanship."

In his memoirs, Tàpies manages to evoke the Barcelona of the 1930s and 40s. He remembered when the anarchists took Barcelona in 1936 being told to wear old clothes if he were walking in the city. And then when defeat came, and the fascists arrived, he recalled that his cultured parents had to have soldiers billeted in their house.

When it was noticed that his father turned off the radio when the fascist hymn Cara al Sol was played, a senior officer came to the family house on Carrer de Balmes and told his father that he must listen to the hymn in future.

In that same book Tàpies offers a key to the puzzle which many tourists ponder as they walk the streets of Barcelona. Where are the Catalans?

The answer is that they don't like downtown; many of them never set foot in the area around the port or the Ramblas or the Gothic quarter if they can help it. In the old days, they left downtown free for newcomers, such as Picasso's family; now they leave it to tourists.

Tàpies's mother was typically interested in moving her family from below Gran Via to above it, and then higher again into the hills above the city, where the air, she believed, was cleaner, and the bourgeois ideal could be worked out in greater peace and with better neighbours.

For Catalans, too, the Pyrenees do not represent a real border with France. There are too many passes in the mountains; they are not hard to cross.

Like Picasso, Tàpies felt a real relief when he arrived in Paris; he has a wonderful description of seeing a French couple kissing on the street in the late 40s; such things would have been forbidden in Franco's Spain.

Barcelona has opened itself to tourism by keeping the tourists between Gran Via and the port almost as though they are prisoners. The building which is dedicated to the work of Tàpies, just above Gran Via on Carrer d'Aragó, is from the 1880s and is one of the early buildings of the Catalan style known as Modernisme.

Tàpies has made it his own by placing wild masses of coiled wire over the roof. The Picasso Museum is down in the old city, in five 14th-century palaces on Carrer de Montcada.

But there are no plaques on the actual houses where they lived, or the places in the city where they had studios. There is much about both of them which belongs not merely in the museums dedicated to them but to the essential spirit of Barcelona.

There is something restless in their legacy which evades easy readings, just as the city itself, as it changes and adapts to things, as it takes in more outsiders and yet remains oddly traditional and almost conservative, evades any simple set of descriptions.

Tàpies's great monument to Picasso, hidden in an unfashionable street, stands for the strength of the connection between the two artists and the city, and the enduring power and mystery of the images they made.

2 April 2011

Letter: Basque question

KEN BRAY

Julian Glover explains "Why prosperous Catalans may beat Basques to the exit" (1 April). Mightn't it be dangerous to have all your Basques in one exit?

Ken Bray

Bath

6 April 2011

First arrests for five years in phone-hacking scandal

● News of the World's chief reporter arrested ● CPS and police row over failure of first inquiry

9 April 2011

Murdoch says sorry as hacking defence crumbles

● Phone crime rife, admits News International ● Settlement with celebrities will cost millions

9 APRIL 2011

Brick by brick

KATHARINE VINER

Jeanne is 27, with a round face that makes her look younger, but she struggles on to the stage. She finds walking difficult, ever since she was tied to a tree and gang raped for many weeks, had surgery to repair the damage, went home and was raped again. She became pregnant during one of the attacks and was forced to give birth in the company of the militias; the baby died. Jeanne finally escaped to the Panzi hospital in Bukavu, at the eastern edge of the Democratic Republic of the Congo. She has had repeated operations on her desecrated lower body. She looks small, shy, defeated.

But then this woman, a victim of the biggest horror story of modern times, in one of Africa's largest countries, steps up to the microphone and starts to speak.

"When you look at me, what do you see?" she asks, with the bold delivery of the born orator, the preacher, the leader. "Do you see me as an animal? Because you are letting animals treat me like one. You, the government, if it was your children, would you stop it? You, you white people: if this violence was happening in your country, would you end it?" She speaks with the kind of fury and focus rarely seen in western politics. Hundreds of other survivors of sexual violence in the audience cheer wildly.

Jeanne (who has requested her last name be withheld for her protection) is not the only speaker here at the opening of City of Joy, a centre for survivors of rape in Bukavu. There is the founder, the New York playwright, author of The Vagina Monologues and activist Eve Ensler. There is Obama's ambassador for women and girls, a prominent congresswoman, someone from the UN. But it is Jeanne who steals the show. And this is the premise on which the centre is founded: that even the most traumatised and brutalised people need not be mere passive recipients of foreign aid, but can in fact become political leaders.

For more than a decade, eastern Congo has become infamous as the "rape capital of the world" and the "worst place on Earth to be a woman". The UN has confirmed these facts. Half a million women, perhaps many more, have been raped since 1998, and in particularly brutal ways. And one response has been the building of City of Joy, a haven where survivors of gender violence who have healed physically (not always straightforward) live for six months and are educated. It is the product of a shared vision that the women don't just need help, they need power. "Eve asked us what we wanted," says Jeanne, the orator. "And we said: shelter. A roof. A place where we can be safe. And a place where we can be powerful. That's what we now have." Jeanne, and women like her, hope to change Congo for good.

The grand opening of City of Joy, in February, is a big party: survivors in celebration clothes dance and sing and bang drums. Some, very badly injured, are carried in. Women who helped construct City of Joy dance with bricks balanced on their heads. Local men taking a stand against sexual violence – the "V-men" (after Ensler's feminist V-Day movement) – make themselves visible with special T-shirts. American donors join a conga line. Women from the stage speak not just of rape but about laws that discriminate against women, the lack of free HIV treatment, what happens to the children of rape. There's a lot of hugging, but the atmosphere is fierce.

The centre's story begins in 1999, when the gynaecologist Denis Mukwege, of Bukavu's Panzi hospital, rang his friend Christine

Schuler Deschryver, a human rights worker in the town. He said he had started to see injuries he had never seen before – women who had been raped in terrible ways, whose reproductive organs had been wrecked, who were suffering from fistulas between the vagina and rectum inflicted not just by gang rape but also by attacks with sticks, guns, bottles. "I said to Christine, this is new," he recalls. "Their vaginas are destroyed. I couldn't understand what was going on."

Everyone in Bukavu knows Christine – she is 6ft without heels (and she's never without heels), mixed race (her father was from a family of Belgian colonisers, her mother a Congolese servant in the tea fields of his plantation), dramatic, demanding. "When Dr Mukwege told me about these injuries, we were very afraid," she says. "And then, in 2000, I was in my office when a woman ran in with a baby girl, 18 months old, her legs both broken back – the baby had been raped. She died in my car on the way to Panzi hospital. I ran into the cathedral with the dead baby in my arms, shouting at God. And that was the day I became a radical fighter."

Bukavu is a ragged, devastated town built on the banks of Lake Kivu in the east of Congo; at one time the Belgian colonisers tried to make it a lakeside retreat, so stunning is the setting. There are no roads, so when it rains the pathways turn to mud. Women (rarely men) stagger beneath gigantic sacks of cassava and charcoal; they sit on the ground with a single tomato to sell. Once a town of 50,000, it is now home to hundreds of thousands, most of whom have fled fighting in the bush to come to the comparative safety of the city.

Congo is the size of all of western Europe, with a very weak state. It is also the poorest country on earth, by GDP, and yet one of the richest in terms of resources – the fertile soil that produces such a lush landscape and juicy avocados brings with it gold, diamonds and precious minerals, with criminals, militias and kleptocrat politicians not far behind. Since colonialism, when King Leopold II of Belgium ran a notoriously genocidal regime in order to plunder Congo's rubber, armies have tried to grab its wealth. President Mobutu, who renamed Congo Zaire and stole a personal fortune of billions, showed that it wasn't only outsiders who could get in on the act. Today's gold rush is over coltan – Congo has 80% of Africa's reserves of the mineral, which is used in mobile phones, laptops, iPads; with the resource in such demand, there's a direct link between the technology consumer boom and the fighting in Congo.

Rape is a feature of war, and is often seen as an inevitability – the second world war general George Patton wrote that "there would unquestionably be some raping". But it is more widespread and more violent in some wars than in others. According to Joanna Bourke, author of Rape: A History, its prevalence depends on how violent a society is already; the disparities between men and women in the culture; whether soldiers fear any kind of punishment for rape; and the extent to which the values that enable mass rape are shared by men on each side of the conflict. On every count, Congo rates disastrously. And there's also a particular problem, what Jean-Claude Kibala, the deputy governor of South Kivu, describes as a "bomb in the middle of society": former child soldiers. "Nobody has a programme for how to deal with them," he says. He tells of a bodyguard who kept falling asleep during the day. "The bodyguard explained, 'When I was a child I was forced to bury a man who was still alive. This image is with me every night and I can't sleep in darkness.' There are people like that all through our society. Destruction and rape are destroying all humanity in the province."

The particular brand of brutality that emerged in eastern Congo in the late 1990s has its roots in the Rwandan genocide of 1994, when 800,000 Tutsis and some Hutus were murdered in three months by Hutu gangs known as the Interahamwe (what they call themselves) or genocidaires (what their opponents call them). When the genocide was stopped by the arrival of the Tutsi exile-led Rwandan Patriotic Front, the Interahamwe fled to eastern Congo, where they established gigantic refugee camps in Goma, a town close to the Rwandan border. Notoriously, the global aid community responded to the refugee crisis with an efficiency that was missing from the response to the mass slaughter of the Tutsis: they fed, clothed and inoculated the genocidaires and their followers, while the few Tutsi survivors mourned their families and scrabbled around for food. The Interahamwe who did not take up Rwandan president Paul Kagame's offer to return home disappeared into the Congolese bush.

The Rwandan genocide was, in the words of French writer Jean Hatzfeld, "enthusiastic processions of ordinary people who every day went singing off to work as killers". Neighbours and friends went out "hunting" Tutsis with farming implements such as machetes and hoes. But it wasn't straightforward murder. As Interahamwe leader Adalbert Munzigura told Hatzfeld in A Time for Machetes: "They needed intoxication, like someone who calls louder and louder for a bottle. Animal death no longer gave them satisfaction, they felt frustrated when they simply struck down a Tutsi. They wanted seething excitement. They felt cheated when a Tutsi died without a word. Which is why they no longer struck at the mortal parts, wishing to savour the blows and relish the screams."

It was these very Interahamwe who imposed themselves on the Congolese people, later reinvented as a militia called the FDLR (Forces Démocratiques de Libération du Rwanda). And over more than a decade of violence, in which power passed from Laurent Kabila to his son Joseph, Rwanda invaded Congo, there was Africa's "first world war", which was played out in Congo (involving Uganda, Rwanda, Burundi, Zimbabwe, Angola, Chad, Namibia and Sudan, and leaving an estimated 5.4 million dead, according to the International Rescue Committee); through all of this, a multitude of new and primarily Congolese rebel militias were formed, and all of them raped women with extreme violence. Which is why Dr Mukwege started to see injuries he'd never seen before.

Rape, devastating everywhere, particularly undermines Congolese society. After being raped a woman is usually excluded by her family and so – when women have the babies and do all the cooking, farming, carrying – community is quickly undermined. Society breaks down. "If you destroy women, you destroy the Congo," Ensler says. "Raping women is the cheapest and most effective way to instil fear in and humiliate a community. It doesn't even cost a bullet."

But is there something deeper at work? Has the epidemic mass rape in Congo got something to do with the country's own history, the result of many years of subjugation, played back? Michela Wrong, in her book In the Footsteps of Mr Kurtz, memorably describes Congo's population as being "marinated in humiliation". Says Ensler: "There is so much rape in men who've been colonised and enslaved. You have to wonder what it's done to these men, to their collective psychological memory." The Belgian colonists were famous for cutting off hands and feet, still a common rebel tactic – Jeanne was forced to watch as her uncle's hands and feet were cut off before he was murdered. Says Ensler: "Centuries of colonialism, slavery and exploitation by the west have come together and are now being delivered on the bodies of the Congolese, most dramatically on the bodies of women."

The particularly violent way of rape that has become current destroys the women's reproductive organs. They can no longer have children (especially terrible in a society in which motherhood so defines being female that the word for "woman" is "mama"). As Mukwege, who has worked for more than two decades with women on the ground in eastern Congo, says, "This will be the destruction of the Congolese people. If you destroy enough wombs, there will be no children. So then you come right in and take the minerals." Here in Congo, in the heart of Africa, home of the origin of man, the rapist wants to stop the human race for good. I was told of a woman being raped who asked the rapist why he was doing it. He replied, "Because I'm already dead." Not for nothing does Ensler describe Congo as "ground zero".

The raped women I spoke to have a straightforward request for how to solve the problem of rape in Congo: get the FDLR (the genocidaires and their descendants) out of the country. A common Congolese refrain is that "rape is not in our culture" – ie, foreign warlords brought it with them – and certainly, returning the FDLR to Rwanda would be a start, as would Rwanda taking responsibility for the other militias in the area it supports.

But it is now much more widespread: brutalised mass rape has become so endemic that the Congolese army, much more populous than the FDLR, reportedly commits most of the attacks. Rape has become normalised – and is only one, dramatic, dimension of a far wider violence taking place throughout the region. "Rape in Congo has tended to attract the headlines," says Carina Tertsakian of Human Rights Watch. "There are also other serious abuses: killings of civilians, arbitrary arrests and widespread looting are all commonplace."

But something is changing. In February, lieutenant colonel Kibibi Mutware and three other Congolese army officers were convicted of crimes against humanity for ordering rape and other crimes in Fizi town, South Kivu, on New Year's Day this year. They were sentenced to 20 years in prison. This is truly a landmark – the first time a senior ranking Congolese army officer has been arrested, tried and convicted for rape crimes. But one case is hardly enough: there has been no action taken against other officers accused of similar crimes also committed that same day, the mass rape of 39 women and one girl in Bushani and Kalambiro villages in North Kivu. And, as Ensler asks: "Will they keep the lieutenant colonel in jail?" But it is, at least, something.

The women of Congo have been hopeful before. Since the late 90s, they have been intermittently fashionable as a global cause in the west; an activist wryly noted that every 18 months or so there's a flurry of media interest, gruesome rape stories are related, each more terrible than the last, and then there's silence. "They come and visit," Schuler Deschryver says bitterly, "and leave me with a pile of business cards." Hillary Clinton, the US secretary of state, visited in 2009. "I made Hillary cry when she came, and it made me full of hope. But then – nothing."

Melanne Verveer, who, in a new role created by Obama, is the US ambassador for women and girls, and who attended the opening of City of Joy, denies that the Clinton visit was followed by no extra money; her aides fluster around me proffering sheets of numbers, proclaiming cash provided ($42m over five years, they say). But Congo is clearly not a priority for international aid: when Ensler went to talk to Michelle Obama about the cause, she got inside the White House before an aide, high up in the Obama administration, informed her that "Congo was not going to be part of the Michelle brand". It is notable that, despite the enormous hope raised in Africa when Obama was elected, both his predecessors, George W Bush and Bill Clinton, showed more interest in the continent.

Although the money for City of Joy is provided by Ensler's movement V-Day (which raises cash through performances of The Vagina Monologues), plus Unicef and various foundations and donors, all are keen to emphasise that the project is owned and led by Congolese women. And their big idea is not aid, but empowerment. If we accept that rape is a violent expression of the power imbalance between men and women, then you prevent rape by helping women get more power. In other words, City of Joy is all about a Congolese kind of feminism.

The programme will be run by Bahati Bachu, a strong-looking woman who carries an air of disbelief that this City of Joy is happening at all, and is a living, breathing rebuttal to those who imagine that feminism does not exist in developing countries. She is 58 (a good age in Congo, where life expectancy is 53) and a longtime women's rights activist, a tough role to take in this harsh place. For International Women's Day in 1999, she asked all the women in Bukavu to stay indoors; they did, and the entire town shut down. She was sacked from her role as regional women's officer as a result. She once threatened to walk bare-breasted through the streets as a protest against women's place in society. "When the rapes started to happen, I denounced it everywhere," she says. "Germany, France. And nothing. I worked for so many years for Congolese women, but eventually I stopped because I was discouraged. But now, with City of Joy, I am seeing the fruit of my work, and others want to join. I will not die before we have a revolution." She does not laugh at this.

Mama Bachu's programme lasts six months. Survivors have "de-traumatisation" sessions; they learn about women's rights ("Some are shocked to hear they have any rights at all," Bachu says), literacy, the economy, accounting, farming, production, business, self-defence, the internet. (Google has donated a £100k technology centre.) Schuler Deschryver says: "Everything is Congolese, not American. So there's no therapy, talking about your relationship with your father." The women asked for small brick houses, arranged like a village, and a place for exercise, "so we can use up our energy and not row in the evenings".

Sixty women will live here for six months, passed on from the gynaecology ward at Panzi hospital, after Dr Mukwege has saved their lives. They come from all over Congo. As the Congolese ambassador to the US, Faudi Mitfu, says, "City of Joy shows that even when a woman has been terribly tortured, she can still stand and build." And, perhaps more hopefully: "Today we build City of Joy. Tomorrow we build our country."

It's almost unbelievable that the poorest country on earth could give birth to a women's movement, just like the incongruousness of the beautiful landscape with the horrific past and present; the terrible damaged lives with the singing and dancing. It's got to have a chance. As Schuler Deschryver says, "There's something you need to know about Congolese women. When we can't walk, we run."

12 APRIL 2011

Brooks faces questioning by police over hacking

18 APRIL 2011

Unstuff your shirts

ALAN RUSBRIDGER

When Daniel Barenboim's hands are not at the piano or holding a baton, they demand a cigar. It is the first thing he mentions as he bustles into Claridge's Hotel on the afternoon of his recent cameo concert at Tate Modern. We will go upstairs to his suite, he explains, and then he can light up.

As if reading his mind, a member of staff shouts down the corridor after him: "Now then, Maestro" (he really does call him Maestro). "No smoking now."

Safely settled into an armchair, Barenboim produces a double-barrelled leather case, lights a very fat cigar and savours the moment. It's 3pm. He's not due at the Tate for four hours. He has not yet decided quite what to play, and is not sure of the acoustic that awaits him in the giant Turbine Hall. He looks tired, but up for a conversation. And a smoke.

A conversation with Barenboim does not take a regular, linear form. If it were a score, it would not resemble a sonata, or indeed anything with a recognisable beginning, middle or end. It is much more like a Sibelius symphony – a multitude of thematic germs, which occasional fuse into a big theme.

So, within five minutes, the thread might go something like this: the shape of the recording industry since the 1980s; the need for new marketing ideas in music, post-internet; the Egyptian and Tunisian revolutions; the Japanese tsunami; the speed of change in the world today; his performances in the West Bank; and the nature of musical communication. There is a connection

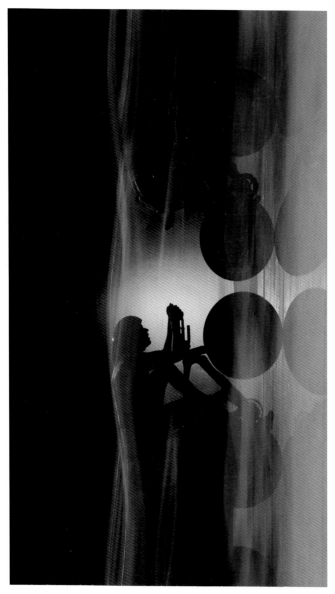

20 FEBRUARY 2011

Speed and symmetry: Great Britain's men's pursuit team at the Manchester velodrome. TOM JENKINS

24 JUNE 2011

Glastonbury: mid-performance, Bono reaches out to grasp Guardian
photographer David Levene's camera. The U2 singer then reversed roles
– taking pictures of Levene from the stage. DAVID LEVENE

Shintona, Japan. Aftermath of the tsunami and earthquake. DAN CHUNG

there, and in time it reveals itself, but there are moments, as with Sibelius, where it's not entirely clear where it's all going.

We start with his new recording deal with Universal. He recalls that he made his very first recording in London ("of all places") in 1954. For years, he was with Deutsche Grammophon ("We did quite a lot of not unimportant things together, like the cycle of the Bruckner symphonies in Chicago"). The Universal deal retains his link with DG, but now he wants to try new things.

The first three discs give a flavour of what's to come: a Warsaw recital of solo piano Chopin pieces; the first recording he has made of the Chopin concertos with the Staatskapelle Berlin; and conducting the West-Eastern Divan Orchestra, which brings together musicians from Israel and Arab countries, in the Schoenberg variations and Tchaikovsky's Symphony No 6.

You could say his primary current obsessions are wrapped up in those three programmes: his rediscovery of Chopin (forbidden to him by his father, who was interested only in the Haydn-Schubert grand tradition); his life in Berlin; and his work exploring the power of music to bridge cultural divides.

But, Barenboim being Barenboim, he first takes a step back before discussing his new recording deal – to talk about recorded sound.

"When the CD came in 1982, it was a completely new departure in the sense that it took [music] completely away, technically speaking, from the human experience, because it was so perfectly recorded."

A spiral of dense smoke drifts up from his chair. I peer up through it, at what may or may not be a smoke alarm.

"It was both the blessing and the curse of the record industry. The blessing, because any technological advance is very positive. It's a curse because it was able to make all the old recordings sound almost like contemporary recordings. Therefore all of us artists were not only in competition with our contemporaries, but with Furtwängler and Nikisch.

"I think now, after 30 years, we must really see what should be done for the future – how to record, what to record, and how to present it. The technical development has been huge, but the presentation, if you want, or to use a more vulgar word, the marketing didn't change that much. I think this evening [at the Tate] is a very small point, but it shows a new departure."

The subject of change leads him to Egypt. And then Japan. The next bit is more linear in my recounting than it was in the increasingly fusty room in Claridge's as he warmed to his theme.

"I don't want to sound melodramatic, but I think that in the last 15 or 20 years, the world has changed so much, in so many ways. And in the last two months, the Egyptian revolution and the Japanese catastrophe – I mean, obviously, not just the earthquake but the atomic menace – shows that we cannot think in the old ways.

"Sixty per cent of the population of Egypt is under 30 years old. In the occupied territories it is 85%. For the first time in history, it was a revolution that happened without leadership.

"What a unique gesture it was that young people were able to create this kind of revolution with the help of the internet and other means of communication. That means we all have to speak of other ways of communication. Can you understand what I'm trying to say?"

I can, but he is on to Japan. "Two weeks ago, I went back to reading what Einstein was writing about the atomic dangers. How many years ago? And how he foresaw all that.

"What the world is saying to us human beings is, 'Don't stick to the old ways, learn to think anew.' And that's what musicians do every day. You don't go out and play Beethoven's Opus 111 without having rethought about it every time you play."

Then come digressions on the uncertain future of the Venezuelan experiment in musical education; why the Palestinians have yet to rise up; the folly of Israel's current political path; how a common love of cuisine might draw Middle Eastern cultures together; and playing Bach in Ramallah.

Performing The Well-Tempered Clavier in the heart of the Palestinian occupied territories in 2007 left a deep impression on him. "It was the quality of listening," he says. "I had the feeling I didn't have to go to them, they were all coming on to the stage to me, in their concentration. This is what music is about" – not, he says, the centuries-old traditions of Vienna or Berlin. "In Ramallah you don't have that. It was one of the most wonderful audiences I ever had for that piece."

This leads Barenboim on to a diatribe against governments cutting back on the opportunities for young people to experience music. This, he thinks, is not only diminishing for them, but for music, which will become limited to a select elite of passionate aficionados "away from the rest of the world, away from the human problems. Therefore you get a community made up of artists and an audience that is an ivory-tower community, because both have lost a great part of the connection between music and everything else."

It's this stranglehold on the future of classical music that Barenboim says he is trying to break. The impromptu concert at Tate Modern – a short recital in an unfamiliar venue – is one tiny example. Within three days of the free concert being announced, 8,000 people had applied for the 400 seats, while 700 more watched a live relay in the hall below. When he was finished, the 1,100 people gave him a standing ovation.

As if to illustrate his point, there was a bitterly divided critical response the following day. One critic was struck by the spell he cast, how no one in the throng stirred as he played: "Sixty years on, he still plays the piano with boyish curiosity, as if the instrument had just been invented."

Another critic expended 900 words sneering at the "legions of crazed fans ... there to witness their Messiah.

"Mention his name in pianophile company," continued the lofty wordsmith, "and it is quickly dismissed." He concluded: "We were ... wrong to attend last night's recital."

Barenboim had begun our conversation with a recollection of an unkind notice by a Guardian critic (of Menuhin, not himself). There may have been a time when he cared about the opinions of "pianophiles" and musical arbiters of ivory tower taste. But, 18 months short of his 70th birthday, he gives every impression of having his eye fixed on new and much more expansive horizons.

20 APRIL 2011

Hideously Diverse Britain: The 'disconnect' on Green Street

HUGH MUIR

We have been discombobulated by immigration, says David Cameron. But, as Vince Cable observed, an election is coming. Even so, standing on Green Street in east London, on a Saturday afternoon, it strikes me that Cameron is right in some regards. There is a disconnect.

Let me tell you about Green Street. When first I came here, more than 40 years ago, it was high street anytown. There was the supermarket but also Marks & Spencer. The high-street banks each had a presence. My mum, dragging me and her shopping trolley, would buy staples from Tesco and Queen's Market, stopping to wave to our white English neighbours: that was fine. But also to chat with church contemporaries, strapping black women in need of guidance/gossip. That was interminable. The West Indian stuff – the yams, green bananas – came from a ruddy-faced Englishman called Hammond. Heckling him about the quality of his yams was part of the theatre.

So what happened? About the time I went to college, the recession ravaged Green Street. The banks drifted away, as did M&S and much of the populace, and into this near corpse of pound shops and charity stores came a life-saving influx, first of Indians, for whom the rents were now agreeably cheap, and then of Pakistani Muslims. They traded there. Bought houses in the surrounding streets. They turned it into the "Bond Street of the east". So where's the disconnect?

Well, at the far end of Green Street stands West Ham United, and what you notice about the influx it generates, from Essex, Kent, Hertfordshire and the other areas of white flight, is that they show little inclination to embrace the new reality. The pie and mash shop does a roaring trade; so do the stalls with burgers and sausages and the KFC. The Duke of Edinburgh pub is full to bursting. But the curry cafes don't see much of a spike. And as the fans head resolutely out again, past the sari shops, the jewellery emporiums, the store selling "Islamic goods", the women in hijab, they do indeed look a little discombobulated. Not hostile. Just otherworldly. They are mostly gone before long and Green Street returns to its latest normal. Plenty of votes in that for Cameron, and he knows it.

23 APRIL 2011

The domestic goddess makes a splash

MADELEINE BUNTING

Earlier this week, a British woman in Australia wore a full head-to-toe black suit, complete with hoodie, to go swimming. Perhaps she thought what she wore on the beach was her own business. How wrong could she be. Wind forward a couple of days and there were already more than 100,000 items on a Google search under Nigella and burkini; the image had been beautifully subverted in a Times cartoon on the op-ed page (it was Nick Clegg's turn to be burkini-ed as he frolicked in the surf with Cameron), and dozens of shots of her unusual swimwear were in newspapers and on websites attracting thousands of hits. Plus several columnists had shared their thoughts on the folly or wisdom of Nigella Lawson's decision.

Lawson's burkini had become a textbook illustration of a Hot, Flat, and Crowded world, to borrow the title of a book by the American globalisation theorist Thomas Friedman. The Hot is self-explanatory, given that the most plausible explanation for the burkini was the Australian sun; Flat, because the speed of the web ensures an audience of millions, even billions, within hours for the smallest detail of someone's everyday life; and Crowded, because for a celebrity, nowhere is safe from the long reach of a paparazzi zoom lens. And, as in all crowds, people want to look and pass comment; a crowded world entails a lot of gossip. It also brings into conversation – or collision – entirely different cultures.

And therein lies the rub. Lawson is an icon of English femininity. She has crafted her own image as carefully as she decorates
one of her fancy cakes. She has offered her voluptuous cleavage
and fine facial features as a way to glamorise the female labour of
feeding family and friends. No longer the sweated brow, stained
hands and soiled apron of mother at the stove, but the effortless-
ness and poise of cashmere cardigans, hourglass figures and – on
one particular occasion which made a big impression on me –
sparkly mascara. Only someone who has turned femininity into a
career would have the time to pull all this off.

But the contradiction thrown up by our crowded world is that
an icon of sexy English femininity turns to a Muslim sportswear
website for help in combating the ageing, carcinogenic ravages
of the Australian sun – or was it to conceal the curves from the
prying eyes of a global audience? Inevitably the commentators
(and so far in my researches, they were all women) pondered on
Lawson's motivation, and whether this decision was a style blun-
der, a "betrayal of her own brand", or a defiant and admirable
insistence on privacy for her body.

What provoked less comment was the extraordinary timing of
Lawson's burkini beach trip, coming only a week after France's
ban on women wearing the burqa and niqab came into force. On
one side of the world, England's finest rose is choosing to don
sharia-compliant clothing, while on the other, one of the fore-
most liberal democracies in the world is bringing the full force of
the law against a small number of women who insist on wearing
their interpretation of sharia-compliant clothing. One prompts
a torrent of witty, playful commentary, the other is accompanied by a bitterly contested debate on the treatment of women in
Islam. At the heart of both stories is an obsession with women's
bodies and how they should or shouldn't be displayed – and the
fierce patrolling of different social conventions governing them.

On a beach, a woman is expected to expose her body, and it's that refusal which has captured attention. Lawson is defying our social conventions to protect herself – her privacy and her skin. And there is a sneaking understanding, even admiration, in many quarters for her gesture. Evident among all the women commenting is a weary recognition of the ordeal of swimwear – the hair removal and fake tans required to meet even minimal standards – which, for the postpartum, becomes a widespread sense of falling short, of failure. And there's an appreciation of how this falls punitively on famous women, whose bodies abroad are scrutinised for extra bulges, cellulite and sag; if anyone is in any doubt as to what Lawson shrewdly dodged, look at some of the harsh judgments on her bikini-clad companion. Few women can fail to understand Lawson's urge to wrap up.

Meanwhile, on the street, a woman is expected to show her face, and when she refuses she now faces prosecution from the state in countries such as France and Belgium. All that distinguishes the two cases of Islamic dress is our beliefs about choice. The assumption is that Lawson chose her outfit, and the assumption is that niqab-wearing women in France are not making a free choice. But how confident can we be of either assumption? Perhaps Lawson would rather the contempt generated by a burkini than the scorn and judgment generated by revealing a middle-aged woman's body – but what kind of constrained choice is that?

Equally, some French niqab wearers use precisely the arguments of individual choice to justify their niqab as a way of ensuring privacy in a culture saturated with the exploitation and commodification of women's bodies. The latter is an uncomfortable reality for many who have been so disempowered that they are only left with irritated impotence: my 14-year-old son asks me why I put up with the huge M&S lingerie billboards plastered over London, and I have no reply. I don't much like the niqab because it eliminates the possibility of street conviviality, but I understand entirely the desire to withdraw from the world's invasive, intrusive attention.

This is the brilliantly subversive conclusion to this random collision of stories in our crowded planet. Unwittingly perhaps, Lawson the skilful image maker has just launched a powerful political statement about how a woman can choose to wear sharia-compliant clothing. Everyone understands her to be an aspirational brand, a role model, an arbiter of taste. In the topsy-turvy chaos of a web world where images and ideas are deracinated, massively projected, manipulated and recycled, Lawson's beachwear has already become iconic – and in a small way, revolutionary. Marianne, the symbol of the French Revolution, stormed the Bastille, breast bared; her 21st-century descendant is burkini-clad.

23 APRIL 2011

The courage of ordinary people standing up to Gaddafi

CHRIS MCGREAL

The Middle East. A man with a car fashioned into a bomb. He disguises his intent by joining a funeral cortege passing the chosen target. At the last minute the man swings the vehicle away, puts his foot down and detonates the propane canisters packed into the car.

It all sounds horrifyingly familiar. Mahdi Ziu was a suicide bomber in a region too often defined by people blowing up themselves and others. But, as with so much in Libya, the manner of

Ziu's death defies the assumptions made about the uprisings in the Arab world by twitchy American politicians and generals who see Islamic extremism and al-Qaida lurking in the shadows. Ziu's attack was an act of pure selflessness, not terror, and it may have saved Libya's revolution.

In the first days of the popular uprising he crashed his car into the gates of the Katiba, a much-feared military barracks in Benghazi, where Muammar Gaddafi's forces were making a last stand in a hostile city. At that time the revolutionaries had few weapons, mostly stones and "fish bombs" – TNT explosive with a fuse that is more usually dropped in the sea off Benghazi to catch fish. The soldiers had heavy machine guns and the revolutionaries, often daring young men letting loose their anger at the regime for the first time, were dying in their dozens as they tried to storm the Katiba.

Then Ziu arrived, blew the main gates off the barracks and sent the soldiers scurrying to seek shelter inside. Within hours the Katiba had fallen.

Ziu was not classic suicide-bomber material. He was a podgy, balding 48-year-old executive with the state oil company, married with daughters at home. There was no martyrdom video of the kind favoured by Hamas. He did not even tell his family his plan, although they had seen a change in him over the three days since the revolution began.

"He said everyone should fight for the revolution: 'We need jihad,'" says Ziu's 20-year-old daughter, Zuhur, clearly torn between pride at her father's martyrdom and his loss. "He wasn't an extreme man. He didn't like politics. But he was ready to do something. We didn't know it would be that."

Ziu may have been unusual as a suicide bomber, but he was representative of a revolution driven by dentists and accountants, lorry drivers and academics, the better off and the very poor, the devout and the secular. Men such as Abdullah Fasi, an engineer-ing student who had just graduated and was in a hurry to get out of a country he regarded as devoid of all hope until he found himself outside the Katiba stoning Gaddafi's soldiers. And Shams Din Fadelala, a gardener in the city's public parks who supported the Libyan leader up to the day government soldiers started kill-ing people on the streets of Benghazi. And Mohammed Darrat, who spent 18 years in Gaddafi's prisons and every moment out of them believing that one day the people would rise up.

Fasi joined the revolution on day two. The protests began after sunset on 15 February outside the police headquarters to demand the release of a lawyer, Fathi Terbil, who was arrested over a lawsuit against the government on behalf of the relatives of 1,200 men killed by Gaddafi's forces at Abu Salim prison in 1996. Relatives of the dead men and lawyer friends of Terbil started to march. As they moved through the city, the crowd swelled and chanted slogans from the Tunisian and Egyptian revolutions. The police attacked them with water cannon and the government unleashed young men wielding broken bottles and clubs against the protesters. All that did was to bring thousands more on to the streets the next day, including Fasi.

"At first we didn't ask Gaddafi to leave," he says. "We just wanted a constitution, justice, a better future. Then they came shooting and beating the people. After that we said Gaddafi must leave."

"I knew I had to go to the Katiba. They were shooting us. In front of me they killed seven people in those four days. The last day was very very hard. People started to get TNT from the other camps and make the fish bombs. Every five minutes I heard a fish bomb explode."

Then Ziu charged the Katiba's gates on his kamikaze mission. What followed wasn't pretty. "[The revolutionaries] were beat-ing Gaddafi people they captured, it's true. When they captured a Gaddafi soldier they said: 'What was this man doing? He was shooting us.' Gaddafi's soldiers wanted to kill anyone. They were using anti-aircraft weapons on humans. It cut people in half. People were angry," says Fasi. So angry that some of Gaddafi's soldiers were lynched. At least one was beheaded.

With the battle of the Katiba won and the revolutionaries in control of Benghazi, Fasi gravitated toward the city's courthouse on the dilapidated Mediterranean seafront, a mix of ornate Italian colonial-era buildings and ugly but functional modern constructs. The revolutionaries had burned the court and the neighbouring internal security offices as symbols of repression. Now they were rallying centres and something of a shrine. Relatives of Gaddafi's many victims over four decades pinned up hundreds of pictures of the dead on the courthouse walls alongside those killed around the Katiba. Ziu's portrait is there as a heroic martyr. While some mourned, others let loose with graffiti plastered across Benghazi declaring that the 42-year nightmare was nearly over.

Benghazians still marvel at their own courage in taking on the regime. Failure would almost certainly have meant execution, years in one of Gaddafi's brutal prisons or exile. Yet otherwise ordinary people inspired each other to take the risk, not for an ideological cause or over some ethnic divide but to enjoy the basic freedoms few have ever known.

Middle-aged men said they stood against Gaddafi because they couldn't bear the thought of their children growing up to face a future devoid of hope. Younger people spoke of a realisation that they could either seize the moment or resign themselves to a half-existence under the tutelage of the next generation of Gaddafis. Even a few weeks later when the regime's tanks were at the gates of Benghazi and the revolution looked as if it might be lost, expressions of regret were rare. The hardcore of revolutionaries

– the female dentistry professor with an eight-year-old child, the accountant with a family in the US, the shopkeeper who wonders where the money to feed his family will come from because the revolution has killed trade – all said that at least they would die as free Libyans.

Few revolutions have been more inspiring. After years of reporting uprisings and conflicts driven by ideology, factional interests or warlords soaked in blood – from El Salvador to Somalia, Congo and Liberia – Libya's uprising seems to me more akin to South Africa's liberation from apartheid. For a start, the once pervasive fear of a hated regime is gone.

From the first days, scores of enthusiastic young revolutionaries, high on the prospect of looming victory, indulged the newfound freedom to finally say what they thought. They churned out screeds listing the dictator's crimes and posters caricaturing Gaddafi as a common thief and agent of Mossad. Some posters imagined him on trial before the international criminal court or strung up on one of the gallows used for public hangings to terrorise the Libyan population.

Revolutionary committees sprang up. Among them was one charged with getting the message to the outside world that Libya 2011 was not Tehran 1979. The savvy revolutionary activists watching CNN and news websites were not slow in recognising the fearmongering in parts of the US media and Congress over what kind of revolution this was.

Almost the only foreigners in Benghazi during the early days of the revolution were journalists. We were feted with free coffee in cafes and regularly stopped on the street and thanked for coming. But reporters were also quizzed by Libyans who picked up on the talk about Islamic extremists hijacking the revolution. Where, they wondered, did the idea of al-Qaida in Libya come from? Couldn't people see what kind of revolution this is?

It is hard not to notice how desperate the core of revolutionaries is to be accepted by the west. It is common enough to run into accountants, oil executives and engineers on the frontline who have studied in Nottingham, Manchester and Brighton. They say they admire Britain and the US. Denunciations of America are noticeably absent, at least on the rebel side of the line. France's president, Nicolas Sarkozy, is a hero in rebel-held areas for recognising the revolutionary administration.

Yet it is also not hard to see why the outside world was uncertain about the revolutionaries. No other country in the Middle East is quite so defined by its leader.

The cult of Gaddafi and his Green Book, his links to terrorism, and the sheer brutality of a regime that publicly hanged students at Benghazi's university for dissent, left little to be admired. The Libyan leader's colourful behaviour, including a taste for Amazonian bodyguards, led much of the world to conclude that he was unstable as well as dangerous. From the outside, there were good reasons to wonder if the collective sanity of the Libyan people had not gone off the rails in those 42 years, especially when Libyans were seen on television in near hysterics as they fanatically waved Gaddafi's green flag and swore to die for him.

"He made us ashamed of our country. He made us ashamed of ourselves," says Mohammed Darrat, the former army officer who, in joining the throngs outside the Benghazi courthouse during the first days of the revolution, committed his first political act since Gaddafi flung him into jail in 1970. "Gaddafi gave this image to the world of the Libyan people as criminals or fanatics. It wasn't true. We knew all along that he didn't speak for us. It was always the people of Libya versus one family, the Gaddafis."

That may not be entirely true. Many Libyans did very nicely out of the regime, at the price of unyielding loyalty to the "brother leader". But it is true that large numbers of Libyans regarded

Gaddafi with contempt. Fasi, 23, grew up listening to his parents
talk of Gaddafi as mentally unstable. "They thought he was mad
– all my family talking about him and what he did in the 70s
and 80s. They regarded him as a criminal for Lockerbie and a lot
of other things. They hated it that the rest of the world only saw
Gaddafi and not the Libyan people," he says.

Fasi was warned by his parents never to repeat such views
outside the house. That didn't stop him. "For my generation, we
were talking about it a lot. You can't say Gaddafi is mad to just
anybody. You can say it to close friends, but not to someone you
don't know properly, in case he's a spy for internal security. In the
last few years we were talking about that a lot among ourselves,
saying we don't want Gaddafi. But none of us expected Gaddafi
to fall. Everybody was waiting for him to die. We left it to God
to deal with him and we told ourselves, whatever happens after,
there can be no one worse than Gaddafi," he says.

Until that day, many young Libyans saw no future in their
own country. They were generally less concerned with Gaddafi's
crimes against his own people – Benghazi was a favoured place
for public hangings of political dissidents – than with the despair
of living in a country where they saw no future. "I had to join the
revolution because we didn't have any hope here," says Fasi. "A
lot of my friends left the country after graduation. You see the
outside, you see the other countries, you see how they live free.
Even if their economies are bad, they are free. That's the point."

For Darrat, the revolution is about something else entirely.
It's personal. He knew Gaddafi from their army days, recognised
the nature of the man and turned against him almost from the
moment he seized power in 1969. "I went to military academy in
Iraq. I saw that revolution and all the suffering there, the crimes,"
he says. "After Gaddafi's revolution I joined a secret group of army
officers. We watched a lot of soldiers in the upper ranks behaving

immorally, harming people because they wanted power. Because of what I had seen in Iraq I thought the same terrible things would happen here. I was right."

Darrat joined a clique of officers planning to overthrow Gaddafi, but after a few months they were betrayed and arrested. "Gaddafi said we were traitors. They showed no humanity. They beat us day after day to obtain information. They smashed my leg and my back. I couldn't walk," he says.

Darrat was sentenced to life in prison. He left behind a wife and four children. Hundreds of other military personnel were also jailed. He describes prison as "very, very bad". After two operations to repair the damage done by the beatings to his legs and back he was immediately returned to his cell without anything to control the pain.

Darrat brings out a picture of his military academy graduation class. In it is one of the army officers who brought Gaddafi to power in the 1969 coup. Another in the group was executed for opposing the Libyan leader. He has no idea why Gaddafi freed him early. "Who knows what Gaddafi thinks," he says. "I don't know how we allowed him to take control of our lives. We could all see what he was."

When Gaddafi seized power he promised to do more for the poor with his distinctive brand of socialism. Wealthier Libyans lost properties. People in rented accommodation were told it now belonged to them. Yet for all the ideological rhetoric a substantial part of Libya's population still lives in poverty.

In a corner of Benghazi rarely seen by its better-off residents is a warren of roughly constructed shacks and containers made into houses. Shams Din Fadelala built his own place from breeze blocks and corrugated iron on a piece of barren land that was once the compound of a German oil company. From the outside, the house does not have an air of permanence. Inside it is immaculately turned out, with china models of flowers and birds on the coffee table.

Fadelala says he had lived much of his life without expectations. Gaddafi's Libya did not encourage hope for a better life. The only real ambition for many Libyans was to stay out of the hands of the dictator's notorious security police and find a job abroad. But Fadelala could not even cling to that small dream. As a gardener in Benghazi's parks, he earns just £90 a month ("I give it all to my wife," he says).

None of that stopped him from supporting Gaddafi. "I had always supported Gaddafi," he says. "There was no one else, so who else could I support? He was the leader."

As Fadelala watched the Tunisian and Egyptian revolutions on al-Jazeera he marvelled at the audacity of the revolutionaries while not entertaining a flicker of hope that the same thing could happen in Libya. "It was interesting but I thought it could never happen here. This is a different country. They didn't have Gaddafi," he says.

The regime calculated that unleashing violence against the protesters would intimidate men like Fadelala from supporting the revolutionaries. It was wrong. By the second day of the revolution, Fadelala was so appalled at the violence that he took the first political stand in his life and went to the courthouse in solidarity with the revolution. "When I saw what was happening, the shooting of protesters at the Katiba, I thought: 'No more Gaddafi'. People were just protesting. He had no right to kill them for that," he says.

Fadelala was not alone. Plenty of Benghazians eyed the uprising with suspicion, worried at the breakdown of order. But Gaddafi's reaction – to slaughter protesters and accuse those demanding democratic freedoms of being drug addicts and members of al-Qaida – revived memories of the most brutal years of the dictator's rule in the 1980s and bolstered support for the uprising.

The revolution has still to be won. Gaddafi controls more territory than the revolutionaries. He managed to get his tanks into Benghazi before western air strikes drove them back. The residents of "free Libya" are in the peculiar position of being the only people on the planet pleading with foreigners to bomb their country.

Yet the uprising has changed everything. The fear of the regime is gone. The revolution has exposed the myth of Gaddafi's invincibility even if he manages to hang on for another few months. Fasi says he now has a reason to stay in Libya. "I really want to share in building this country," he says. "It's a dream to be the best country in the world. We can be that now. I think it needs democracy, and this country is rich. Democracy and oil, that's all we need."

27 APRIL 2011

The Middleclass letters: Kate Middleton writes home to Mummy

CATHERINE BENNETT

ST ANDREWS 2001

Dear Mummy,

Are you sure this is the right place? I haven't seen Him anywhere. But St Andrews is amazing and everyone in hall is amazing, with such an amazing sense of humour. If you are a chav you have to have a nickname, for example I am called Kate Middleclass, but I don't mind really because they are all quite plump. History of Art is amazing. If we are wrong it is not too late to change to somewhere I might be happier, apparently there are more Etonians at Exeter than at Eton!

love, Kate

PS I really need a Barbour.

Dear Mummy,

Do hang on about Exeter because Mummy you were right! I had only been under that desk in the library for two weeks when he turned up, then I dropped my books and you would love his hands, they don't show up on the fridge magnet. Then by chance we were both in Tesco and by chance we reached the checkout at the same time and if you look at June on our calendar, he was wearing that exact sad but sweet expression. And when he was helping me up after I fainted I saw he had my favourite Pot Noodle, the prawn'n'Marmite! I think it was a sign that I should definitely give St Andrews a try.

love, Kate

PS If Steve rings it's over.

Dear Mummy,

The pole was a brilliant idea but I have not seen him for ages. Have you ever been beagling? Jonty Dorchester is mad about beagling as well as being William's cousin but it costs 1,500 a term because of the dogs.

love, Kate

PS Please get me some tweed, it's urgent.

Dear Mummy,

Thank Daddy for the cheque. I went beagling and you would love it apart from the dogs. I met Rollo Porchester and Jago Upminster and Jonty got hog-whimpering and undid my Barbour(!) and all I was wearing underneath was a tiny vest! Apparently William prefers shooting.

love, Kate

PS Do you think Uncle Gary could source a gun?

Dear Mummy,

Don't worry about the gun because HE almost ran me over on his bicycle! Goodness knows how, I just happened to be resting in the road in that little skirt you sent. Apparently History of Art was way too intense so he has switched to Geography! But Mummy he was with this awful Georgiana Gough-Coutts-Anstruther-Stourton-Howard-Vane-Tempest-Kitchener-Byng-ffoulkes-Ferrers-Astor-Prynne-Thynne-Stuart-Willoughby-de Walden-Spencer-Fitzherbert-de Bliquey-Smith, I have forgotten the rest, but you would hate her and he hardly looked at me even though I found my blouse had somehow fallen off in the emergency. I said do call me Kate and Georgiana said it was the shortest name she has ever heard for someone who actually had the choice of a longer one.

love, Catherine

PS Please send my GCSE geography textbook.

Dear Mummy,

I won't change to geog because it was snowing and William was in Tesco when he slipped on a banana I had accidentally just dropped and he said hi, it's Kate Middleclass isn't it and I said Catherine actually. Then he said what ghastly weather we're having which is amazing because I had been thinking the exact same thing then he noticed I was shivering in this tiny vest and offered me his jacket!!! Then Georgiana said oh dear, don't they teach you how to put on your coat in History of Art? Because I was actually holding it! But I said I was on a dare not to wear it from Jonty and it turned out they are practically inseparable! William said how about we all get together for bridge, and I said I much preferred swimming and he looked definitely intrigued.

love, Catherine

PS I need a new bikini. White?

Dear Mummy,

Tell Daddy thanks for finding the house, you would love it. I asked William and Georgiana, who has gained some weight recently, she does not like to swim like William and I. Then there are Jonty and Geordie Scarborough and Guy Money-Scumbagge and they were all so thrilled when I told them about my pole-dancing exercises, even if they definitely will NOT be allowed to watch! Then when Georgiana saw her room also had the washing machine in it she changed her mind, so it is just I and the boys and the beagles can have the utility room.

love, Catherine

PS Tell Pippa I asked, but nobody seems quite sure about Harry and Chelsy.

Dear Mummy,

Honestly I have done everything you said. William says my ironing is legend and he adores my Tesco's Finest Beef Wellington. We both love swimming and apple and mango J2O. But now he is out with Georgiana, who does not even like pot noodles, while I write his essay about stalactites. So I wonder if I should have gone to Exeter with Nico Doncaster and Rollo Living-De'ath because everyone at St Andrews is engaged now, except for the younger sons and National Trust tenants.

Kate

PS Georgiana asked me to model at the Uber-Hotties of St Andrews fashion show even though she knows I am not an honourable, which is history in the making she says.

Dear Mummy,

You are so clever, of course it was Georgiana's trick but I got there early and swapped the chicken suit for a see-through skirt they had all been fighting over. It was quite loose round the waist so I pulled it under my arms and afterwards William said I am truly babelicious which is practically a proposal don't you think? Then somehow my real clothes had vanished so I had to keep the dress on all evening. Isabella left early so Willie came home with me and I showed him my pole-dancing.

love, Catherine

PS How is Daddy's shooting?

Dear Mummy,

Those hot pants sound amazing but I think the other mothers will mainly be in dresses. See you at graduation!

love, Catherine

PS Please tell Daddy the flat has to be crawling distance from Boujis or there is basically no point.

LONDON 2004

Dear Mummy,

Willie's family are amazing. Prince Philip asked me to show him how to work a till! Then Princess Anne asked me how you jump over a counter! Andrew does this trick where he undoes your bra with one hand.

love, Catherine

PS Ask Daddy to move some of the tubs because Willie is going to visit in his helicopter!

Dear Mummy,

The Jigsaw job is amazing but I hate not seeing Willie now Georgiana has split up from Rollo. You should have seen her in Boujis Mummy, she was practically naked and so drunk on fascist-sexmaniacs, which is this amazing mixture of vodka, Limoncello, Night Nurse, Lucozade, cider, raspberry juice and gallons of vintage Krug. Willie loves it but I generally stick to herb tea in case anyone needs their stomach pumped which is a fairly regular occurrence when Harry is around!

love, Catherine

PS No, he hasn't.

Dear Mummy,

I hardly miss working because I am so busy looking after Willie's uniforms and going to Boujis is also quite demanding because of the hours, but rewarding because the boys do need protecting from some of the awful girls, especially after they have drunk lots of McFascistsexmaniacs which is this amazing cocktail of whisky, ginger ale, Grand Marnier, cherry juice, Calpol, sake, Chateau Margaux 1976, Pepsi and gallons of vintage Krug. We have not heard from Georgiana since I accidentally sprayed her with Mace. The answer is still no.

love, Catherine

PS Please do not ask me again.

LONDON 2007

Dear Mummy,
  No.
  love, Catherine
PS I told you not to ask me again.

Dear Mummy,
  Yes I know you had had me by my age. And no. I got the pole out, but still no. So I will do what you said. It seems an awful risk but at least Jonty Dorchester is still free and sadly his father is unwell.
  love, Catherine
PS Camilla says hang in there because it worked for her.

Darling Mummy,
  You genius! Am enclosing the lucky hot pants for Pippa because after I accidentally fell on the floor underneath Jonty Dorchester, who has just inherited by the way, Willie said he suddenly realised what love means. So tomorrow we're going on holiday for a year with Rollo and Geordie and Jago and Guy, all the girls are busy, and I will be in touch as soon as IT happens!
  love, Catherine
PS Camilla says has Pippa ever thought of changing her name to Philippa? Because two syllables is still a short name.

CLARENCE HOUSE 2010

Dearest Mama,
  I know the ring is creepy but Prince Charles is so mad about recycling and I'm sure Camilla is right about knees under the

table first, equality later. And I hate to go on but please remind Pippa about my curtsey! I appreciate it is a little formal but it is what people expect and one may as well get accustomed. Especially with Harry still on the market.

Your loving daughter,

Catherine.

PS Mama, for the announcement, not your jeans-and-boot look PLEASE.

PPS If Princess Anne gets tricky at the reception just find Uncle Gary or kick her up the bum. After Friday 29th we take precedence.

30 APRIL 2011

Let them watch Kate: storming of the palace, British-style

MARINA HYDE

Whether it was history repeating itself as history, or farce repeating itself as farce, depends entirely on your point of view. The marriage of His Royal Highness Prince William to Catherine Middleton was washed down by that cocktail of fevered excitement and irate lack of interest that constitutes public opinion these days – so consider it a day when the country split into two, with each side accusing the other of madness. Much like a standard marital row, in fact.

But along with binge-drinking and misplaced self-regard, royal occasions are something at which Britain is undeniably world-class, and anyone still poised for a republic is advised to put down their knitting needles.

As the cameras trained on the Queen's rather shabby net curtains, awaiting the couple's balcony kiss, one costumed well-wisher told the BBC the crowds had initially been held back. "But in the end," she explained, "the people just pushed the barricades down and rushed towards the palace." And that's as close to the French Revolution as we're going to get – a sort of love-storming of the Bastille.

It all read like a recipe for the perfect British day: worries about the weather, lots of mentions of Princess Di, and a chance to talk about the class system. Even the Germans obliged by having a pop at us, with Der Spiegel's London correspondent wondering "why this eccentric nation continues to worship the Windsors".

The answer, perhaps, is because there is no quality more English than the country's ability to suspend its disbelief again and again – be it in the buildup to a World Cup quarter-final, or when faced with the latest iteration of the House of Windsor story. People know that most of the royal family's recent marriages have been fairytales. Grimm.

But something allows the excitement to rebuild, and anyone who begrudged the gazillions who camped out to spend their day cheering and waving flags had a sobering televisual alternative: ITV2's back-to-back screening of The Only Way is Essex.

As for the marriage ceremony, it was watched by luminaries from the Beckhams to the Bercows to the alleged former head of the Bahraini torture service. To the left, the king of this; to the right, the queen of that. The last time Carole Middleton had to proceed down an aisle this intimidating she was pushing a trolley and uttering the dreaded words "I'm afraid we've run out of the chicken."

But for all the confected snobbery about Kate's origins, and her black sheep uncle Gary, the bourgeois preoccupations of the buildup could never have withstood the big guns of the occasion.

In truth, there is scarcely a piece of British heritage so vulgar or outrageous that it cannot be somehow softened and folded into this most oddly enduring of myths.

During his apprenticeship on Savile Row, the late Alexander McQueen famously sewed "I am a cunt" into the lining of a suit jacket being made for Prince Charles. Yet today, the newest member of the House of Windsor was dressed by the house of McQueen, itself renewed dazzlingly by the succession of Sarah Burton.

At Westminster Abbey itself, two establishments fought for prominence. The Beckhams – who you'll recall sat on thrones at their own wedding – queued like hoi polloi to get in, while megastar Elton John travelled in steerage at the back of the nave, miles behind various ancient but unidentifiable aristos who haven't been playing with a full order of service since the old king was on the throne. The telly cameras immediately overrode their protocol function, and were far more interested in cutting to the celebs than any of the more recherché foreign dignitaries.

Thus it was possible to see that neither the Queen nor Victoria Beckham knows the words to Jerusalem off by heart, with both filmed relying intently on their order of service.

Incidentally, we must doff our plastic coronets to the choice of William Blake's brilliantly mad and mystical hymn of nostalgia for something that never really existed, but which does bring the neck hairs to attention on the big occasion. The only reading was from Romans. "Bless those who persecute you," intoned Kate's brother James, pausing to allow the reference to the press to sink in. "Bless and do not curse them."

Most overused phrase of the day? "A very modern love story", followed by telly commentators' dreary emphasis on the fact that William and Kate were "very down-to-earth people", as though all the nation wanted out of a monarchy were a former accessories buyer for Jigsaw and a groom spawned in the hellfires of the

House of Windsor, but now merely keen to make his name as a mid-ranking air-sea rescue operative.

The day frequently couldn't make its mind up. On the one hand, loyal subjects were supposed to be impressed that minor royals had forgone horsedrawn carriages and were being shuttled in minibuses. On the other, they were expected to develop a sudden yet obsessive interest in state arcana – the provenance of gold altar plates, the engraving of a ceremonial bridle, the fact that the Green Drawing Room at Buckingham Palace opens into the White Drawing Room. We're all supposed to be semioticians now, so do feel encouraged to speculate on what Prince Harry calling himself "best man" as opposed to the more traditional "supporter" means for modern Britain, or what Samantha Cameron's failure to wear a hat means for your local Sure Start centre.

As for what's next, you need hardly ask. ITV's coverage of the wedding kicked off at 0600 hours, and it took all the way until 06.16 before sofa-based royal expert Eve Pollard had declared firmly: "We want an Olympics baby."

So there you have it. Royal uterus watch begins today.

4 MAY 2011

The truth about Bin Laden's last hours

DECLAN WALSH

By the time Pakistani soldiers lifted the cordon around Osama bin Laden's house in the garrison town of Abbottabad, triggering a media stampede, the most obvious traces of its infamous resident had been effaced.

The American soldiers who had swept in aboard four helicopters on Sunday night had scoured the three-storey building, taking away computer hard disks and a trove of documents – as well as Bin Laden's bloodied body, which was later buried at sea.

The following day, Pakistani intelligence – angered at not having been informed of the raid, and embarrassed that it took place under their noses – made a second sweep. Tractors carted away furniture and other belongings. But it was impossible to erase every trace of the drama that ended the manhunt.

Beyond the gates, children in flip-flops and salwar kameez fished chunks of blackened helicopter debris from the surrounding fields, flung there after a US helicopter that failed to take off was blown up by its own soldiers.

One boy produced a jagged, soot-encrusted chunk of metal, perhaps part of an exhaust, from a drain. "This is silver!" declared 12-year-old Yasser. A nervous-looking intelligence official, loitering nearby, grabbed the child by the hand and led him away.

Fascination with the raid was not confined to Abbottabad. In Washington, fresh details were being revealed by the White House, some which contradicted the earlier version of the demise of the world's most wanted man.

In the hours after Bin Laden's death, US officials briefed that he had put up a fight and shot at the Seal 6 team that stormed the second and third floors of his hideout. Other details suggested he used one of his wives as a human shield.

The White House confirmed that neither was true. Bin Laden was unarmed, was shot in the head and chest, and his wife had been wounded in the leg while rushing towards the special forces before he was killed.

The administration was considering whether to release the photos of the Saudi fugitive's body to counter claims in the region that he had not been killed at all. "There are sensitivities about the appropriateness," said spokesman Jay Carney. "It is fair to say it is a gruesome photograph."

CIA director Leon Panetta told NBC that the government had been talking about the best way to release the photograph. "I don't think there was any question that ultimately a photograph would be presented to the public," he said.

Another shifting narrative concerned the property itself. Up close, Bin Laden's house, a tall, unlovely piece of architecture, towering over the policemen guarding the gate, was not quite the million-dollar mansion described by officials. The walls were high, certainly, but not unusually so for north-western Pakistan, where privacy is jealously guarded. The paint was peeling, there was no air conditioning.

But it was the only house in the neighbourhood with barbed wire and surveillance cameras. And it towered over its only neighbour, a small, ramshackle dwelling made of rough bricks with plastic sheeting for windows. The people inside were scared and apprehensive.

Zain Muhammad, an elderly man perched on a rope bed on the porch, said Pakistani soldiers had come in the night and taken away his son, Shamraiz. He produced a photo of a smiling man with a moustache in his early 40s. "I've no idea where he is. The soldiers won't allow us to leave, not even to fetch water." The family did harbour some suspicions about the house 10 feet away, however – and in particular the pair of secretive, security-conscious brothers who owned it.

"They told us they had to protect themselves because they had enemies back in their home village. They had to screen off the house to protect their women. A lot of us thought they were smugglers," said Abid Khan. Stranger still, the two men had two cows and some goats, but had no discernible source of income.

Construction started around 2004. A year later Bin Laden moved in, according to US officials – perhaps around about the time of the devastating Kashmir earthquake that killed 73,000 people in October of that year. As the wounded flooded into Abbottabad's military hospital a mile away – so many that doctors set up a tent on the main lawn – the Saudi fugitive and his clan were settling into this house down the road.

There had been great speculation about his whereabouts. Across the border in Afghanistan, US soldiers distributed matchboxes with Bin Laden's picture and details of a $25m bounty.

In Pakistan, the US embassy paid for expensive television ads appealing for information. "Who can stop these terrorists? Only you!" implored a voice as images of Bin Laden and 13 henchmen flashed across the screen.

The then president, Pervez Musharraf, insisted the Americans were wrong. His security forces had "broken the vertical and horizontal command and communication links of al-Qaida" in Pakistan, he boasted. "There are a lot of people who say that Osama bin Laden is here in Pakistan," he said. "Please come and show us where."

In Abbottabad, the two Pashtun brothers had finally completed their house, less than a mile from the Pakistan Military Academy where Musharraf himself had been trained.

One of them was Bin Laden's courier, the man trusted to take his messages to the outside world. CIA officials subsequently learned his nom de guerre from an al-Qaida militant picked up in Iraq: Sheikh Abu Ahmed al-Kuwaiti. US officials described him as a Pakistani brought up in Kuwait.

To the locals, however, he was simply a Pashtun businessman with an identity card issued in Charsadda, north of Peshawar. He and his brother seemed to be known by several names: Arshad and Tariq Khan, but also Rasheed, Ahmed and Nadeem. The gas bill was in the name of the elder brother, Arshad Khan, presumed to be the "courier" sought by the Americans. Oddly, the house had four separate gas connections. They kept largely to themselves, coming and going in a small white Suzuki van and a red jeep. But they joined in with the everyday rituals of life, condoling the bereaved, celebrating weddings and births. It may have been a necessary part of the cover story; to have done otherwise might have aroused greater suspicion.

"They weren't chatty," said Rasheed, a 32-year-old local shopkeeper, lounging behind his counter, who said he sold the brothers salty biscuits and chewy toffees when they arrived with their seven children. He refused to believe they had any links to Kuwait. "We absolutely believed they were Pashtuns," he said.

But the young trader did notice one strange thing. Seven years earlier he had worked on the house as a labourer when it was being built, and had wondered why the brothers insisted that the walls should be 3ft thick.

In the end, the two brothers were Bin Laden's downfall. The CIA learned of Arshad Khan's identity four years ago, and after a two-year search traced him to the Abbottabad area.

Then, last August, a Pakistani working for the CIA spotted one of the brothers as he drove his Suzuki van from Peshawar, leading them to the house. In February, the CIA became convinced Bin Laden was inside, leading to last Sunday's raid.

The two brothers were killed in the opening moments of the assault, according to the CIA, along with Bin Laden and one of his sons, thought to be Khalid.

Many details, however, remain blurred. US officials amended their initial version to reveal that a woman who was killed during the raid on the compound was not Bin Laden's wife.

It is also not clear how Bin Laden, who was cornered in a third-floor room now marked by a shattered windowpane, resisted as the US soldiers barged into his room.

President Barack Obama insists the Navy Seals would have detained him if they could, but it is hard to imagine US officials would have relished either a trial or the spectacle of the al-Qaida leader being held in Guantánamo Bay.

Bin Laden's erstwhile neighbours, now in the gaze of the world's media, congregated outside his house. Some seemed angry, others bemused. One bearded man scolded his friends for speaking to the foreign press; others seemed to relish the attention, presenting themselves for detailed interviews about their brushes with the neighbour they never knew. A few displayed pro-Osama bravado. "I would have opened fire on the Americans myself if I had to defend him!" declared one man.

Others worried about more material problems. "It's going to destroy property prices in this area," muttered one. And there was a surreal moment when an Osama lookalike – a man with a thin face, a large white turban and a full, scraggly beard – turned up at the front gate, triggering laughs and a flutter of camera shutters.

But there was no sign of life from a nearby property, about 50 metres from Bin Laden's back wall, with a high perimeter wall and two watchtowers. Neighbours said it had been built three years ago by a man whose family has long owned property in the area. The nameplate read: Major Amir Aziz. Locals said he was a serving Pakistan army officer. Despite repeated rings on the doorbell, he refused to answer.

It is unclear what will happen now to the house that Osama built. It has become an embarrassment for Pakistan, a reminder of the fact that the world's most famous fugitive managed to live in suburban comfort, apparently undetected, for up to six years.

Some fear it could become a shrine of sorts for al-Qaida supporters, and so it may be destroyed. But failing that, it may simply be rented out again. It is, after all, an attractive property – spacious, well located, and fully fitted with advanced security features. In fact it's just the sort of house that is favoured by security-conscious US diplomats elsewhere in Pakistan. Perhaps they might consider taking it.

6 MAY 2011

Seven lessons from 7/7

ESTHER ADDLEY

1. The line between life and death is very thin, and very arbitrary

Patrick Barnes and Philip Beer travelled together from Bore-hamwood every morning, but on 7 July 2005, the service was slow and they got to the Piccadilly line 15 minutes later than usual. They were standing face to face, holding on to a bar, when Barnes felt as if he had been hit on the head with a brick. It was a moment or two until he came round to hear the screams. Barnes shouted through the smoke for his friend, whom he couldn't see: "Are we going to die?" "No," said Beer, "everything's going to be fine."

In the smoke and confusion, Barnes was able to stagger from the scene, but he couldn't find his friend. Beer, wedged tightly against him when the bomb exploded, died in the carriage.

Again and again, the shattering testimonies of the witnesses to 7 July have underlined how very thin the line was between life and death, and the apparent arbitrariness of who survived and who did not.

Catherine al-Wafai, sitting five feet from the suicide bomber Mohammad Sidique Khan on the Edgware Road train, walked off the tube in a daze and made it all the way home, wearing only one shoe. Philip Duckworth, standing next to Shehzad Tanweer near Aldgate, was blown from the carriage and staggered from the scene, with just a small piece of the bomber's shin bone in his eye. Others who were further away from the bomb sites, however, did not make it.

In some cases survival depended on the chance intervention of others. Martine Wright and Andrew Brown both lost legs in the Aldgate bomb but their lives were saved because they were sitting near the carriage door, and because Elizabeth Kenworthy, an off-duty police officer who climbed into the carriage, was able to reach them, tie tourniquets around their limbs and keep them calm. The young man rolling on the floor a little further into the carriage appeared much less badly injured, so she was "very, very upset" to learn that Richard Ellery had died.

Others made it thanks to reserves of will that they probably had no idea they had. Philip Patsalos, a university professor, recalled feeling his leg after the King's Cross blast and finding it "rather mushy". "I started thinking to myself, I've got to stay alive, I'm going to die here." He concentrated on counting his breaths in and out, keeping himself calm. When the emergency services arrived, he was so still they walked past him, thinking that he too was dead.

"I said, 'Sir, help me, I'm dying,'" he told the inquests. "Did he respond?" asked the lawyer. "Yes."

2. 7 July was a global atrocity

For much of the past five months, a number of news organisations have reported the 7 July inquest largely in their London news bulletins, as if only the capital had been attacked. But it is not merely the fact that this was the biggest terrorist assault in British history, barring Lockerbie, that makes 7/7 an atrocity against the entire country – and much further afield. The timing and location of the bombs, attacking commuters at rush hour on London's socially levelling transport network, meant that they killed both bankers and students, cleaners and consultants, many from far beyond the capital.

Ellery, a shop assistant at Jessops in Ipswich, was visiting for a one-day course. Michael "Stan" Brewster worked for Derbyshire county council and was in the capital for a conference. Jennifer Nicholson commuted from Reading, James Adams from Peterborough, Adrian Johnson from Nottinghamshire. Marie Hartley died on a day trip from Lancashire.

The attacks also acutely illustrated London's status as a global microcosm in which, with brutal irony, different cultures habitually live, work and travel together in peace, side by side. The dead of 7 July had origins in at least 23 countries: Montserrat and Mauritius, Kenya and Poland, Sri Lanka and New Zealand and Ghana.

Sam Ly's family had fled Vietnam for Australia as refugees in the 1970s; he had travelled to London on a working holiday. Atique Sharifi's parents were killed by the Taliban when he was a child; he came to Britain in 2002, unable to speak any English, to earn money to support his younger sister in Afghanistan. Gladys Wundowa had worked in a salt mine as a child in her native Ghana to raise money for her siblings; she became a maid for a Lebanese family, moved to London, found work as a cleaner and had embarked on a course in housing management when she died. Two thousand people attended her funeral in her home village in Ghana.

It wasn't only London that mourned.

3. Crises turn some people into heroes

How would you react if the railway carriage or bus in which you were travelling was destroyed by a suicide bomb? Would you flee, mindful of your family and your own survival? Would you dare walk down a tube tunnel towards a loud bang, not knowing whether the line's electric current was off? Would you climb into a smoke-filled carriage filled with scenes of unspeakable carnage? For those following the inquests, those questions have been unspoken but ever present.

It is not easy to predict what makes a hero. Certainly many of those who risked their lives to help on 7 July had experience, or some professional training, in trauma situations. Adrian Heili, whose intervention almost certainly helped to save the life of Danny Biddle, who lost both legs, an eye and his spleen in the Edgware Road blast, had served with the Austrian army in Kosovo. Group Captain Craig Staniforth, an RAF wing commander, smashed a window in his undamaged train, which had pulled up alongside the bombed Edgware Road carriage, and swung from the handrails to climb into the wreckage to help desperately injured survivors. He talked to John Tulloch, who had serious head injuries, telling him about his daughter's university applications in a desperate bid to stop him going to sleep.

Others, however, were not professionals. Events organiser Steven Desborough was being evacuated from the Aldgate train, when he turned – "I don't know why" – and climbed into the wrecked carriage. He cradled 24-year-old Carrie Taylor in the moments before she died.

"There were people that walked on and I don't blame them," Desborough was careful to say, and of course many of those who left may have calculated, rightly, that they were unable to help and would only be in the way. Others were in profound shock. It is difficult to explain the impulse that prompted a number of passengers at Aldgate to pause to take photographs of the scene even as Dr Gerardine Quaghebeur was fighting to save lives; they may not now be able to explain it themselves. But given the scale of the atrocity, and the challenges facing the emergency services in arriving at the bomb sites, there is no question that some, perhaps many, passengers' lives were saved directly because of the actions of their fellow commuters.

"I don't think you can sum up my debt of gratitude," Wright has said of Kenworthy. "People like that don't come around that often, and if it wasn't for her I would be dead."

4. The bombers were ordinary, silly young men, as well as evil murderers

Shortly before 1am on 6 July, Jermaine Lindsay, who the following day would murder 26 people on the Piccadilly line train, received a text message from Khan, the plot's ringleader. The message, though menacing in retrospect, is almost comical in its content. The pair, their texts showed, had taken to referring to each other as characters from the 1980s television programme The A-Team, and riffing on tough guy BA Baracus's fear of flying.

"Yo BA big nackers," texted Khan, "you on dat plane or wat. fool."

Lindsay replied: "I ain't getting on no plane fool."

Khan may not have known at the time that Lindsay, who was married with a young child, had invited his 17-year-old girlfriend to spend the evening of 6 July in a hotel with him in London, where he promised her they would "spend some quality time together and ... have some bad boy room service".

The pair had met at a boxing club in their home town of Aylesbury after he winked at her. They had been on a handful of dates, going for a drive to a nearby lake in his Fiat Brava, or to Milton Keynes to wander round a shopping centre. On that occasion he asked her if she knew how to get hold of a gun, since he was going to London with some mates "to teach some people a lesson".

Throughout the inquest a vivid and unsettling picture has emerged of the four bombers, who – as well as being murderous plotters directed by phone calls from an as-yet unidentified terrorist mastermind in Pakistan – were also banal, sometimes silly, often very ordinary young men.

Tanweer also had a secret girlfriend whom he had met as a teenager, and courted by taking for late-night drives in his car. She knew of his obsession with cricket and jiu-jitsu, but thought he wasn't particularly religious. They had moved apart but stayed in contact, and got together again in early 2005. She felt he loved her, she said, and they made plans for the future, though she was puzzled by the blond tones in the hair on his head and arms – in fact, they had been bleached by the hydrogen peroxide he had been preparing in the bomb factory. The night before the bombings he played cricket with friends in a nearby park.

Khan, too, was a complicated character, greatly respected in the primary school where he was a learning mentor, though teachers had expressed concerns about his hardline views. The man regarded as a father figure was at the same time using his position to try to convert children as young as 11 to his brand of radical Islam.

Shortly after the 9/11 attacks, the inquests heard, when he was still a young teenager, Hasib Hussain had passed a note to his fellow school pupils which read: "You're next."

Hussain, 18 when he died, had told his teachers that he wanted to go to university, but dropped out of school a week before it was due to finish at the end of June 2005. A week after that he murdered 13 people on the number 30 bus.

5. Though many individuals were heroic, the emergency response fell short

PC Dave Hill, normally employed as a diplomatic protection officer for the Metropolitan police, was driving with colleagues along the Thames when they heard reports of unexplained explosions at Edgware Road. They raced to the scene, where Hill entered the tunnel and climbed into the mangled carriage – "because I was there". The officer, who wept while recalling the scenes he had witnessed, may have directly saved a number of lives through his actions; he was far from alone among emergency-service professionals in acting without a second thought to save others.

But, however inspiring the individual acts of heroism performed by police officers, firefighters and paramedics, the uncomfortable truth is that the emergency services' response to 7 July was hampered by delays, communication failures, tactical confusion and a jobsworth adherence to protocol that at times defied common sense.

Again and again, survivors spoke of the appalling wait for rescuers, even as they felt themselves slipping ever closer to death. Fire crews did not arrive at Edgware Road until an hour after the attacks. The first paramedic on the scene called urgently for ambulances; he learned later that ambulances from two stations nearby had not been dispatched. Paramedics intended for Russell Square were sent to the wrong location, meaning they also arrived almost an hour after the attack.

Firefighters arrived at King's Cross station at 9.13am but did not go to the scene of the blast until 9.42am because of communication protocols. Police and firefighters were forced to use runners between tunnels and station concourses because their radio system at the time did not work underground.

Most worrying, perhaps, was what emerged at the inquest about the "Gold" command centre at London Ambulance Service headquarters. This was a scene of barely contained chaos, in which staff could not log on to computers, messages were scribbled on pieces of paper and subsequently lost, and a single operator was handling every 999 call and radio message relating to the four bomb sites. Three hours after the first attacks, the inquest heard, those in charge of the ambulance response were still unclear about how many bombs had exploded and where. Ambulances were not even dispatched to Tavistock Square, scene of the bus bomb, until 52 minutes after the blast.

The ambulance service was also forced to admit that it "did not provide a complete picture" to a London Assembly inquiry in 2006 into the emergency response, giving an account which suggested a speedier and more efficient response than had actually taken place. "There was no intent to deceive," insisted an ambulance spokesman.

6. We may never know how much MI5 knew before 7 July

One of the most dramatic images to emerge from the inquests was not an image of a bomb scene, but a grainy, black-and-white surveillance photograph of Aldgate bomber Tanweer, which MI5 sent to US secret services in the months before the attacks to be shown to a key al-Qaida informant. The informant, Mohammed Junaid Babar, had not identified the image as being significant, it emerged in evidence – perhaps unsurprisingly since the original, which very clearly showed the bomber with Mohammad Sidique Khan, had been cropped so badly as to render Tanweer unrecognisable and cut out Khan altogether. Babar had been involved in training Khan in a terrorist camp in Afghanistan.

MI5 had no explanation for the poor quality of the image. "One of my children," tartly noted inquest counsel Hugo Keith, "could have done a better job."

Witness G, the security service spokesman giving evidence anonymously, acknowledged in court that MI5 had allowed a committee of MPs to be misled over its classification of suspects, and had not told the MPs about the original, good-quality picture.

But if the spokesman, under cross-examination, did shed some light on MI5's involvement, to many of the bereaved families his evidence was distinguished more by what it did not reveal. It was known before the inquest, for example, that Khan came on to MI5's radar on at least eight occasions before the bombings, dating back as early as 2001. The witness cited limited resources, unsophisticated computer systems, even Khan's common name, as explanations of why the dots had not been joined. Repeatedly, he said the service had improved its systems since the attacks and would be unlikely to miss such connections again. But he did not elaborate how and why.

At one point, almost as an aside, Witness G told the court that he was confident Khan could have been identified as a trained jihadist in March 2005, four months before the bombings, had agents chosen to investigate a major lead. They did not, he said, for a "proportionate and reasonable" reason. However, he was unable to disclose what that was, he said, "for national security reasons".

7. Inquests have their limits

After a process of more than six months, during which more than 300 people have given evidence in person and a further 200 by statement, 1,173 pieces of evidence have been disclosed and at least 16 separate legal teams have had their say, all involved will hope that the coroner will have made significant strides towards uncovering the full story of 7 July.

But however admirable, in the minds of many bereaved families, Lady Justice Hallett's management of the inquest process has been, questions are certain to remain even after she delivers her verdicts. Legal rules tightly circumscribe the powers of coroners, whose principal role, of course, is to rule on cause of death. It is not yet absolutely certain how much scope she will consider she has under "rule 43" to make recommendations to prevent further deaths.

Some of the bereaved families believe that the end of the inquest should represent the close of the period of inquiry. But others have pressing questions that they insist still have to be answered. A number of family members feel that the security services were allowed to sidestep important questions during the inquest process, and that the witness who gave evidence on MI5's behalf was not pushed by the coroner or her barrister to give full answers.

Some relatives question Witness G's assertion that the failure to follow up intelligence about the 7 July bombers was due to limited resources, or question why Babar, who remains the only person to be convicted in relation to the bombings, served only four years in a US prison before being released.

Some years ago lawyers representing survivors and the bereaved families launched legal action to force the government to hold an independent inquiry into the attacks. Those proceedings were stayed while the inquest process was ongoing; they could be reactivated, dependent on the coroner's findings and potential recommendations. It may not be over yet.

7 MAY 2011

Lib Dems slapped, punched, kicked, knifed and left for dead

JONATHAN FREEDLAND

A year ago, the country was plunged into a weekend of murky uncertainty after a general election that nobody won. This time, there was no fog or confusion – only dazzling clarity. It illuminated a battlefield in which Alex Salmond stood tallest, master of all he surveyed, closely followed by a grinning David Cameron, whose plan for dominating the decade took another step forward. Far, far behind, picking his way through the corpses of his mown-down troops, was a bloodied Nick Clegg. And, all around them, the landscape of a Britain that could be about to change drastically – even breaking in two.

The day brought three outcomes whose scale was breathtaking. Most expected the Scottish National party to triumph in Edinburgh, but few predicted it would crush its opponents so comprehensively, winning an overall majority under a PR system designed 12 years ago to thwart just such a possibility. Never let it be said again that PR produces indecisive outcomes, while first past the post guarantees certainty: in Scotland and Westminster it's the other way around.

The second knockout result came in the AV referendum, with a thorough walloping of the alternative vote. The unmistakable victims of that, and of the rest of the day's voting, were the Liberal Democrats. The party was not just given a bloody nose by the electorate: it was slapped, punched, kicked and finally knifed before being left for dead. Flattened in Scotland, the Lib Dems lost half their councillors in England, their share of the vote reduced to numbers so meagre they were last seen back when the party was known as the SLD and mocked as "Salads".

Defeated politicians always talk of "lessons learned" in such circumstances, so here's one. Personalities matter, now more than ever. Voters may piously tell phone-in programmes they care only about the issues, but the last 24 hours have confirmed that that's bunk. The SNP swept the board largely because Scots saw Salmond as a natural first minister, while his Labour opponent was anything but: Gray by name, grey by nature.

In the 21st century, candidates for the biggest jobs need vivid, stand-out personalities. Labour take note: they can have as many policy reviews as they like, but if the British public don't warm to Ed Miliband it will all be in vain. This personalisation of British politics cuts both ways. Few deny that the Lib Dem wipeout and the AV defeat were a repudiation of Clegg. The no campaign calculated that the mere sight of the Lib Dem leader's face on their leaflets would turn millions off voting reform – and their calculation paid off.

The immediate impact will be on the coalition. Lib Dems now understand exactly why the Tories were so eager to make that "comprehensive and generous offer" a year ago this weekend. It was not so much a power-sharing arrangement as a blame-taking one: the Lib Dems' role is to be the Conservatives' human shield and on Thursday they played the part perfectly. They took the heat while the Tories remained unscathed, their share of the vote unchanged since 2010, with even some council gains in England. For the senior partner, coalition is working out very nicely.

Conventional wisdom says Clegg will now demand a consolation prize or two, goodies to soothe his battered party and keep it content with coalition. But Cameron has no pressing reason to be emollient. For what leverage does Clegg have? He can't threaten to walk out, knowing that in an early general election only annihilation awaits. The Lib Dems are now hostages in this coalition, chained to the cabinet table, fated merely to hope that something turns up between now and 2015.

That is but one measure of Cameron's strength. His victory in the no campaign is another. Even Lord Mandelson praised him for his "bold leadership", conceding that it was the prime minister's eventual intervention on AV that made the difference. Above all, Cameron has now secured the long-term future of a first-past-the-post system that ensured virtual Tory hegemony for most of the last century. The shrivelling of the Lib Dems helps him further still, as onetime tactical Lib Dem voters head back to Labour – thereby splitting the anti-Tory vote and letting the Conservatives win. That's how the Tories picked up seats yesterday.

But surely the most significant consequence of 5 May will be the SNP's ability to stage a referendum on Scottish independence, at a time of its choosing. Again, the received wisdom and polls say such a vote will be lost. But they said the same about the SNP – or any party – winning 65 seats in Holyrood. And now the SNP has 69. Besides, Salmond is probably the most accomplished political operator and performer in these islands. I would not bet against him.

And if he won a referendum and the union that has lasted three centuries were to break up? Obviously, the cultural and constitutional impact would reverberate for generations. But the narrower electoral consequences would endure too. An independent Scotland would deprive Labour of its most solid base, all but ensuring a permanent Tory majority in Westminster.

That is the sharpest lesson for Labour, on what was a tepid night for the party at best. It can no longer rely on Scotland; it has to be competitive in England. Otherwise, the future is clear, but it is definitely not orange. The future is blue.

7 MAY 2011

When refs attack.
Or just use your nickname

THE SECRET FOOTBALLER

According to the Terminator films, man-made machines will arrive sometime in the future where they become self-aware and take over the world. Given the speed at which football embraces technology, it's safe to assume that referees will be the last human sacrifice. In the meantime we will have to hope that we can produce a few more officials like Howard Webb, who has the task of taking charge of Manchester United and Chelsea on Sunday.

Many referees lay claim to one archetypal dictator-like trait (self-confidence) while exhibiting all the hallmarks of another (self-delusion). What rankles most with players during a game is a referee who is clearly enjoying being the centre of attention, and not, I hasten to add, because we feel that they may be detracting from the main event, namely us. This is because a referee who displays this behaviour generally blows his whistle more than is necessary, impinges on the flow of play and is wholly unapproachable from the outset.

This showmanship could be the result of a few things: either the teams he is refereeing have given him a hard time in the not too distant past or, just as likely, the referee in question personifies his performance. Whatever the reason, some games have certainly been ruined by these flaws. For the record, Rob Styles embodied all of those characteristics.

Some referees are over-friendly and refer to the top players by their nicknames and to other players, who perhaps don't command the same aura, by their surname. Thinking about it as I have over the years, it must be in our human nature to want to buddy up to those who are at the top of the tree and, in turn, try to please them.

I have seen many decisions given that I don't think players from smaller teams would necessarily have got, and when you throw into the mix the consequences of not giving a decision to a "big" player that then results in a goal for the other team or incurs the wrath of that player's manager in the media, then one can see how a referee might have one eye on Monday morning's headlines before he steps on to the pitch.

This human element in referees gives players all the encouragement they need when trying to steer a match in their favour, from cracking jokes in the tunnel with him to applauding when he gives a decision their way – especially if it should have gone to the other team – or putting a reassuring hand on his shoulder. Yet an aggressive approach can be just as effective. If a referee gives any indication that he may be unsure or weak then he will come in for some fairly heavy-handed tactics, from physical contact to the worst abuse.

Webb, who for my money is the best referee we have, once showed me first-hand how he refuses to take any nonsense from players. After a series of free-kicks given against us, I ran towards him to remonstrate, shouting and swearing as I went. As I got to him, he swivelled round and poked a sausage-sized finger into my midriff. Winded, I found myself in the desperately uncomfortable position of being doubled over, while at the same time crying with laughter inside at the thought of anyone in the street where I grew up finding out that a referee – and a copper no less – had taken me down with a single prod of a finger. He finished me off by saying in an eerily calm voice: "Don't talk to me like that." Sometimes it is better to admit defeat. The shame, however, lives on.

I can't say that I am particularly proud of losing my cool and swearing at referees. It is very difficult to get across just how angry you can become on a football pitch, but swearing is a weakness – a sign that the brain isn't working fast enough to construct a decent sentence and get your point across.

There are a couple of refs who swear as much as some of the players, telling us to fuck off if we go near them and worse. It isn't a problem, but it does stand out as a markedly different approach and makes booking a player for dissent more tricky.

Of course, there are occasions when players, and managers for that matter, go completely over the top and make a referee's job virtually impossible. The Football Association wastes money on its flawed Respect campaign in a token attempt to look as if it is being proactive, but it does not offer any of the referees the real protection that they so badly need for them to do their job.

I believe that fitting all officials with a microphone, with the full knowledge of the players, managers, coaching staff and fans, would go a long way to ending the abuse they take. I'm pretty confident that players would think more than twice about swearing at any official if they thought everyone could hear them. I know I would.

In 1989 David Elleray wore a microphone in a match between Millwall and Arsenal. After he judged that Tony Adams's shot hadn't crossed the line, the Arsenal captain was overheard calling Elleray the C-word. If there is one word that you never call a referee it's "cheat". Adams, it is safe to assume, would have spoken to Elleray a little differently had he known he was being recorded.

At least it looks as if there may be some relief on the horizon for officials. It is widely anticipated that goalline technology will be with us in time for the 2012-13 season, which should help to stem some of the conflict that we see every time an official has to make a decision like the one at Stamford Bridge last Saturday.

Not enough time for machines to gain self-awareness between now and then but certainly long enough for the players.

9 MAY 2011

Watching Seve in his prime was a life-affirming experience

RICHARD WILLIAMS

In good times and bad, Severiano Ballesteros never failed to remind us of why we fell in love with sport in the first place. Watching him play in his gorgeous prime, swept along on gusts of glory, improvising with an artist's instinct and touch, was an infallibly life-affirming experience. Watching him during the long years of decline was a reminder of mortality.

His death deprives us of a golfer whose appeal reached out far beyond the game's own constituency. He was a handsome man and, as he chased down five major championships, a handsome sight. In later times, before he belatedly called it a day, the hopeless thrashing of his dark-eyed attempts to revive that lost genius drew crowds willing him to recover the rapture of his youth.

Everyone in this line of work has favourite Seve stories, tales of encounters with a man in whose hands sport turned into the thing it is supposed to be: a matter of risk and romance, of danger and daring. The first of mine comes from a time when his descent from Olympus was gathering pace.

It was back in the spring of 1994, on a day when black rain was falling on the practice day for the Spanish Open in Madrid. Ballesteros, 20 years into a professional career that had begun at 17, was working on the practice green with a coach called Mac O'Grady, a 43-year-old ex-pro from Minnesota whose methods combined the findings from his own research into the neurobiological aspects of the golf swing with mind-management techniques that appeared to have been drawn from the wilder shores of Californian psychotherapy.

A week earlier Ballesteros had won his first tournament in two years, the Benson & Hedges Open at St Mellion, ending a headline-making barren spell of 50 events with only four top-10 finishes and 17 missed cuts. Hoping to find out if the recovery was real and he was finally on the way back, I walked in his footsteps with the voluble coach for company. O'Grady's words gave a glimpse of the lengths to which a top sportsman will go in the attempt to become reacquainted with the gifts that once came naturally.

Here's the sort of thing he said, delivered with the tongue on rapid-fire, punctuated by sleeve-plucking and eye-locking and scribbled down more or less accurately while following his client up hill and down dale: "Seve has one mission. Salvage. That's it. To get things stable. He's the captain of the ship. The bullion's in the hold and it's pulling out of the harbour on the Spanish Main. In his youth he felt invulnerable. He had his adventures and he couldn't wait to get back to give the spoils to Queen Isabella. But now in his old age of 37 he realises that he can't carry the whole world on his shoulders. Three years ago he hit the rocks, the ship sank, and all the gold went down with it. But it's all still there, at the bottom of the sea, waiting."

Later, in the locker room, Ballesteros was more interested in looking back at his 15 pars during that final round at St Mellion than in discussing his game in terms of carrying bullion back to Queen Isabella. He thought he had glimpsed the one quality that always eluded him, even in the major-winning days, when his genius could still overpower the more erratic elements of his game. "Consistency is what gives you the victory," he said.

"When you're playing consistently, you can have a bad day and still score OK. What I find most difficult as I get older is to focus on the game. For me there's more than just golf now. When I was 20, there was nothing else. Now I have a family, I have businesses. And also, of course, the body doesn't react as well as it did at 20."

So now, at 37, what was his motivation? "A lot of people follow me. They're pulling for me. When I go to a tournament and I see the people who've come to watch me, that motivates me a lot. I feel like I must do something extra to make sure they enjoy it. When you enjoy it, the motivation's there."

But it wasn't just about the mind. He had recently returned from an Arizona clinic, where five weeks of intense treatment had failed to achieve more than a temporary easing of the chronic back condition that was slowly and insidiously bringing about the downfall of a champion. Nothing that O'Grady or any other coach could say or do would restore the light of Ballesteros's once blazing talent to anything like full beam. And, like a lot of relationships in his life, the one with O'Grady, which began so promisingly, was corroded by suspicion and ended in acrimony.

A few weeks later, however, there was a moment that no one present will ever forget. It was during the 1995 Ryder Cup at the beautiful Oak Hill course outside Rochester in New York State, and on a bright and blustery Sunday the European captain, Bernard Gallagher, ignored Ballesteros's wayward form and sent him out to face Tom Lehman in the opening match of the singles round. Soon Seve was clattering around the course in a fury of scattergun tee shots, attended by a small but devoted gallery.

At the 5th he sliced his drive so badly that it cleared a stream and landed yet again in thick rough, this time with a stand of tall trees between his ball and the green. Knowing that he would not take the safe option, his audience clustered around him in a semicircle, close enough for him to feel their breath on his neck as he surveyed an obstacle as big as your average cathedral. Seve extracted the 9-iron from his bag, swished it a couple of times, took a long, deep breath and planted himself over the ball. The wind dropped. Birds ceased their song. Then Seve gave a mighty heave and the ball exploded from the face of his club before soaring high over the trees.

He was on the move before it had cleared the highest branches, following his shot like a gun dog on the scent, chased as it dropped in the heart of the green by the cheers that no one present wanted to stop. And, from a position of almost ludicrous unlikeliness, he got up and down.

Those cheers were his companion through more than 30 years of triumph and disaster. One can only hope he heard them in the very darkest hours, on sleepless nights far away from the golf course, when he still wondered if he could turn back the pitiless forces of decay and, through sheer force of will, call the magic back to life.

24 MAY 2011

Rule-breaking love rat lets cat out of bag

SIMON HOGGART

An MP yesterday suddenly named Ryan Giggs as the prominent footballer who had obtained an injunction.

The MP cannot be named, by me at least, since he is, prima facie, guilty of a breach of parliamentary convention, if not the law. He is also a family man, and a self-admitted "love rat". My ruling is that he has suffered enough and it would not be in the public interest, or in his and his family's interest, for me to name him and so expose him to further abuse.

The MP stood up during a brief session devoted to injunctions and the privacy law. The attorney general, Dominic Grieve, had already announced there would be a committee of both houses devoted to the matter. This is the government's usual way of saying "shut up, will you, while we try to work something out". John Prescott – sorry, m'lord Prescott – sat in the gallery alternately scowling and laughing.

John Whittingdale, who chairs the culture, media and sport committee, said you would need to be living in an igloo not to know the name of the footballer; there was, he said, a real danger of making the law an ass. (Some might think it was already too late to fret about that.)

David Davis was worried because last week's report by the master of the rolls (not the man who chose Lord Irvine's famously expensive wallpaper, but the chief civil judge in the country) seemed to imply that injunctions should apply to parliament as well as to the media.

Grieve made it clear that nothing would affect parliamentary privilege. But he didn't promise that the media could report what was said. This would be truly weird and a politician's worst nightmare; MPs could use the rules to expose wrongdoing but no one else could know about their zealous work. Unless they used Twitter.

Then came the moment. I was slightly surprised that the Speaker called the MP, who I can reveal sits for a Midlands constituency and isn't exactly the hunkiest he-man in the House, not that that narrows the field much, frankly.

The MP has form, and has tried to break injunctions before. But if he had not been called, he would have barged in on a point of order later, so perhaps Mr Bercow had no choice.

The MP rose to say that about 75,000 people had named Ryan Giggs on Twitter. "It is obviously impractical to imprison them all, and with reports that Giles Coren also faces imprisonment..."

The Speaker leapt up. The thought of Giles Coren's Prison Feasts, a 13-part series on BBC1, was too much. He slapped the MP down, saying these occasions were for discussing principles, "not seeking to flout, for whatever purpose!" We were shocked. Mr Bercow had used a transitive verb without an object. Can parliament sink any lower?

We were left to ponder the true meaning of these events. Rich footballer has affair – two days' wonder in the tabloids. Rich footballer spends a fortune to conceal affair – this one will run for years.

25 MAY 2011

'You must discover the character behind the face'

STEVE BELL

Hitting 60 gives you plenty of food for thought. Having a retrospective exhibition at the same time gives further cause for astonishment. How did I ever manage to draw that small, without glasses or artificial aids? How did I manage without scanning and email? Well, everything went by train. How did I manage with four young children snapping at my heels? I used to work at night, when they were all tucked up. My oldest son, born the year I started working for the Guardian, is now 30 with ankle-biters of his own. He's grown – but have I?

There is no defined career path to becoming a cartoonist. I came to it almost in reverse. I have loved cartoons, drawing and having a laugh, but the notion of doing it for a living didn't take root until very late. I had studied art, but I found the idea of being an artist risible. (Monsieur L'Artiste was one of the first characters I ever drew at university.) So I started out as a teacher, but the stress was unbelievable. I knew things had gone too far when being off to have my wisdom teeth taken out felt like a relief. What I craved was a job where I could shut myself in a room and talk to myself, sometimes very loudly and in a variety of accents.

With my girlfriend Heather's encouragement, I handed in my notice and followed my friend from university, Kipper Williams, into the daunting world of freelance cartooning. I had no portfolio and no contacts, other than those Kipper gave me, and no plan, other than the fantasies engendered by my infinite sense of entitlement. It was the second-best decision in my life. The best was to marry Heather, which I did that same year, in 1977.

While I was teaching, I had been drawing strip cartoons and illustrations, unpaid, for Birmingham Broadside, the city's answer to Time Out. I had introduced a character called Maxwell the Mutant: having been exposed to deadly radiation, in the grand old comic book tradition, Maxwell would mutate into someone unexpected every time he drank a pint of mild. Since 1977 was a Jubilee year, he naturally mutated into the Queen. His deadly adversary was Neville Worthyboss, a thinly veiled and rather inadequate caricature of the then Tory leader of Birmingham city council, Neville Bosworth. Despite my ambition and self-belief, I knew I needed to work on my caricatures. I never realised they would become a life's work.

Through dogged persistence (I still cherish my rejection letter from the Beano), I found work writing and drawing children's comics. My first professional effort in print, for IPC's Whoopee comic, was Dick Doobie the Back to Front Man; he sank without trace after a few months in 1978. But I was learning – and I had been paid.

At a leftwing publication called the Leveller, I introduced a strip about a really obnoxious supreme being, Lord God Almighty. But I wanted to draw comics about politics. I tried Time Out repeatedly, which in those days had a leftwing slant, but there was nothing going. Then I went to the magazine's offices for about the fifth time in 1979, immediately after the election of Margaret Thatcher, and saw the news editor, Duncan Campbell. He said they were looking for a comic strip to tackle the new Tory government. Would I like to submit a rough idea? I rushed home, grunted, strained and produced a pencilled rough of an allegorical strip where the animals were the people and the farm management were the government. They wanted one every fortnight; naturally, it became known as Maggie's Farm.

This was a huge break, but my Maggie needed work. I'm not someone who has an easy, natural talent for quick caricature, as Gerald Scarfe and Martin Rowson do. I take my time. It isn't simply a question of getting the likeness: you have to discover the character behind the face. My early Thatchers are no more than press photos rendered into line drawings, but then the woman herself was not yet a fully formed personality. The Iron Lady with Churchill's Trousers was an image that she consciously worked on, along with the darkening of her hair and the lowering and slowing of her voice. For a long time, though, I couldn't identify what it was about her that really got to me. What her government was doing was very, very nasty, but there was something else as well.

I came to realise, while drawing her over the first year of her government, that she was deranged, but in a very controlled way, and this was expressed in her eyeballs. Her utter self-belief, her total conviction of her own rightness, went way beyond arrogance. She was mad. Perhaps I subconsciously empathised with her for this. Even so, I hated her more than any other living being. Within a couple of years, she had managed to triple unemployment, slash services and lay waste vast tracts of British industry.

When I saw Thatcher for the first time, in October 1980, at the Conservative conference in Brighton, I was horrified and intrigued. The crowd was terrifying; the whole occasion felt like a gathering of the undead. This was where she unveiled the deathless phrases: "You turn. If you want to. The Lady's. Not. For turning." The delivery was leaden. It was like a bad stand-up comedian addressing a particularly slow audience. Tory audiences are well turned-out, shiny and simple-minded, and in all the years I have been studying them, nothing whatever has changed.

The Guardian had informed me, in 1978, that they wouldn't be using my work in the foreseeable future. But in 1981, we had a newborn son and a mortgage in the offing. So in desperation I sent off more stuff. It paid off. In November 1981, the first If... strip appeared. Within six months, the ludicrous Falklands war had broken out, and since all imagery emanating from the Task Force sailing south was so rigidly controlled by the Ministry of Defence, the kind of surreal graphic speculation that only a cartoon strip can provide came into its own.

Nine years later, I was still hard at it when Thatcher fell from grace. It was great fun to draw a visual commentary on the fall as it happened. Her neck had thickened, her shoulders broadened, her quiff solidified. The eyeballs were wilder than ever: one hooded, one roaming free. Thanks to the wonders of fax, I was now able to draw a cartoon for publication the following day without having to go into the office (I had moved to Brighton). I produced my first big comment-page job on the day of Geoffrey Howe's devastating resignation speech, then another on the day Thatcher quit.

It was a horrendous amount of work, but it was addictive. With the arrival of John Major, and the outbreak of the Gulf war, I was sucked into doing two, three, then four large cartoons for the comment page a week, as well as the daily strip. I was so delighted at not having to draw Thatcher any more that caricaturing Major came quickly and easily, as light relief. The logic was simple. He was one more useless Tory, only he was superuseless. He became Superuselessman, wearing not sleek red briefs over a bright blue body stocking, but Y-fronts over a grey suit. Major's slow death went on for far too long: by 1997, I was overjoyed to be drawing the blazing underpants sinking into the Thames, never to be seen again – except when they reappeared on Edwina Currie's head in 2002.

Tony Blair took longer to capture. It wasn't until stalking him at the Labour conference in Blackpool in 1994 that I noticed he had a little mad eye of his very own: politically and visually, he was channelling Thatcher. What Blair did was the appearance of conviction; what Gordon Brown did was the appearance of substance. Ten years of Blair gave way to the quick-quick-slow death of Brown. It was like drawing a crumbling cliff face, or the north end of a southbound cow.

At David Cameron's first conference as Tory leader, in Bournemouth in 2006, there was a sudden outbreak of pale blue skies, puffy clouds and trees waving in the breeze. The massed simpletons were still there, seething in the blue shadows, but they looked increasingly baffled. Then Cameron himself came on stage and burbled sweet nothings about the NHS. They didn't believe a word of it and Cameron didn't either, but he was channelling Blair. He had all the hand movements, the stiff, deliberate podium body language, and he could do sincerity almost as well as the master. But he's smoother and doesn't appear to possess any hair follicles. It turns out he is made of translucent pink rubber.

Saddest of all is Nick Clegg, a rather poor clone of Cameron, who in turn is a tribute act to Blair, who is himself channelling Thatcher. And who was she channelling? Her father, Alderman Roberts, the grocer of Grantham town? Winston Churchill? Adolf Hitler? Beelzebub? Who can say?

Am I getting cynical in my old age? I don't think so. I have a strong feeling that I was born cynical and that, somewhere within me, a dewy-eyed idealist has always been struggling to get out. I have been lurking under the podium, drawing politicians so closely for so long, that I have almost come to like them. I don't think they are any more venal and corrupt than we are. They talk bollocks because we talk bollocks – and because it's their job. Yet sometimes they say something that pushes a button and lights up the room. It is a rare skill and it doesn't happen often. Mostly, it is a slow slog through cliche and soundbite, followed by a slaughtering at the polls. What is worse is that many of them actually enjoy being done over satirically, since it shows that at least one person is paying them attention.

These men and women are professional idealists and I take my hat off to them. Then I kick them up the arse. Because it's not what they say or what they are, or even what they say they are, that gets my goat: it's the things they actually do to us in our name.

27 MAY 2011

Inglorious end for feared general who became feeble old man

JULIAN BORGER

Just before dawn yesterday, 16 years after Ratko Mladic became a fugitive, a dozen police and government cars drove into the village of Lazarevo and put a quiet, discreet end to one of the world's longest manhunts.

It was over so quickly and noiselessly that almost all the inhabitants of the northern Serbian village slept right through – the very opposite to the intense violence that marked the end this month of his fellow fugitive at the top of the world's most wanted list, Osama bin Laden.

Like Bin Laden, the 69-year-old Bosnian Serb had grown old beyond his years in hiding. He was balding and his left arm was paralysed as a result of a stroke several years ago. It is also thought he was suffering from kidney problems. A Serbian government official described him as "hardly walking and seriously ill". Another said: "He was looking much older than anyone would expect."

Rasim Ljajic, a government minister in charge of co-operation with the Hague war crimes tribunal, said "Mladic looked like an old man" when he was arrested.

"One could pass by him without recognising him," Ljajic said. "He was pale, which could mean he rarely ventured out of the house, a probable reason why he went unnoticed."

Ljajic said Mladic had two guns in his possession, but did not resist the arrest and "was co-operative".

He was arrested by civilian police, who had accompanied agents of the Security Information Agency (known as the BIA) and the Serbian War Crimes Prosecutor's Office, who had tracked Mladic down.

He had been under surveillance in Lazarevo for at least two months according to Serbian official sources. They were watching an old man called Milorad Komadic who looked a lot like the notorious general they had been looking for. There was the limp arm, the height, the face, and the blue eyes. Apart from the pseudonym – perhaps deliberately similar to the real name so that it would be easy for an old man to remember – there was no attempt at disguise.

Mladic's political master from the Bosnian war, Radovan Karadzic, was arrested two years ago on a bus in Belgrade. He had been living as Dragan Dabic, a new-age healer, and had grown a long beard and tied a top-knot in his hair, as a thin disguise.

His general, with whom he had orchestrated the worst crimes in Europe since the second world war, had made no such efforts. He had grown no beard, nor dyed his hair. He was hiding in plain sight in his cousin Branko's house. Branko was one of several Mladic family members living in the village, and his house had reportedly been searched several times before.

The village is surrounded by the long thin fields that are the mark of the strip-farming techniques still used in that part of the world. Lazarevo lies on the open plains of the Vojvodina, near the Romanian and the Hungarian borders, an area that has long been an ethnic melting pot.

The Mladic clan were among a wave of Bosnian Serbs who have been migrating there since the second world war, so it was a relatively comfortable place for the old general to hide. In a reflection of local feeling someone had hung up a sign in the village yesterday that said: "Ratko – Hero".

It seems the 16-year manhunt came to an end not because

Mladic made a mistake, but because time and politics had moved relentlessly against him. One by one, the layers of protection, political and physical, that he had wrapped around himself, fell away, leaving a vulnerable old man.

The ultra-nationalists inside the Serbian security apparatus who had shielded him so assiduously had grown old and retired. Others had been arrested or levered out of their positions by a new generation of Serbs who came into office along with President Boris Tadic, and who were focused on modernising Serbia and dragging it into Europe.

Before then, Mladic had lived something of a charmed life for a hunted man. He slipped from public view in 1995 when Nato forces first arrived in Bosnia, leading to the signing of the Dayton peace agreement. But for the first few years after the war, he was under minimal pressure. The Nato forces patrolling Serb areas made only token gestures towards looking for Mladic, Karadzic and the other war criminals. On the few occasions they knocked on the right door, their quarry had already gone, often tipped off by leaks emanating from Nato member states.

Richard Dicker, the director of the international justice programme at Human Rights Watch, said: "Certainly Nato dropped the ball in carrying out its obligations to carry out the arrests of indicted war criminals. It was a disgraceful history. There was a several-year period when Karadzic would cruise through checkpoints quite openly."

Dicker said that changed when Tony Blair came to power in 1997, ordering a more robust search for the fugitives. The SAS took a leading role in tracking them down, along with US special forces under a young, rapidly rising officer called David Petraeus. Mladic and Karadzic, however, escaped the dragnet, with the help of elaborate evasion methods provided by their contacts in Slobodan Milosevic's government.

One senior officer involved in the search described how his unit had tried to follow Karadzic's wife in the hope she would lead them to him. She set off one day in a black Audi with dark windows and the Nato special forces shadowed her. But she disappeared into a covered car park.

"He waited for her to come out, but instead six identical Audis drove out and all went in different directions and we lost her," the officer recalled.

Ultimately, however, it became impossible for Mladic and Karadzic to stay in Bosnia, and both moved to Serbia with the help of their friends in Belgrade.

In the Milosevic era, Mladic was a hero to the Serbian officers with whom he had served in the Yugoslav national army. He lived for several years in the army's Topcider barracks and moved around quite openly in Belgrade, being seen at an international football game in 2000, and at his brother's funeral a year later.

He was guarded by a gang of about 50 armed men, mostly paramilitaries. When he turned up at an event, they would form a cordon around him, even blocking off roads in the manner of a small paramilitary force. It was also said that Mladic himself carried a few hand grenades, intending to blow himself up if anyone tried to grab him. The message was clear enough: Mladic could only be seized at a very high price in blood.

The pressure mounted on Mladic when Milosevic was ousted in a popular uprising in October 2000, and was replaced by a popularly elected and charismatic prime minister, Zoran Djindjic, who vowed to turn the country westwards. In 2002, his government signed an agreement with the Hague tribunal for the former Yugoslavia, to turn over Serb war crimes suspects. But that agreement was reached before Djindjic had anything like full control over the security forces. It turned out he was vulnerable to Mladic. In March 2003, Djindjic vowed to arrest the former general to help clear the way to EU membership. A few days later he was assassinated by a sniper with links to organised crime and the Serbian secret police.

Under Djindjic's nationalist successor, Vojislav Kostunica, the hunt continued in theory, but it was half-hearted at best. Mladic moved out of the barracks and into a warren of flats in drab communist-era blocks along Belgrade's Sava river, according to a report in the New York Times last year. Secret police officers admitted they had known all along where he was, but had received no orders to grab him.

But Mladic's days on the run were numbered with the election of Tadic in 2008, as Serbia turned west once more. Tadic put Sasa Vukadinovic in charge of the BIA and he set to work purging and reorganising the agency with a single aim.

He told the Serbian parliament last year that catching Serb war crimes suspects was the BIA's "absolute priority", but in fact it took Vukadinovic two years to turn the agency into a truly effective unit.

"This has been a long process of organisational evolution," Dicker said. "They could not go after Mladic before without risking a serious backlash if not an attempted coup coming from within the security forces."

In an effort to help Vukadinovic, MI6 and the CIA sent officers to Belgrade dedicated to the hunt for the suspect. The presence was acknowledged publicly in 2009 by the foreign minister, Vuk Jeremic.

Announcing Mladic's arrest, Tadic acknowledged the investigation was not over entirely. The last Serb fugitive, Goran Hadzic, a former ethnic Serb leader from the Krajina region of Croatia, is now the focus of the agency's efforts, but Tadic said the BIA would also be targeting the network which supported Mladic, possibly including state officials.

The hunt for Mladic, which reached its zenith with no gunfire and hardly any fuss, has mirrored the transformation of the Serbian state. Arguably, with the arrest of an old man in Lazarevo, Serbia entered a new era as a modern European state.

27 MAY 2011

Letter: Kitchen cabinets

LINDA McDOUGALL

I was fascinated to get a look at Cameron's new Downing Street kitchen (Eyewitness: No 10 Downing Street, 26 May). I thought it looked comfortable, practical and a bit like mine. Tom Meltzer (Shortcuts, G2, 26 May) is hypercritical and probably doesn't spend much time in kitchens.

I have a bookcase in mine for recipe books and whatever I happen to be reading, and I have an iPad for looking at recipes online and sending the odd impulsive email like this one (just like the Camerons I am smart enough to keep the cover on when I am not using it).

Our pots, cups and glasses are on shelves just like Sam and Dave's. Our oven gloves bear similar battle stains. Unfortunately, having the right kind of kitchen does not seem to have advanced my husband's political career at the same speed as Dave's, but I am very hopeful that we are on the right track.

Linda McDougall
Kitchen keeper for the MP for Grimsby

31 MAY 2011

Chav: the vile word at the heart of fractured Britain

POLLY TOYNBEE

That word slips out. This time it was used by a Lib Dem peer on the Equality and Human Rights Commission. Baroness Hussein-Ece tweeted: "Help. Trapped in a queue in chav land. Woman behind me explaining latest EastEnders plot to mate while eating largest bun I've ever seen." When challenged, she said she hadn't meant chav in any derogatory way. Of course not. But take a look at the venomous class-hate site ChavTowns to see what lies beneath.

She would presumably never say nigger or Paki, but chav is acceptable class abuse by people asserting superiority over those they despise. Poisonous class bile is so ordinary that our future king and his brother played at dressing up and talking funny at a chav party mocking their lower-class subjects.

Wrapped inside this little word is the quintessence of Britain's great social fracture. Over the last 30 years the public monstering of a huge slice of the population by luckier, better-paid people has become commonplace. This is language from the Edwardian era of unbridled snobbery. When safely reproduced in Downton Abbey, as the lady sneering at the scullery maid or the landowner bullying his workers, we are encouraged to look back smugly as if these shocking class differences were long gone. The form and style may have changed – but the reality of extreme inequality and self-confident class contempt is back.

That brief period between 1917 and 1979, when British wealth, trembling in fear of revolution, ceded some power, opportunity and money to the working classes, is over. There is now no politics to express or admit the enormity of what has happened since the 1980s – how wealth and human respect drained from the bottom to enrich and glorify the top.

Public perception of the shape of society has been so warped that most no longer know how others live, where they stand in relation to the rest, who earns what or why. By deliberate misrepresentation, drip, drip, week after week, the powerful interests of wealth deliberately distort reality. The best weapon in the class armoury fosters loathing of a "feral underclass" – its size vague and never delineated, relying on anecdotes of extreme dysfunction, of which any society has plenty. One sneer cleverly elides millions of low-earning workers in equal chav contempt for all living on an estate, drawing any benefit – even if in work – as cheats, addicts and layabouts. That's the way to divert resentment from those above, to those below.

Here's a prime example. On this quiet bank holiday weekend, Iain Duncan Smith's department deposited a dirty little non-story on the doormat of his favourite newspapers. Headlined "No More Excuses", the press release lists "the 10 top worst excuses used by benefit cheats". They include "I wasn't using the ladder to clean windows, I carried it for my bad back", and "It wasn't me working, it was my identical twin".

There are no figures to say how many people put up the sort of ludicrous pleas heard daily in any magistrates court. Department for Work and Pensions figures are anyway wobbly. Last year David Cameron declared war on benefit fraudsters, calling in special agents to deal with £5.2bn of fraud and error in the benefits bill – worth, he said, 200 secondary schools and 150,000 nurses. Cathy Newman's excellent Channel 4 FactCheck found £1.5bn of that was fraud and the rest error.

This latest DWP press release says fraud is now £1.6bn. That's a walloping sum – but let's put it in proportion. It's still only 0.7% of the benefits bill. Many a company would be proud of such a low loss from theft. The attorney general's National Fraud Authority found £38.4bn lost to fraud last year. Most fraud is in the finance industry – £3.6bn – though it's only 9% of the economy. That's more than is stolen in retail – a larger sector. Meanwhile, £15bn was officially caught in tax fraud, while estimated tax avoidance is £70bn.

But never mind, benefit stories are eye-catching and they do the job intended: they make us mean and ungenerous, stifling protest at Duncan Smith's monumental £18bn benefits cut. Such tales spread a wider loathing of a whole perceived class, of anyone on benefits. With most of the poor in work, that includes battalions of the low-paid whose miserable pay is topped up by tax credits to stop them starving. But a few choice anecdotes are worth a ton of statistics. That ladder! Ha!

I am on the circulation list for all DWP press releases, so why didn't I get this one and why wasn't this tacky rubbish put up on their website? "We only sent it out to a couple of our key contacts," said the duty press officer yesterday – that was the Mail and the Telegraph. "It was a soft consumer story, a PR story we sold proactively, so we didn't sell it any wider." So that's how Iain Duncan Smith does it these days, "selling" to friendly buyers only.

Anecdotes smearing all on housing benefit or tax credits help make the working class disappear. In his 1997 triumph, Tony Blair declared class over, we're all middle class – except for a "socially excluded" lumpen rump. "The new Britain is a meritocracy," he declared – not as a future goal but as a fact. So who are the 8 million in manual jobs and the 8 million clerks and sales assistants who make up half the workforce?

In my book Hard Work, I reported on the remarkably strong work ethic of those in jobs paying little more than benefits, the carers and cleaners doing essential work well, despite lack of money or respect. In Unjust Rewards, David Walker and I charted how since the decline of the unions people have lost their bearings on class and incomes: the mega-wealthy are clueless about ordinary earnings and even the poor are misled into thinking their pay is quite middling.

Aspiration and social mobility are the useful mirage, laying blame squarely with individuals who should try harder to escape their families and friends, instead of seeking great fairness for all. It suits life's winners to pretend this is a meritocracy: we well-off deserve our luck, anyone can join us if they try.

A superb and angry new book, Chavs, by Owen Jones, published next week, pulls together the welter of evidence on the demonisation of the working class. Read it for a strong analysis of the conspiracy to deny the very existence of a working class, even to itself. New Labour colluded with this vanishing act but Ed Miliband's espousal of the "squeezed middle" may be tiptoeing towards giving a voice back to the great disappeared.

Summer

Next time you see a photo of an unhappy male face but can't place the source of your revulsion, try this quiz ...

HADLEY FREEMAN

To quote those wise sages of human behaviour, Salt'n'Pepa, let's talk about sex. That is no random reference, for it does seem that a certain gospel from Sage Salt and Prophet Pepa has been doing the rounds among high-profile men, judging from their kamikaze approach to pushing it, to quote the holy text, into the most poorly chosen of places.

Oh, for the days when a sex scandal meant a handsome young president discreetly smuggling a Hollywood actress into the White House. Somewhere in the interim, sex scandals stopped being vaguely sexy and are now more akin to an episode of The Jeremy Kyle Show. Back in ye olden days pre 26 May, the unfortunately named congressman Anthony Weiner was best known for his admirable rant last summer against Republicans who voted against providing healthcare for the 9/11 recovery workers who have suffered health problems since. Post 26 May, any past professional achievements have been obliterated, for he will always be known as yet another example of nominative determinism.

Late last month a photo of what I shall coyly describe as a physical expression of male excitement was sent from his Twitter account to a 21-year-old woman. Weiner then put the passion he once used to defend 9/11 workers into denying that he sent a photo of tented underwear, but was decidedly less clear whether the photo is of him, suggesting that either he takes photos of the Weiner wiener and keeps them on his computer or he cannot recognise his own body. This is what is known as a lose/lose situation.

On Monday of this week, more Weiner photos emerged, proving, among other things, that he is the Mrs Slocombe of American politics with his predilection for feline-based puns, and he eventually confessed all. The only person who can see an upside to this whole farrago aside from the cheap-shot, pun-obsessed journalists like myself is Arnold Schwarzenegger. One can almost hear his familiar voice on the wind: "Thank you, Anthony. Thank you." On the same day Weiner finally confessed, Dominique Strauss-Kahn pleaded not guilty to attempted rape of a hotel maid, an accusation that, Jon Stewart pointed out, is "like a live action metaphor. The head of the IMF trying to fuck an African? It's like he's posing for his own editorial cartoon."

This came just the day after another allegation about Ryan Giggs. Giggs may have accomplished the impressive feat of topping the football league of stupidity with his recent antics, from attempting to sue the concept of gossip to, it was claimed this weekend, having an affair with his sister-in-law.

If all that weren't enough to have the whole world cross its collective legs, here comes John Edwards, bringing a retro feel to the current trend of sexual stupidity. Last week Edwards was indicted by a federal grand jury, and prosecutors claim that he spent $925,000 in donations to keep his mistress and their child hidden during his 2008 presidential campaign. Rarely would $925,000 have been worse spent, and I say that as a regular watcher of MTV Cribs. Just in case this story is looking relatively a bit vanilla, Edwards' wife was then suffering from cancer.

If I were sex, I'd look for a better PR because, frankly, whoever is looking after its image has not been doing a very good job recently. Sex is being flaunted by a very non-aspirational demographic, and now sex is suffering from brand fatigue; it is the Gap of procreational pastimes.

Moreover, if it is true, as is so often claimed, that any time anyone-other-than-a-Caucasian-man does something like, say, become editor of the New York Times or president of the United States, they then represent their entire gender, race or religion, then straight Caucasian men really need to seek out better representation. Their public faces are letting them down.

It is difficult to keep track of so many revolting men doing so many revolting things. So next time you see a photo of a self-pitying male face but you can't quite place the source of your revulsion, do the quiz, below, and all questions should be resolved.

1. Does this sex scandal involve a man who is so lazy that when he decided to engage in some extramarital behaviour he simply turned to the woman who was cleaning his bedroom? If yes, go to question two.

   If no, go to question three.

2. Does this sex scandal involve more national stereotypes than a Tintin cartoon?

   If yes, go to question three.

   If no, go to question three.

3. Did the man give the woman any money?

   If no, and the answers to questions one and two were yes, you are looking at a picture of Dominique Strauss-Kahn.

   If yes, and the answers to questions one and two were, respectively, yes and no, you are looking at a picture of Arnold Schwarzenegger.

If yes, and the answers to the previous questions were no, go to question four.

If no, and the answers to the previous questions were no, go to question four.

4. Are there embarrassing sexytime photos?

If yes, you are looking at a photo of Anthony Weiner (and hopefully just a photo of his face).

If no, go to question five.

5. Will these shocking accusations upset his wife?

If the answer is probably but she can't say now because she has sadly since passed away, you are looking at a photo of John Edwards.

If the answer is probably but she may not say because she is a Wag and they can be a very tolerant species, you are looking at a photo of Ryan Giggs.

10 JUNE 2011

Philip at 90: still the strength behind the throne, in spite of the gaffes

STEPHEN BATES

It is a fair bet that the Duke of Edinburgh, celebrating – or, more likely, enduring – his 90th birthday this morning, will not settle down with a copy of the Guardian to read this article.

Accosted once by Polly Toynbee at a Windsor Castle reception and asked whether he ever read the paper, he snorted: "No fear."

But it is not just us. He does not like any media. He believes it went to pot when Rupert Murdoch landed.

"It is almost pathological," says the broadcaster Gyles Brandreth, who is a friend. "And yet he was the first royal to give an interview on television, trying to be innovative. He thinks it has become all negative, all about his gaffes. He says it doesn't bother him, but it annoys him and leaves him contemptuous."

Broadcasters have sent the most innocuous representatives to interview him for this anniversary – Alan Titchmarsh and Fiona Bruce – and both have been barked at, their most genial questions batted back with exasperation.

Brandreth said: "Here is a man of 90 who still does 300 engagements a year, and in 60 years has never been late, never gone to the wrong place, never dressed in the wrong uniform, and there have been five occasions in all that time when he has cried off because of illness."

And yet, compared with all that, admits Brandreth, the pile of cuttings about his gaffes is weighty. Ah yes, the gaffes. It is a long list, some clearly magnified in the telling.

There was him, 25 years ago, telling a group of British students in China that they would end up "slitty-eyed"; the suggestion that an old-fashioned fuse box must have been put in by an Indian; and the question to an Australian aboriginal leader in 2002, asking whether he still threw spears.

Three weeks ago in Ireland, the local press fell into earnest discussion about whether his remark – "that sounds very Irish" – after someone made a convoluted explanation constituted another gaffe. They decided it did not.

The endless recycling apparently makes the duke cross, particularly the alleged remark to a group of Cardiff children standing next to a steel band in 1999: "Deaf? If you stand near there no wonder you're deaf."

He points out he never said it. His mother was deaf and he is a long-term patron of the Royal National Institute for Deaf People, so instinctively it is not the sort of thing he would ever say. Too late: it is in the press cuttings.

What he is, say friends, is questioning. Not for him the platitudes and passivity of the Queen. After 60 years, he wants a conversation, to provoke answers, to fill dumbstruck silences, to ward off tedium.

Ministers, called to preach before the royal family at Balmoral, report daunting lunchtime conversations afterwards with the duke beadily dissecting the flaws in their sermons. His study library, containing 11,000 books, includes works of comparative theology and other more surprising texts, such as the poetry of TS Eliot. "Don't tell anyone," he barks. But he has read them.

Friends say those who tend to be put out by his brusqueness are from the officer class, and facing a grilling they were not expecting.

The duke himself does not see the need to apologise, or explain, or emote. It is generally not what people of his generation do, and resilience and emotional reticence was something he learned early.

Born on Corfu in 1921 into the Greek royal family – christened Philippos, though he, like the rest of them, was of Danish and German ancestry – he and his family fled when the monarchy was overthrown the following year. They were rowed out to a British ship, as a Guardian letter-writer noted this week, and he was placed in an orange box.

A peripatetic and lonely childhood followed. Abandoned by his father, who went to live in the south of France, his mother confined to an asylum following a breakdown, his older sisters marrying Nazis, he was shuffled between relatives and educated in spartan boarding schools in Germany and Scotland before training for the British navy, in which he served during the second world war.

Asked by an interviewer about his childhood at home, he retorted: "What do you mean 'at home'? You get on with it. You do. One does."

He will be used to the sneers about Phil the Greek, but his initiation into the British royal family in the aftermath of the war was demeaning. He was, the courtiers thought, no gentleman and, worse, "little better" than a German; the diplomat Harold Nicolson noted him down as "rough, ill-mannered, uneducated and ... probably not faithful".

A bit too Teutonic, it was said. A footman gleefully reported that his naval valise contained no spare shoes – his only pair was holed – or pyjamas, or slippers.

A new biography says he did not feature in Queen Elizabeth's first-11 of suitors for her eldest daughter. Then, once married to his besotted bride and with his career as a naval officer taking off, he was forced to give it up when his wife ascended the throne, becoming the new queen's consort and pledging at the coronation to be her "liege man of life and limb and of earthly worship".

He was condemned to a lifetime of walking a few paces behind, making conversation, shaking hands, inquiring politely, not making waves, avoiding controversy. He could not even pass his surname to his children. He was, he said, "nothing but a bloody amoeba".

He has stuck at it and developed his own interests: the Duke of Edinburgh's award scheme to encourage young people to volunteer for community service and engage in teamwork and outdoor strenuousness, which has had four million teenage participants over the last 55 years (he still attends many of the ceremonies to give out gold awards); the presidencies of the World Wildlife Fund and the National Playing Fields Association as well as others.

These are not perfunctory duties. Peter Westgarth, chief executive of the award scheme, says: "He does not suffer fools gladly. You don't make flippant remarks. He will challenge you. But he supports you, too – he's helpful and positive and knowledgable."

David Nussbaum of WWF UK adds: "He questions to provoke and to get spice into the conversation. If you have that lively a mind at 90, you are doing well."

Today will be a working day, with a reception for the centenary of the RNID at Buckingham Palace in the morning, a dinner for the colonels of the Household Division in the evening. On Sunday there will be a family celebration and service at Windsor. The Queen says he has been "my strength and my stay all these years". But for how much longer can he keep it up?

14 JUNE 2011

When life is finally squeezed of all its juice, Terry Pratchett finds there's tea on tap

SAM WOLLASTON

I never knew there was so much tea involved in death. "Would you like a cup of tea?" Peter Smedley asks Sir Terry Pratchett, before they settle down to talk about dying. Peter – a lovely, brave, old-fashioned man who has a splendid wine cellar and used to drive sports cars and fly aeroplanes – has motor neurone disease. "It's a beastly, undignified business," he says, Britishly. Soon he'll go to Dignitas in Switzerland to die. Terry, who has Alzheimer's disease,

24 JULY 2011

Memories and mementoes: the pavement outside singer Amy Winehouse's home in Camden, London, after her death.

PAUL BROWN/REX

26 MARCH 2011

Riot police in the West End of London after a march against public sector cuts broke up into sporadic violence. FELIX CLAY

23 AUGUST 2011

Tripoli. Joyous Libyans after the storming of Muammar Gaddafi's compound in the heart of the city. SEAN SMITH

11 JULY 2011

Looking cheery: Rupert Murdoch is driven away from his central London base. Over the next two weeks he lost key executives, closed the News of the World, was forced to withdraw his bid for outright control of BSkyB, and saw the launch of one judicial inquiry, two parliamentary inquiries and two new police inquiries into phone hacking. LUKE MACGREGOR/REUTERS

is thinking about assisted dying too. Meanwhile he's making this extraordinary film, Terry Pratchett: Choosing to Die (BBC2).

As well as Peter, Terry talks to a woman who helped her husband, the Belgian writer Hugo Claus, die. Hugo had a cigarette even though he'd given up, and they sang a song together. "He died singing," she says. And Terry visits a young man called Andrew who's also going to Dignitas. Andrew has multiple sclerosis which, though he seems disturbingly OK, he describes as "like walking down an alley that's getting narrower, with no doors." All these people speak very well about dying.

As does Pratchett, as you'd expect. "I'd like to live life as long as I can squeeze the juice out of it," he says. He too goes to Dignitas in Switzerland, not to die this time, just for a look around, and to say goodbye to Peter and Andrew who have gone there to die. This is where tea comes back into it. Ludwig Minelli, the Dignitas founder, offers Terry more tea. Ludwig has an enormous collection, more than 50 different kinds, and describes himself as a "tea-ologian". I think he's used that one before. So Terry has more tea, in one of the cheery, brightly coloured cups of the Dignitas house.

It's a funny place. Not a lovely chalet in the mountains, with meadows and edelweiss and the sound of cowbells, as you might hope for; but a strange blue prefab on a Zurich industrial site. There are a couple of "escorts" to help you through your final hours. Erika is warm and helpful and provides tea and hugs when required; Horst is a lugubrious-looking man with a pipe that he smokes out on the balcony in the snow, and when the moment comes, he films it all on his digital camera – for legal reasons probably.

Peter, the lovely brave old boy with motor neurone disease, invites Terry to be there for his death. This is not the first time assisted dying has been shown on television, but it's probably the most touching and intimate. Would Peter like tea or coffee, asks his wife, a glamorous woman with pearls who once fell for a dashing young man with sports cars and aeroplanes. "I'm going to have coffee, darling," he says. Is he sure he wants to die today? Yes, quite sure, he says, calm as you like.

After all the paperwork, he swallows the first of the two clear liquids he has to take. Would he like some tea, asks Erika. No, thank you, he says. Shut up about the tea. He has a chocolate instead, and takes the second liquid and his wife strokes his hand.

Everything about this moving but not over-sentimental film really makes me think assisted death for the terminally ill is not just a good idea but a human right (more importantly Pratchett feels the same and the news at the weekend was that he's signed up). But there's a moment, when the poison takes its grip, when it's very hard to watch. For a very short time Peter's not calm, he's uncomfortable and in pain, he wants – but doesn't get – water. It lasts only a few seconds, then he's asleep, but it's not nice. That would frighten me, I think, but I'm not brave like Peter. And I'd like to go somewhere nicer than a dreary industrial estate in Zurich, even if it does have nice cups and 50 varieties of tea on offer.

18 JUNE 2011

Albania's 'second greatest living writer' was a hoax, but does it really matter?

IAN JACK

The Albanian writer Jiri Kajane, who is about to die this morning aged 65, found more literary success abroad than he ever did at home. The Stalinist regime of Enver Hoxha was no place for free spirits, and Kajane could count himself lucky that his satirical drama Neser Perdite (Tomorrow, Every Day) earned him no more than a ban from the ministry of culture. In 1981 the play had one performance in Tirana. Thereafter, Kajane stuck to short stories that were to make his small reputation in the west. Long after Hoxha's death in 1985, Kajane felt his position too precarious for him to publish work in Albania. By the end of the last century he was more famous in Chicago than he was in his birthplace, Kruje, the small hill town recognised in Albanian history for its resistance to the Ottoman empire and Italian conquest. It was a paradox he enjoyed.

Kajane's stories were only very slyly political. Most featured two protagonists, a narrator known only as the Deputy Minister of Slogans, and his friend Leni, the sous chef at the Hotel Dajti. Against a grey background of travel restrictions and shortages, the stories followed the two friends helping each other through the universal problems of love, family and boredom. Many US editors liked and published them. In the 1990s, they appeared in serious literary journals such as Glimmer Train, the Chicago Review and the Michigan Quarterly Review. A high point was his inclusion in The Killing Spirit: An Anthology of Murder-for-Hire, which was published by Canongate in 1996 and two years later by the Overlook Press in New York.

In that book, Kajane's story took its place alongside pieces by Ian McEwan, Joyce Carol Oates, Patricia Highsmith, Graham Greene and Ernest Hemingway. A review by Time Out Scotland declared him "Albania's second greatest living writer" (after Ismail Kadare, later to win the Man Booker International prize).

I first came across his stories in 1998, while editing Granta. They came by post to the heap of unsolicited contributions known as the slush pile, which my colleague Sophie Harrison read diligently. Most slush comes from creative writing students, who were then mostly from the US and tended to copy Raymond Carver. But more original things could be found, and one day Sophie said, "Have a look at these, they're interesting."

They were. It's difficult to say why. What I remember now is their laconic strangeness, which may be what had appealed to his US publishers. Much of the attraction of writing from eastern Europe vanished with the Berlin Wall. The stimulant of oppression was no longer there; Big Macs had replaced the secret police. But Albania wasn't Czechoslovakia. It looked, by comparison, remote and mysterious – and here sang a new and mysterious voice.

We debated buying a story for the magazine. We even wondered if Kajane had more that could be published as a collection. We needed to get in touch, but our only route lay through his translator, Kevin Phelan, from whom the submissions had come. Phelan said Kajane wasn't easy to pin down, but he himself might be passing through London soon. He was sure Kajane would be thrilled at the idea of a collection. A meeting was arranged, and so one afternoon Phelan turned up in the office from Heathrow, in transit (as it turned out) between Nairobi and Washington.

The denouement will now be obvious, but before the meeting it seemed no more likely than discovering that Syria's leading lesbian blogger, Amina Abdallah Araf al Omari, was a married, middle-aged American called Tom MacMaster living in Edinburgh. Photographs and biographical details of Kajane, after all, appeared in the contributors' notes of serious US journals. We needed to meet or at least talk to him before we could publish – a condition none of his publishers, before or after, seems to have made. Phelan then confessed that Kajane didn't exist. Phelan and a friend, Bill U'Ren, had invented him. The two had met as creative writing students at the University of California in Los Angeles.

Phelan had made a couple of short trips to Albania in the 1980s. U'Ren had never been. As young writers, they'd discovered that their stories, which then had contemporary US settings, attracted little attention; perhaps too playful to fit the fashion for trailer-park realism. Albania changed everything.

Phelan's revelation was transfixing, and nearly as unbelievable as how he and U'Ren earned a living. Phelan was an FBI agent, at that moment returning from investigations into the bomb that destroyed the US embassy in Nairobi, killing more than 200 people; he produced ID to prove it. U'Ren (according to Phelan) worked as a psychological coach to a baseball side, the San Diego Padres.

Reader, what to do? We dropped our interest in Kajane, of course, but did we have a duty to unmask Albania's second greatest living writer as a couple of guys exchanging thoughts and sentences in California? I telephoned the editor of a US magazine that had taken Kajane's stories to ask if she thought the author really existed. "I darn well hope so," she said. After that, I did nothing. It seemed too righteous, and a little smug, to tell so many publishers they'd been had. And at our meeting Phelan had asked a good question: if we liked the stories when we thought an Albanian had written them, why did we like them less when we knew their true authorship?

Fiction isn't the false non-fiction of Tom MacMaster – it has a different purpose – and you might argue fictional authorship is simply just another device that helps promote what fiction always wants, which is believability. In a later Kajane story, the chef Leni has written some stories that he's trying unsuccessfully to sell to the editor of a British literary magazine. "It's just that they're not very Albanian, if you know what I mean," says the editor, Ian James (aha). "Love and relationships and family concerns, these are all fine ... but where is the lone hero fighting a struggle against mind-numbing governmental tyranny?"

That wasn't the problem. The problem was that I believed the stories came from authentic Albanian experience – a difficulty, I admit, that has never bothered us when it comes to Daniel Defoe's lack of marooning experience. But Defoe didn't pretend to be Man Friday.

As I write, the collected stories of Jiri Kajane are still available online (Winter in Tirane, aka Some Private Daydream) with the "second greatest living Albanian writer" emblazoned on the cover, and Phelan and U'Ren credited as the translators. U'Ren is now an assistant professor of creative writing at a liberal arts college in Baltimore. Phelan still works for the FBI in California – from an office, he told me this week, which has a good view of Google's ever-expanding headquarters.

This seems appropriate. Online publishing and its offer of geographical blankness and authorial pseudonymity have made hoaxes easier than ever. They allow writers to pretend and to play, and they have a long and irrepressible history – think of the teenage Thomas Chatterton posing as a medieval monk, Thomas Rowley – of which Kajane is a distinguished example. It seems a shame, almost, to assassinate him.

20 JUNE 2011

'Don't be surprised if Athens burns. And don't be sorry'

ADITYA CHAKRABORTTY

Athenians used to stop off at Syntagma Square for the shopping, the shiny rows of upmarket boutiques. Now they arrive in their tens of thousands to protest. Swarming out of the metro station, they emerge into a village of tents, pamphleteers and a booming public address system.

Since 25 May, when demonstrators first converged here, this has become an open-air concert – only one where bands have been supplanted by speakers and music swapped for an angry politics. On this square just below the Greek parliament and ringed by flashy hotels, thousands sit through speech after speech. Old-time socialists, American economists just passing through, members of the crowd: they each get three minutes with the mic, and most of them use the time alternately to slag off the politicians and to egg on their fellow protesters.

"Being here makes me feel 18 again," begins one man, his polo shirt stretched tight over his paunch, before talking about his worries about his pension.

The closer you get to the Vouli, the parliament, the more raucous it becomes. Jammed up against the railings, a crowd is clapping and chanting: "Thieves! Thieves!"

There is another mic here, and it's grabbed by a man wearing a mask of deputy prime minister Theodoros Pangalos: "My friends, we all ate together." He is quoting the socialist politician, who claimed on TV last year that everyone bore the responsibility for the squandering of public money. Pangalos may have intended his remark as the Greek equivalent of George Osborne's remark that "We're all in it together", but here they're not having it. "You lying bastard!" they roar back. "You're so fat you ate the entire supermarket."

This is an odd alloy of earnestness and pantomime, to be sure, but it's something else too: Syntagma Square has become the new frontline of the battle against European austerity. And as prime minister George Papandreou battles first to keep his own job, and then to win MPs' support for the most extreme package of spending cuts, tax rises and privatisations ever faced by any developed country, what happens between this square and the parliament matters for the rest of the eurozone.

The banner-wavers here know this. In the age of TV satellite vans and YouTube, they paint signs and coin slogans with half an eye on the export market. Papandreou's face is plastered over placards that congratulate him in English for being "Goldman Sachs' employee of the year". Flags jibe at the *rive gauche*: "The French are sleeping – they're dreaming of '68."

Most of the time, the anger is expressed sardonically. A friend shows me an app on her phone that gives updates on the latest political and industrial actions – its name translates as iStrike. But it's not hard to see how this situation might boil over.

"Are you an indignado?" I ask Nikkos Kokkalis, using the term coined by young Spanish protesters to express outrage at José Luis Rodríguez Zapatero's austerity plans, now swiped by the Greeks. "I'm a super-indignado," he almost shouts. A 29-year-old graduate who lives with his parents, Nikkos has never done a proper job – just menial tasks for a website and an internship for a TV station. "There are 300 people over there," he waves at the MPs' offices. "Most of them make decisions without asking the people."

For their part, protesters with salaries and wrinkles are fuming at the spending cuts already inflicted on them. Chryssa Michalopolou is a teacher who calculates that her annual pay has already gone down by the equivalent of one and a half months, while her living costs have shot up, thanks to rising taxes and inflation. Does she buy the government's line that it needs to trim the public sector? "After 15 years' service, I'm only on €1,200 (£1,056) a month," she says. "I didn't see any boom; I simply paid my taxes and now I am being punished."

On display here is more than a personal grievance; it also reveals a glaring truth that politicians across Europe have so far ignored. In their efforts to hammer out a second loan agreement for Greece, eurozone ministers are focusing on the differences between bond swaps and bond rollovers, the tensions between Berlin and the International Monetary Fund and the European Central Bank or how far continental banks can withstand another massive shock.

Taken for granted in these negotiations is that the Greeks (and, by implication, the Irish and the Portuguese) must accept more austerity. Yet in Athens, whether on the streets or even at a policymaking level, these technical details barely figure on the agenda. It's not just that the terms are different, the entire debate is too. Here, the argument concerns how much more austerity the Greek economy, its people and even the government can take – because all three are already at breaking point.

When Greece was all but locked out of the financial markets last May, Papandreou accepted a €110bn loan from Europe and the IMF. The idea was that the money would tide the country over for a year, in which time his government would at least start sorting out its public finances. For Angela Merkel, Nicolas Sarkozy and the rest of Europe, the loan came with some pretty tight strings attached: they charged the Greeks interest well above the official eurozone rate, and set demanding budget targets for the Pasok socialist government.

A year in, and the deal is not working. Greece has been in recession for two years, and on official forecasts this will be its third. When I ask Athens University economist Yanis Varoufakis to describe the economy, he shoots back one sentence: "It's in freefall."

Sitting on the balcony of his flat behind the Acropolis, he throws out some statistics: 50,000 businesses went bankrupt last year, industrial production fell 20% and will drop another 12% this year. Unemployment has surged, so that one in six of the workforce don't have a job. These are the sort of figures associated with a depression, and the predictable result is that the public finances are getting worse. Greece's debt has ballooned to 153% of GDP; on Varoufakis's projections, even if ministers manage to make all their promised cuts, the government will owe three times the entire national income.

Behind these numbers lie the stories of a society in distress. One man talks about his daughter who works in the in-store restaurant of a large supermarket outside Athens; at closing time, she and her workmates have started giving out unsold meals to the newly unemployed – the 21st-century equivalent of a soup kitchen. An employee of a local council notes that they pick up 17% less rubbish than a year ago, simply because people have cut back on food. The owner of an art gallery tells me her son has just started his first job; holding a master's in accountancy, he works six hours a day in a mobile-phone shop.

The lazy accusation to hurl at Greece is that it had a bloated public sector and so was bound to come a cropper. Not so, says Varoufakis: the country has a public sector in line with the rest of Europe (although, nearly everyone I speak to agrees, one that does not work as well), but takes in taxes some 35% below where they should be.

Wealthy Greeks have always treated the country's tax system like a church collection plate: what they give is strictly optional. This gap was covered up for as long as the Greek state could get cheap credit; then in 2008 it became glaringly obvious. The other problem covered up during the boom years was the rotting away of the industrial base. That too is now the subject of angry public discussion.

I take a tour of the shipbuilding yard in Perama, just outside Athens. Greece has the largest commercial fleet in the world, and yet Perama is utterly silent. There is a rusting hulk, abandoned a few years ago, when those who commissioned it could no longer afford to pay for it. A decade ago, this yard employed 7,000 workers – now it has around 500. There was a time when assembling small cargo vessels was seen as pedestrian work; last year, the yard was contracted to build two boats, and the jobs were fought over. A few minutes away lives Tassos Alexandris, who was laid off from Perama in 2008. The hall of his flat is decorated with needlepoint; inside are pictures of the Virgin Mary put up by his wife, Nikki. She is ill, and his 26-year-old daughter has worked for six months in her entire career. How do they make ends meet? Nikki snorts with laughter.

"The electricity connection is inside the flat; otherwise the board would have cut us off," begins Tassos. His mother-in-law lives upstairs and, while he is too ashamed to ask her for food, she allows him to raid her fridge at night. They had a small green Citroen, but couldn't afford to keep it. Now he runs a motorbike, although with no plates and no taxes. "I can't sleep at night for worry," he says. "It has affected every part of our lives: personal, sexual, the lot." How many families in this block do they think are in a similar situation? Nikki tots them up: "80%."

Tassos doesn't just support the protesters of Syntagma; he thinks they will go further. "Don't be surprised if Athens goes up in flames," the 50-year-old says. "And don't be sad, either." His words initially sound melodramatic, but the anger keeps coming up. "Politicians now walk around with bodyguards," says Aris Chatzistefanou, the co-director of Debtocracy, a film about the Greek crisis that has become a sensation. He quotes a newspaper report of how restaurateurs are taking down those cheesy framed photos of dining politicians, of how one government spokesman went to dinner a few weeks ago only for the rest of the restaurant to start shouting "You are eating the blood of the people".

The anger against the austerity and the politicians imposing it is palpable; whether it will translate into political success is debatable. Papandreou may be one of the most hated men in Greece, but there is no mainstream politician who has an alternative to acting under creditor's orders. This isn't about an electorate taking on a government, either, but the impossible political arithmetic of disparate groups of Greeks on one side versus the IMF, the European Central Bank and 16 other eurozone members on the other.

Run that by the protesters of Athens, though, and even the older, more pragmatic ones have an answer. "We may lose," one grey-haired trade unionist said to me. "But what matters is how you lose."

20 JUNE 2011

Cameron and Co flock to pay homage at Murdoch's party

21 JUNE 2011

Obituary: Brian Haw

CRAIG TAYLOR

Brian Haw, who has died aged 62 after being treated for lung cancer, was a tenacious peace campaigner who in 2001 took up residence in Parliament Square, beneath a banner that read "Stop Killing My Kids", and refused to relinquish his patch for nearly 10 years.

Haw travelled from his home in Redditch, Worcestershire, to Westminster on 2 June that year, moved to publicise the effects of British sanctions on Iraq. Days of praying and fasting turned into months of protest as Haw outlasted others who had brought their temporary grievances to the pavement opposite the Houses of Parliament. Soon, he was no longer protesting about sanctions, but against the buildup to the war in Iraq, then the war itself, and the occupation that followed. When he finally left the pavement in March 2011, he was still warning onlookers and passersby of the effects of the conflicts in Afghanistan and Iraq.

Haw was born in Woodford Green, Essex, and grew up in Whitstable, Kent, where he had his first experiences of an evangelical church at the age of 11. His father, a wartime sniper in the Reconnaissance Corps, had been one of the first to enter the Bergen-Belsen camp after it was liberated and his experiences were partly, Haw said, what led him to take his own life when his son was 13. Haw was apprenticed to a boatbuilder, then joined the merchant navy and eventually saw the Suez Canal and Bombay, "and if those people were here now, they'd say: 'Is all this pavement yours? You're living like a king'," he said in 2002.

His camp at Westminster varied in size over the years and was labelled both an eyesore and an integral patch of democracy. Day after day, it was home to a man whose life was protest, and whose talent was survival in a harsh landscape of exhaust fumes and police scrutiny. Haw spent hours speaking to supporters, detractors and those who stood quietly surveying photos of dead Iraqi children. His battered banners became a visual counterpoint to the usual tourist snaps of Whitehall. Their variety and colourful insistence was not lost on the artist Mark Wallinger, who won the

2007 Turner prize with a piece entitled State Britain, a recreation of Haw's display.

Haw was guided by his fervent Christian beliefs, and aided at times by practical pieces of equipment, including a cheap megaphone. No one who worked in Whitehall, from the prime minister down, could remain unaware of his presence. His shouted slogan, "45 minutes, Mr Bliar", was so loud it led to objections by MPs. In 2002, Westminster city council tried unsuccessfully to remove Haw's camp, but his greatest legal challenge came in 2005 when the Serious Organised Crime and Police Act was passed, banning any public protest within one kilometre of Parliament Square. Particularly troubling for Haw was Section 132, which would allow police to remove any permanent protesters in the square. ("Serious organised crime?" Haw asked. "Do they really think I'm the Godfather?") Haw won an application for judicial review of the act as it required all protests to have authorisation from the police "when the demonstration starts", and his had already been going for a long time. He gained permission to stay, subject to conditions regarding the size of his display.

His closest supporters, who furnished Haw with sandwiches and cigarettes over the years, would class him as another in the line of tenacious Christian protesters bearing witness. Haw himself was puzzled that so few others could spare the time to come to Parliament Square. He saved some anger for those who thought a single march in 2003 would force the government to stop its involvement in Iraq. In his view, if 100,000 people had arrived and refused to move for a week, war would have been averted. It wasn't so hard, Haw said, just to come and sit in front of this place and protest.

Haw was uncomfortable speaking about the practical nature of his life on the pavement. Questions about survival, sleeping habits, showers, the fumes and police presence were often ignored or deflected. Over the years his skin became leathery. His nose was broken twice. The 10 years took their toll, and some questioned whether his protest had become ineffective.

What was impossible to question was Haw's combination of friendliness and bloody-mindedness, his insistence that it was not impossible to be heard, to challenge courts, to remind those in power of the consequences of their actions. Haw angered some, mystified others, and continued to prowl the pavement, even on crutches, wearing a hat covered in badges, with slogans such as "Keep My Muslim Neighbours Safe". Years into the protest, the battered hat looked as if it was more badge than corduroy.

"I don't mind them," Haw said in 2002 when asked about the mice that appeared in the square around dusk. He pointed a finger towards parliament. "It's the rats over there on the other side we have to look out for." Haw was father to seven children with his wife Kay, who divorced him in 2003.

Brian William Haw, peace campaigner, born 7 January 1949; died 18 June 2011

27 JUNE 2011

'Like you, Tim, I'm not much of a musician'

TIM DOWLING

On the train I tell myself I won't write about the mud. There's always mud, I think, and everyone always writes about it. Let's just say the going is extremely soft, even liquid. The ground sucks at your boots when you walk and, once you've crossed a few hundred metres of it, it sucks at your soul a little, too.

When people talk about Glastonbury in terms of numbers, the scale of it can be hard to fathom. I can't really picture 137,000 people, or imagine the throughput of the 3,200 toilets laid on to accommodate them. But there is one statistic that struck me with a certain force: over the three days no fewer than 2,200 acts were scheduled to perform. Whether anyone watched them or not, several thousand people will be able to say they played Glastonbury 2011. And when I turn up early on Saturday morning, I mean to be one of them. I am going to play the banjo at Glastonbury.

Finding someone to play with proves more challenging. Despite some cajoling from the Guardian music desk, Noah and the Whale do not wish to be associated with, or photographed anywhere near, a banjo. Instead I manage to book a brief jam session with the Fisherman's Friends, a sea-shanty group from Cornwall, under a giant giraffe. I can't see why an a cappella group would need banjo accompaniment, but I am not in a position to be choosy. Unfortunately they are, and I'm left standing under the giraffe by myself. Later they reschedule for 6pm.

I am obliged to strike out on my own. Although I would like to claim toting a banjo around a huge muddy festival as an additional hardship, I can't. Everybody's carrying stuff. Parents are happily hauling pushchairs through the mire. People are walking around the site in wedding dresses. I pass a man wearing butterfly wings, Spock ears, a purple feather fascinator and a high-visibility vest.

I decide the Stone Circle – a sort of catch-all spiritual focal point on a rise at the southern edge of the site – might be a good place to kick off my Glastonbury career, but it soon becomes clear that anyone seeking to draw attention to themselves in the circle faces impressive competition. I climb up on one of the stones and play for a bit, but no one comes near. Some festival-goers appear to be attempting to commune with the other stones, either by leaning against them or laying on hands. On the stone directly opposite, four people dressed as Teletubbies are having their picture taken. Around the campfire at the centre of the circle all one hears is a series of sharp staccato gusts, as balloons are filled with nitrous oxide and sold to punters by enterprising, red-faced men. It's sort of peaceful.

After about 20 minutes a small child with a painted face clambers up on the stone beside me and listens while I play.

"How many Glastonburys have you been to?" I say, trying to make small talk.

"Six," he says. I notice he has something written on his forearm.

"It's my first one," I say. "What's that written on your arm?" He grabs hold of his wrist and reads it out carefully.

"Please. Return. This. Child. To…"

I have to go, because I'm appearing with Billy Bragg, who has graciously consented to let me play a song with him in his regular 3pm slot, Bill's Big Roundup, on the Left Field stage.

"The song is called Way Down Yonder in the Minor Key," he told me when I spoke to him on the phone the previous Thursday. "But don't listen to the recording, because I don't play it that way any more. You need to find the version I play live. Your best bet is a YouTube clip from a Canadian children's programme called Peggy's Cove, where I'm singing it to a puppet lobster."

"OK," I said.

"It might have been a crab, I don't know," he added.

It was a lobster. After watching the clip several dozen times, I think I've memorised the chords, as well as all the lobster's lines, but as I approach the backstage area behind the Left Field tent, my hands are shaking. I once drove two hours through a blizzard to see Billy Bragg play, and the prospect of meeting him would be very exciting were it not alloyed with a sense of impending doom. He pulls his guitar out of his case and talks me through the song's basic structure. It's simple enough, but I get a bit lost in the run-through.

"The thing is, Tim, I'm a bit like you," he says. "Not much of a musician." I pause to admire the way he has welded a charming bit of self-deprecation to an insult so neatly that at first I mistake the whole thing for a compliment. During our brief rehearsal I never once play the song right.

I wait backstage while Bragg begins his show, which immediately follows a debate on the future of green employment. On stage with him are Emmy the Great and singer-songwriter Leon Walker, late of Dartmoor prison, who Billy met though his campaign to provide musical instruments to offenders, Jail Guitar Doors. I am, in every possible sense, out of my depth.

After their third song I get introduced, I walk out, I sit down and, well, I'm afraid I don't remember too much after that. I'm pretty certain I missed the passing A chord in the first chorus (I've always assumed that "passing" is in its musical sense more or less synonymous with "optional") because every time it came around again Bragg turned and gave me a quick, hard stare to make sure I didn't forget again. Later I also recall something Bragg said to Leon about me just before we went on. "We're treating him as a musician today, not a journalist," he said, sounding as if he'd only just decided it. "Bring him in gently, he's one of us."

I'll take that – if I never play Glastonbury again, I can be content with the memory of Billy Bragg's extreme generosity. Which is just as well, because the Fisherman's Friends cancel our six o'clock. I am left to wander the site. In the Craft Field I see a stall where people are taught how to build ovens out of cob, an ancient, handmade clay-and-straw building material. This strikes me as odd, since the whole festival already seems like a giant machine for churning straw into wet clay with the feet. We're all making cob, hundreds of acres of it, smooth and oven-ready.

In a dystopian urban mockup called Shangri-La, I am suddenly surrounded by nurses in platinum blond wigs, who prod me and look into my eyes. They tell me I have a virus. They recommend tequila.

I realise I haven't seen much music. I slog over to see Pulp at the Park stage, where the mud is so sticky that to stand still is to risk permanent cementation. As the sun sets, the woman next to me offers me something brown and homemade from a lemonade bottle.

"What is it?" I say.

"After Eight vodka," she says.

"Oh, no thank you," I say. There is a long pause while we listen to Pulp.

"So what do you do?" I say. "Just crush up After Eight mints with vodka?"

"No, I melt them," she says.

"Actually, I think I'd better have some of that."

This begins a chain of events that I could probably summarise as more drinks. My legs turn to lead. I watch Coldplay's set on a hospitality bar telly. Glastonbury runs on a 24-hour clock, but I do not. I find myself listening to people who are drinking whisky at 2.30am complain of being defeated by tiredness. I decide it's time to find my tent while I still can. It sits directly under a guard tower – tower R2 – where a watchman's walkie-talkie brings news from around the festival all night. "We have a very distressed individual wishing to leave the site," it chirps at 4am. This makes it hard to sleep, but I find it reassuring to know that if I become distressed in the night – a distinct possibility – I need only shout up to him.

The next morning the sun has dried the mud into leathery lumps and rolls. At midday I wander off to the Pyramid stage – my first visit – to see the Low Anthem. At this hour it's easy to get to the front of the stage, where security guards are handing out cups of water. I notice the Low Anthem have a banjo on stage. That's at least two banjos, out of just 2,200 performers. I think I smell a trend.

28 JUNE 2011

Where is the anger now?

ANDY BECKETT

Just off a stairwell at the University of London Union, last winter one of the nerve centres of the student anti-cuts protests, there is a small, locked room. "Free Education For All," read the old placards piled carelessly on a windowsill. "Protest/Strike/Occupy." Stacked more neatly on the floor, like firewood, are hundreds of unused placard handles.

Has the anti-cuts movement just been biding its time in recent months, while the coalition's poll ratings have steadied and mass protests have almost ceased? Or has a certain momentum been lost?

This Thursday's planned strikes, the first big, overtly political ones since the coalition took office more than a year ago, should clarify the state of play somewhat. But what is already obvious, though not much remarked on, is that opposition to the government's radical policies – policies for which it has provocatively little electoral mandate – has not developed in the ferocious way many people thought it would. Are most Britons simply not that angry with the coalition? Or is it that modern political anger has its limits?

Seven months ago, the students who had just stormed the roof of Conservative party headquarters sent a text to journalists. "We are against all cuts," the occupiers announced. "This is only the beginning." Strikingly, within hours a government source described the disorder in London that day in exactly the same terms: "This is just the beginning. This is the first of a series of protests by various sections of society against what we are now doing. This sets the benchmark for other protests."

A fortnight on, after another turbulent student march, it was the turn of the head of the Metropolitan police, Sir Paul Stephenson, to forecast "disorder on the streets" as Britain entered a "new period" of political ferment. Through the winter and into the early spring, evidence of this apparent change kept coming: campus occupations on a scale not seen since the 1970s; the involvement of schoolchildren, and of young Britons of all classes, on the student marches; the massive all-ages anti-cuts demonstration in London in March; even the attack during the December student march on a Rolls-Royce containing a startled Prince Charles and Camilla – a world-turned-upside-down moment worthy of a revolutionary propaganda film.

"In November and December there was this euphoria of dissent," says Mark Fisher, a leftwing blogger and academic. "It made you think a new thing was coming." In March, the radical publisher Verso rush-released a book, Springtime: The New Student Rebellions, on the unrest in Britain, the rest of Europe and the Arab world. "There is a new mood in the air," declared the introduction. At Verso's 40th anniversary party in London in November, intense-looking participants from ongoing student occupations met excited veterans of the legendary youth insurrections of the 60s.

But then the great British revolt went a bit quiet. A plan to turn Trafalgar Square in London into a centre of resistance like Tahrir Square in Egypt came to nothing. The campus occupations ended. At the May local elections, the Liberal Democrats were mauled but the Conservatives did much better than expected. The wedding of Prince William and Kate Middleton in April suggested that much of austerity Britain was still keener to gawp at rather than attack luxurious royal vehicles. Meanwhile, the spring's unusual glut of sun and bank holidays and huge non-cuts-related foreign news stories also helped change the British political atmosphere. Just at the moment the long-dreaded cuts began to take effect, with the start of the current financial year, they almost disappeared from the front pages for the first time in many months.

"It's not that the anger has gone away, but without the constant flashpoints provided by the student protests, it feels more dissipated," says Fisher. Owen Jones, another well-connected young leftwing writer, says: "The danger is just to have one-day [actions], almost to release a bit of anger, make the point, do some media-friendly protest-as-theatre, then go home – with no sense of where the protests go next."

University College London had the winter's most high-profile student occupation. The grand square room the students held for a fortnight – talking to journalists, hosting sympathetic academics and celebrities, and turning the walls, according to an admiring London Review of Books article, into "a sort of slogan competition" – now looks as if the occupation never happened. The walls are slogan-free and spotless. The chairs are back in rows for the room's usual round of exams and dinners and conferences. Outside in the main quadrangle, the occupation's banners are gone, and students wander about in graduation gowns: non-political life goes on.

Since January, pollsters have noticed this lull. "We expected to see more anger," says Tomasz Mludzinski of Ipsos Mori. "The net satisfaction ratings for the government are holding up pretty well."

In the 70s Edward Heath, a more moderate Tory prime minister than David Cameron, infamously had ink thrown at him and a cigarette stubbed out on his neck by enraged voters. During Margaret Thatcher's premiership in the 80s, Morrissey and Elvis Costello wrote songs longing for her death, Margaret on the Guillotine and Tramp the Dirt Down ("... when they finally put you in the ground / I'll stand on your grave and tramp the dirt down"). Heath and Thatcher's modest backgrounds, and Thatcher's gender, made some people readier to hate them. Cameron's old-fashioned male ruling-class aura, depressingly, prompts more deference and acceptance.

In recent months, the double-digit leads Labour sometimes enjoyed over the Tories in the winter have disappeared, to be replaced by a flimsier advantage. The Conservatives' ratings remain remarkably steady, at around the 36% they won in the general election. The proportion of voters worried about losing their jobs or being directly hurt by the cuts is, according to YouGov, slightly smaller now than it was in January.

"We've had at least 18 months of everyone telling us, 'It's going to be hard,'" says Laurence Janta-Lipinski of YouGov. "There's been some very good perception management by the government." Cameron, famously, used to work in PR. Others, too, have had things to gain from issuing apocalyptic forecasts: police chiefs shielding their budgets from the cuts; unions wanting to show their continuing political relevance; newer anti-cuts groups wanting attention; and a media hungry, as ever, for national crises.

Meanwhile, Cameron's U-turns – starkly different from Thatcher's behaviour in office – have made his government's policies look like bargaining positions rather than actual ambitions.

Political anger needs a focus, and the coalition presents a moving target.

Polls also show voters deeply split over who is responsible for the cuts and the feeble economy: besides the coalition, they blame the bankers, Gordon Brown's government and the global economy. The parliamentary expenses scandal has also cast a long shadow, spreading a paralysing disillusionment with politics in general, evident in the poor performances of all three main parties in the 2010 election.

Ed Miliband's time as Labour leader has done little, so far, to unite and energise the coalition's enemies. But his frustrating silences and missed open goals in the Commons are only part of a bigger problem. As a political vehicle and way of thinking, the British left has been losing ground for three decades. Even the fiery Mark Serwotka, head of the Public and Commercial Services Union and one of the instigators of Thursday's strikes, conceded in this paper last December: "The union movement today is different from that of the early 1980s – the last time we faced such an attack on the public sector. Membership is barely half what it was, and anti-union laws constrain us." Labour local authorities, too, lack the legal loopholes – and the political confidence – that enabled Ken Livingstone's Greater London Council to act as a rallying point against Conservative policies in the 80s. Instead, with expressions of regret, and fierce but usually short-lived protests outside their council chambers, current Labour authorities have voted the government's cuts through.

In 2009, shortly after the financial crisis, Fisher published Capitalist Realism, a punchy but dispiriting book about the collective gloom created by a malfunctioning market economy and a shrinking left. Across the west, he wrote, there is a "widespread sense that not only is capitalism the only viable political and economic system, but also that it is impossible even to *imagine* a coherent alternative". A related sense of resignation underlies public attitudes to the cuts: seen as "unfair" by a two-to-one margin in all YouGov's recent polls, but also seen as "necessary" by the same margin. The sociologist Richard Sennett produces a good metaphor for the dread and passivity that has frequently been the British national mood since the general election: "It's the snail pulling into its shell."

Thirty years ago next month, another economic slump and austerity government helped provoke Toxteth in Liverpool into the fiercest of the many riots of the Thatcher era. Toxteth is still poor: most of its eerily half-empty landscape of huge, often derelict Victorian properties, waste ground and boxy council estates is in the most deprived 1% of neighbourhoods in the country. The area remains profoundly alienated from the Conservatives, without a Liverpool MP since 1979. But residents seem more resigned than in the 80s. "The north always gets hit worst by cuts," says a pensioner in one of the few remaining shops, who has been in Toxteth since the 40s. "People are angry. But they're really scared of losing their homes, their jobs."

A newsagent in the street where the 1981 riot started says: "This government can't manage a thing. But when I get into debt, I blame myself first, the government second." As we talk, a stream of customers ask him the prices of the cheapest sweets and sugary drinks: modern British escapism in action.

"In the 80s, you could get 100,000 people on the streets in Liverpool against the Tories," says Tony Nelson, a long-standing Liverpool trade union and community activist. "Those days are gone. People are watching Jeremy Kyle on TV all day. There is anger among the unemployed, but community groups like us, we're keeping a lid on it for now." But, he goes on: "The government needs to be very careful: they're thinking of taking funds away from the community groups. People in this city have always had a disrespect for authority. If there's one place where something kicks off, it'll be here."

There are two ways that street unrest can badly damage a government. One is for the government to appear to have lost control, as with Heath and the miners' strikes of the 70s, which led to power cuts and the police being swamped by mass pickets. The other is for protests to crystallise a wider dissatisfaction, as with the poll tax march and riot of 1990, which showed how out of touch the Thatcher government had become. In other circumstances, anger can fizzle out – or even backfire. The 1981 inner-city riots, the 1984-85 miners' strike, and the immense 2003 anti-Iraq-war march all temporarily shook governments, but left them even more publicly determined not to change course. In each case, they won a general election not long afterwards.

So far for the coalition, the protests have been awkward rather than fatal. But it is more vulnerable than most recent governments. There is potential for splits both between and inside the coalition parties in response to well-organised opposition. The government's many U-turns have made further campaigns against its policies likely. There is the economic situation: Britons are among the gloomiest of all westerners about their economy, according to Ipsos Mori. And there is the fact that austerity governments across the world are losing elections. In many ways the coalition, with its lack of a proper majority or mandate, and its faithful adherence to the free-market economics discredited by the financial crisis, resembles a cartoon character that has run off a cliff and, any moment, may feel the force of gravity.

"After two years of this government, will the public be as forgiving? I don't think so," says Vidhya Alakeson of the Resolution Foundation, a thinktank which this year has been running focus groups of economically stressed voters. She has found her interviewees "partly ignorant" about the impact the cuts will have on them, and "partly grateful to still be staying afloat" financially, for now, but also "a bit sad" at "losing out on options" they expected to have. After the seemingly endless boom of the Blair years, says Alakeson, "I don't think those expectations have gone away." And frustrated public expectations can be lethal for governments.

Often, it is not until the second or third year that a British government's poll ratings collapse. And Britain, like other rich democracies, is only just emerging from a long depoliticised era, dominated by the technocratic ideas explored in Adam Curtis's recent BBC2 documentary series All Watched Over by Machines of Loving Grace, and by what Fisher calls the "debate and comment" culture of cathartic but politically impotent radio phone-ins and internet forums. The anti-coalition actions so far have at least re-established the idea that protest can be meaningful, and even enjoyable. And just as the cuts are turning out not to be the overnight apocalypse many feared, but a quieter, more relentless erosion, so the protests may not hurt the government immediately, but eat away at its perceived legitimacy for years until its rickety structure suddenly folds.

"There's a huge, slow momentum building," says a spokesman for the rising activist group UK Uncut, which is scheduled to meet unions for the first time to discuss co-ordinated anti-government protests. "So far, UK Uncut has done single-day actions, but it will definitely have to look again at that model. There is some way to go in getting the Daily Mail readers who are outside their local library protesting at cuts and, say, striking teachers to link up."

Yet few doubt that interesting times are coming. On Newsnight a fortnight ago, a British political veteran gave his little-reported view of the prospects for unrest in Europe and beyond. "There is enormous discontent among young people," he said, "about long-term unemployment, about the extent of economic problems ...

We will see political movements for change – not just in the Arab world." And as he concluded his remarks, the foreign secretary William Hague looked intriguingly calm.

5 JULY 2011

News of the World hacked Milly Dowler's phone during police hunt

NICK DAVIES AND AMELIA HILL

The News of the World illegally targeted the missing schoolgirl Milly Dowler and her family in March 2002, interfering with police inquiries into her disappearance, an investigation by the Guardian has established.

Scotland Yard is investigating the episode, which is likely to put new pressure on the then editor of the paper, Rebekah Brooks, now Rupert Murdoch's chief executive in the UK, and the then deputy editor, Andy Coulson, who resigned in January as the prime minister's media adviser.

The Dowlers' family lawyer, Mark Lewis, issued a statement yesterday describing the News of the World's activities as "heinous" and "despicable". He said the Dowler family was now pursuing a damages claim against the News of the World.

Milly Dowler disappeared at the age of 13 on her way home in Walton-on-Thames, Surrey, on 21 March 2002.

Detectives from Scotland Yard's new inquiry into the phone hacking, Operation Weeting, are believed to have found evidence of the targeting of the Dowlers in a collection of 11,000 pages of notes kept by Glenn Mulcaire, the private investigator jailed for phone hacking on behalf of the News of the World.

In the last four weeks the Met officers have approached Surrey police and taken formal statements from some of those involved in the original inquiry, who were concerned about how News of the World journalists intercepted – and deleted – the voicemail messages of Milly Dowler.

The messages were deleted by journalists in the first few days after Milly's disappearance in order to free up space for more messages. As a result friends and relatives of Milly concluded wrongly that she might still be alive. Police feared evidence may have been destroyed.

The Guardian investigation has shown that, within a very short time of Milly vanishing, News of the World journalists reacted by engaging in what was standard practice in their newsroom: they hired private investigators to get them a story.

Their first step was simple, albeit illegal. Paperwork seen by the Guardian reveals that they paid a Hampshire private investigator, Steve Whittamore, to obtain home addresses and, where necessary, ex-directory phone numbers for any families called Dowler in the Walton area. The three addresses Whittamore found could be obtained lawfully on the electoral register. The two ex-directory numbers, however, were "blagged" illegally from British Telecom's confidential records by one of Whittamore's associates, John Gunning, who works from a base in Wiltshire. One of the ex-directory numbers was attributed by Whittamore to Milly's family home.

Then, with the help of its own full-time private investigator, Glenn Mulcaire, the News of the World started illegally intercepting mobile phone messages. Scotland Yard is now investigating evidence that the paper hacked directly into the voicemail of the missing girl's own phone. As her friends and parents called and left messages imploring Milly to get in touch with them, the News of the World was listening and recording their every private word.

But the journalists at the News of the World then encountered a problem. Milly's voicemail box filled up and would accept no more messages. Apparently thirsty for more information from more voicemails, the paper intervened – and deleted the messages that had been left in the first few days after her disappearance. According to one source, this had a devastating effect: when her friends and family called again and discovered that her voicemail had been cleared, they concluded that this must have been done by Milly herself and, therefore, that she must still be alive. But she was not. The interference created false hope and extra agony for those who were misled by it.

The Dowler family then granted an exclusive interview to the News of the World in which they talked about their hope, quite unaware that it had been falsely kindled by the newspaper's own intervention. Sally Dowler told the paper: "If Milly walked through the door, I don't think we'd be able to speak. We'd just weep tears of joy and give her a great big hug."

The deletion of the messages also caused difficulties for the police by confusing the picture. It also potentially destroyed valuable evidence.

According to one senior source familiar with the Surrey police investigation: "It can happen with abduction murders that the perpetrator will leave messages, asking the missing person to get in touch, as part of their efforts at concealment. Anybody who destroys that evidence is seriously interfering with the course of a police investigation."

The paper made little effort to conceal the hacking from its readers. On 14 April 2002 it published a story about a woman allegedly pretending to be Milly Dowler who had applied for a job with a recruitment agency: "It is thought the hoaxer even gave the agency Milly's real mobile number ... the agency used the number to contact Milly when a job vacancy arose and left a message on her voicemail ... it was on March 27, six days after Milly went missing, that the employment agency appears to have phoned her mobile."

The newspaper also made no effort to conceal its activity from Surrey police. After it had hacked the message from the recruitment agency on Milly's phone, the paper informed police about it.

It was Surrey detectives who established that the call was not intended for Milly Dowler. At the time, Surrey police suspected that phones belonging to detectives and to Milly's parents also were being targeted.

One of those who was involved in the original inquiry said: "We'd arrange landline calls. We didn't trust our mobiles."

However, they took no action against the News of the World, partly because their main focus was to find the missing schoolgirl and partly because this was only one example of tabloid misbehaviour. As one source close to the inquiry put it: "There was a hell of a lot of dirty stuff going on." Two earlier Yard inquiries had failed to investigate the relevant notes in Mulcaire's logs.

In a statement, the family's lawyer said the Dowlers were distressed at the revelation. "It is distress heaped upon tragedy to learn that the News of the World had no humanity at such a terrible time. The fact that they were prepared to act in such a heinous way that could have jeopardised the police investigation and give them false hope is despicable," Lewis said.

The News of the World's investigation was part of a long campaign against paedophiles championed by the then editor, Rebekah Brooks.

The behaviour of tabloid newspapers became an issue in the trial of Levi Bellfield, who last month was jailed for life for murdering Milly. A second charge, that he had attempted to abduct another Surrey schoolgirl, Rachel Cowles, had to be left on file after premature publicity by tabloids was held to have made it impossible for the jury to reach a fair verdict.

Surrey police referred all questions on the subject to Scotland Yard, who said they could not discuss it.

The News of the World's parent company News International, part of Murdoch's media empire, said yesterday: "We have been co-operating fully with Operation Weeting since our voluntary disclosure in January restarted the investigation into illegal voicemail interception. This particular case is clearly a development of great concern and we will be conducting our own inquiry as a result. We will obviously co-operate fully with any police request on this should we be asked."

8 JULY 2011

The scandal that closed the News of the World

● Murdoch axes paper as hacking crisis engulfs him ● Labour presses for Rebekah Brooks to quit

13 JULY 2011

Andy Hayman stars at phone-hacking committee session

SIMON HOGGART

The star of the marathon committee session on phone hacking was undoubtedly Andy Hayman, the then top copper who was in charge of the first inquiry that led nowhere.

He must be given his own sitcom, a blend of Life On Mars and Minder, starring Hayman as Del Boy. One of the MPs called him "a dodgy geezer" to his face. Put it this way: I wouldn't let him sell me a cheap Rolex, if I wanted to know the time.

His evidence followed other high-ranked plods. As usual John Yates was given a toasting by the committee (he must be a masochist; nothing stops him coming back for more). The chairman, Keith Vaz, told him that his evidence had been "unconvincing", and he could expect to be summoned again. We half-expected him to say: "Ooh, yes, please!"

But to the committee, he was George Washington compared with Mr Hayman. I've seen a few incredulous MPs in my time, but nothing like this. Through most of Mr Hayman's evidence they were either rolling with laughter, or favouring him with a cold, sardonic glare. Or both.

Mr Vaz asked about the fact that he had taken a job as a columnist with News International, the very firm he had been investigating. "That is a private matter for me and the Times," said Hayman primly, to startled surprise.

They asked about his private life. Was it true he'd been hacked over that? "'Aven't got a clue," he replied. It turned out this was one of his catchphrases, along with "dunno", "can't remember", "can't recall" and "that was four or five years ago!"

"All this sounds more like Clouseau than Columbo," said Vaz, in what may have been a microwaved soundbite.

Mark Reckless pointed out that both he and the former DPP were now working for News International. "Do you wonder how that looks to the public?"

Hayman: "It could look bad."

Vaz: "We all think it looks bad."

Julian Huppert, a Lib Dem, said that some of what he said was "quite incredible". Mr Hayman snapped into "who, me? I swear on my baby's life..." mode.

"OK," he said, "beat me up for being upfront and honest!"

The Tory Michael Ellis, his voice swooping up and down with astonishment, said: "You made a judgment call to accept hospitality from the people you were investigating?"

Hayman: "Yeah." (Mocking laughter.) He added: "Not having the dinner would have been potentially more suspicious than to have it." (Louder laughter.)

"I dunno why you're laughing ... we would never, ever have a dinner that would compromise the investigation."

(I wonder what would have happened if he had troughed with a top stolen car dealer. "I do hope you find the lobster Newburg and foie gras to your taste, Basher.")

Nicola Blackwood, a Tory, looked faint. "I feel I've fallen through a rabbit hole," she breathed.

Stephen McCabe, Labour, wanted to know why Hayman had ridiculed John Prescott when he said his phone had been hacked. Vaz: "You said he was ranting and there was no evidence. You said that if he was right, you would eat your words."

Mr Vaz asked if he should pass him a piece of paper, and for a moment we thought he was going to force Hayman, physically, to eat his words.

Lorraine Fullbrook, another Tory, asked outright if he had ever accepted money from NI.

You would have thought she'd accused him of being a predatory paedophile, not someone who had conducted a hopelessly inadequate inquiry into a firm which had wined and dined him, and then given him a well-paid job.

"Good god!" he exploded. "Absolutely not, I can't believe you suggested that! That is a real attack on my integrity!"

Keith Vaz concluded: "Normally I would sum up the evidence, but on this occasion, it speaks for itself." And he didn't mean it in a kind way.

14 JULY 2011

The sky falls in

GUARDIAN LEADER

It is a measure of how much has been achieved in this revolutionary week that by the time David Cameron set out details of the inquiry into media and police standards on Wednesday lunchtime, and News Corporation announced it was dropping its bid for BSkyB soon after, both things seemed natural and unavoidable. A wave of public and political contempt is reshaping the landscape. At the start of the month no senior politician dared defy Rupert Murdoch. Now, all of them have. Party leaders united around the terms of the inquiry and the Labour-sponsored Commons debate – itself presaged by the collapse of the deal it had been arranged to condemn.

Wednesday brought a drama in four acts. At prime minister's

questions Mr Cameron sought unsuccessfully to rid himself of the taint of proximity to the News International executives who oversaw phone hacking, of which more in a moment. In his Commons statement, the prime minister set out the terms of an inquiry into media standards of extraordinary scope and potential. By mid-afternoon, News Corporation pulled the plug on the BSkyB deal: a victory for plurality over the power of a rootless corporation. In particular it was a success for Ed Miliband, whose decision to break with News International has become the definitive act of his leadership so far. Finally, Gordon Brown delivered a powerful speech whose justified moral outrage was only equalled by its divisive consequences in the chamber.

Mr Brown presented himself in retrospect as a white knight who stood up to the Murdoch empire, only to be let down by the timidity of others. Not everything at the time was like that. The Brown government was far from pure in its dealings with the press. But the former prime minister was on firmer ground when he questioned Mr Cameron's record. The prime minister's response raised further significant questions about his slapdash approach to phone hacking and the appointment of Andy Coulson as his media adviser.

In February 2010, this paper ran a story which should have given Mr Cameron pause for thought. For legal reasons it contained only limited details of the News of the World's decision, while Mr Coulson was editor, to employ a private investigator who had served a seven-year sentence for perverting the course of justice and who had been charged with conspiracy to murder. Believing that Mr Cameron should be made aware in private of the full details, the Guardian passed them to his senior adviser, Steve Hilton.

In the Commons, however, Mr Cameron told MPs that the Guardian passed no significant private information about Mr

Coulson to his staff. That is incorrect. Second, he suggested that the Guardian had been able to put all the significant facts of the story in the public domain at the time. That is incorrect, too. Third, he claimed that the fact that the editor of the Guardian, Alan Rusbridger, did not mention the story to him at two later meetings implied it was not important. That is an evasion: the first meeting followed the private warning and the second took place after Mr Coulson had resigned. Mr Cameron could have been in full possession of the facts, and acted on them, had he chosen to be. Instead he gave Mr Coulson a job in Downing Street.

This matters because at the core of the whole affair lies the shoddy and secret way in which some powerful media groups have dealt with political leaders from both main parties. In this, Mr Cameron may not even be the greatest sinner. But he happens to be the prime minister who must address all what has gone on. He cannot do so properly while he continues to evade the truth of his own past dealings.

The world is changing. Mr Murdoch's spell has been broken. The BSkyB deal is off. The inquiry can lead to a cleaner, more plural, future. Mr Cameron is trapped by his past.

15 JULY 2011

Gordon Brown now suffers that incurable syndrome: ex-PM

SIMON JENKINS

No animal in the political jungle is more awful in its misery than an ex-prime minister. With the blood of past battle still congealed on its back, it howls through the haunts of old, reeking of stale breath and stale headlines, a putrefying hulk of resentment, hopelessness and revenge. It grabs friend and foe alike by the neck and cries: "Fools, the lot of you. I was right all along. Now look at the mess you have made."

Gordon Brown rose in the Commons debate on Wednesday and caused a buzz of excitement. Someone had left the cage door open and the beast was loose. Was the man who bestrode the exchanges for a decade about to render his account on the deficit, the credit crunch, the Afghan war or his views on Tony Blair?

The answer was no. The issue that roused those mighty haunches from the benches was whether Brown's phone had been tapped. A man who had inexplicably paid court to the Murdoch press, attended Rebekah Brooks's wedding and even organised her birthday now accused her of "law-breaking on an industrial scale". The Sun has emphatically denied it used illegal methods to gain medical details of Brown's baby, but Brown knew he was on the side of angels and wanted no excuses. He was incandescent at the cabinet secretary for denying him a full judicial inquiry into his outrage.

There is no known way of retiring from the highest power with dignity. Every nation handles its statesmen in retirement differently. Kindly dictatorships shoot them or send them into exile. Some democracies bury them in pompous thinktanks with pompous titles. America declares its ex-presidents instant history and gives them foundations, staffs, limousines and memorial libraries.

Britain has never worked out what to do, because prime ministers were assumed to have country estates to which to retreat. The House of Lords is a happy retirement home, where ageing statesmen can still sniff the air and touch the hem of power, with a modest pension and a memoir advance.

But there is no way of handling the rage. Since the second world war, only Attlee, Churchill, Douglas-Home and Wilson can be said to have left office in relatively good order. Eden and Macmillan left sick. Heath, Major and Blair left afflicted by failure. Thatcher and Brown left in a maelstrom of skulduggery and treason.

The closest to perfection was Alec Douglas-Home, who led his party to a creditable defeat in 1964, and then returned in glory to a distinguished period at the Foreign Office in 1970. A Scots grandee, he was once heard at Pratt's, the London club, chatting about what to do with ex-prime ministers, having apparently forgotten he was one.

Douglas-Home appears to have been immune to what David Owen – in his study of leadership pathology, In Sickness and in Power – called the "hubris syndrome". Analysing the psychological impact of power on a leader's personality, Owen pointed out that these people, with huge doses of daily adrenaline, are in a perpetual state of post-traumatic stress disorder. The public presentation of men such as George Bush and Tony Blair might be that "of affable guys who can be trusted". Yet their inner hubris was "a great menace to the quality of leadership and the proper government of the world".

The unnaturalness of a senior politician's life, the lack of normal relaxants (other than alcohol), and the aloofness from family and friends, creates a disorder of which medical science is largely ignorant. As Owen points out, this omission is a serious matter that surely merits as much study as does ordinary illness.

To the end, Macmillan and Callaghan demonstrated the well-known feature of the syndrome, the fantasy that they would one day be "called back" to save their countries. Heath was sure Margaret Thatcher would make such a mess that he would return to power. Indeed, on the eve of the 1979 election Thatcher's aides were so convinced she would lose that they asked Heath to share her last pre-election party broadcast, reducing her to a fury of frustration and tears.

Throughout her premiership Thatcher had to put up with Heath sitting just below the gangplank in a permanent state of sullen resentment. Making the best of it, she said that he was an ever-present warning of a mistake she should never repeat. When Heath eventually published his memoirs, he waddled to the podium at the Millbank reception, gazed over the audience and began, with the merest twitch of a smile: "The sulk is over..." It was not.

But then Thatcher gave as good as she got. Soon after her fall she travelled to open a hotel in Warsaw, lecturing an adulatory audience on the wonders of being Polish. She went into complete orbit and was even told she should run as Poland's president, a suggestion that left her glowing with ambition. Such moments of recalled glory were rare, and she soon sank into resentment at her overthrow, muttering about treachery and "never having lost an election". Though Major had always served her with total loyalty, she was dreadful towards him, flirting with Blair in 1997 when he blessed her as "a radical, not a Tory". She even assured the nation just before the poll that Blair "is a man who won't let Britain down".

Probably it is just that prime ministers – like most people – revert to some former identity in retirement. Douglas-Home became a courteous Borders grandee, whose addiction to field sports ensured he would never stray into commenting on his successors. Callaghan took to his Sussex farm, regretting that as an old sailor, "I never had a Falklands war to fight".

Major never lost his thin skin and sensitivity to criticism. I was sitting one balmy day watching cricket at Lords when a figure slid into the seat beside me, his identity shielded by the sun. "You were quite wrong about me," the man said nervously, "quite wrong." It was John Major, still fuming about something I had written, and long forgotten, years before. Major has at least settled into a profitable retirement doing what he does best, which is talk.

Blair's life since leaving office has appeared to mimic the film The Ghost. It showed him moving between cold, shoreline villas devoid of books, staffed by lonely secretaries and faceless men with earpieces. Everywhere was a numbing security and silence. The Blair character's retinue of cosmeticians and historians seemed to rebuild his past as often as they did his face. Life after political death was for him a world cruise of pseudo-peacemaking, with a suite and a secretary in every trouble spot. Blair is today like Henry II, still doing penance for the death of Becket.

Hubris syndrome is probably incurable, the occupational disease of power. But it must have its uses. Ex-prime ministers should always have a place in the upper house, there to dispense such wisdom as is sometimes the product of experience. I would gladly hear Blair and Brown reflect, under due cross-examination, on their past deeds. The one duty owed by youth to age is sometimes to listen.

18 JULY 2011

Met chief quits over hacking

19 July 2011

'Everybody got carried away with this power that we had. No one caught us'

NICK DAVIES

At a time when the reputation of News of the World journalists is at rock bottom, it needs to be said that the paper's former show-business correspondent Sean Hoare, who died yesterday, was a lovely man.

In the saga of the phone-hacking scandal, he distinguished himself by being the first former NoW journalist to come out on the record, telling the New York Times last year that his former friend and editor, Andy Coulson, had actively encouraged him to hack into voicemail.

That took courage. But he had a particularly powerful motive for speaking. He knew how destructive the News of the World could be, not just for the targets of its exposés, but also for the ordinary journalists who worked there, who got caught up in its remorseless drive for headlines.

Explaining why he had spoken out, he told me: "I want to right a wrong, lift the lid on it, the whole culture. I know, we all know, that the hacking and other stuff is endemic. Because there is so much intimidation. In the newsroom, you have people being fired, breaking down in tears, hitting the bottle."

He knew this very well, because he was himself a victim of the News of the World. As a showbusiness reporter, he had lived what he was happy to call a privileged life. But the reality had ruined his physical health: "I was paid to go out and take drugs with rock stars – get drunk with them, take pills with them, take cocaine with them. It was so competitive. You are going to go beyond the call of duty. You are going to do things that no sane man would do. You're in a machine."

While it was happening, he loved it. He came from a working-class background of solid Arsenal supporters, always voted Labour, defined himself specifically as a "clause IV" socialist who still believed in public ownership of the means of production. But, working as a reporter, he suddenly found himself up to his elbows in drugs and delirium.

He rapidly arrived at the Sun's Bizarre column, then run by Coulson. He recalled: "There was a system on the Sun. We broke good stories. I had a good relationship with Andy. He would let me do what I wanted as long as I brought in a story. The brief was, 'I don't give a fuck'."

He was a born reporter. He could always find stories. And, unlike some of his nastier tabloid colleagues, he did not play the bully with his sources. He was naturally a warm, kind man, who could light up a lamp-post with his talk.

From Bizarre, he moved to the Sunday People, under Neil Wallis, and then to the News of the World, where Coulson had become deputy editor. And, persistently, he did as he was told and went out on the road with rock stars, befriending them, bingeing with them, pausing only to file his copy.

He made no secret of his massive ingestion of drugs. He told me how he used to start the day with "a rock star's breakfast" – a line of cocaine and a Jack Daniel's – usually in the company of a journalist who now occupies a senior position at the Sun. He reckoned he was using three grams of cocaine a day, spending about £1,000 a week. Plus endless alcohol.

Looking back, he could see it had done him enormous damage.

But at the time, as he recalled, most of his colleagues were doing it, too.

"Everyone got overconfident. We thought we could do coke, go to Brown's, sit in the Red Room with Paula Yates and Michael Hutchence. Everyone got a bit carried away."

It must have scared the rest of Fleet Street when he started talking – he had bought, sold and snorted cocaine with some of the most powerful names in tabloid journalism. One retains a senior position on the Daily Mirror.

"I last saw him in Little Havana," he recalled, "at three in the morning, on his hands and knees. He had lost his cocaine wrap. I said to him, 'This is not really the behaviour we expect of a senior journalist from a great Labour paper.' He said, 'Have you got any fucking drugs?'"

And the voicemail hacking was all part of the great game. The idea that it was a secret, or the work of some "rogue reporter", had him rocking in his chair: "Everyone was doing it. Everybody got a bit carried away with this power that they had. No one came close to catching us." He would hack messages and delete them so the competition could not hear them, or hack messages and swap them with mates on other papers.

In the end, his body would not take it any more. He said he started to have fits, that his liver was in such a terrible state that a doctor told him he must be dead. And, as his health collapsed, he was sacked by the News of the World – by his old friend Coulson.

When he spoke out about the voicemail hacking, some Conservative MPs were quick to smear him, spreading tales of his drug use as though that meant he was dishonest. He was genuinely offended by the lies being told by News International and always willing to help me and other reporters who were trying to expose the truth. He was equally offended when Scotland Yard's former assistant commissioner, John Yates, assigned officers to interview him, not as a witness but as a suspect. They told him anything he said could be used against him, and, to his credit, he refused to have anything to do with them.

His health never recovered. He liked to say that he had stopped drinking, but he would treat himself to some red wine. He liked to say he didn't smoke any more, but he would stop for a cigarette on his way home. For better and worse, he was a Fleet Street man.

19 JULY 2011

Yates of the Yard quits over 'gossip'

20 JULY 2011

Coached out of a tight corner

NICK DAVIES

At one point yesterday afternoon, the Murdochs were asked what coaching they had received in preparation for the hearing. "We were told to tell the truth, to be as open and as transparent as possible," came the reply. It was a little more sophisticated than that.

Their performance strongly suggested that the besuited consiglieri in the row behind them had earned their fees. There were signs of two kinds of advice – a PR strategy and a legal defence. Both were all about crafting an escape from a tight and unpleasant corner.

The foundation stone of the PR strategy was humble apology. James Murdoch interrupted his first answer to say how sorry he was, how great his regret was. Rupert Murdoch interrupted his son's apology to make his own. "This is the most humble day of my life," he said. Twice. PR consultants around the planet would spot the soundbite there, uttered by Mr Murdoch but written surely by an expert.

They continued to apologise at all available intervals. Rupert, in particular, volunteered that he had been absolutely shocked, appalled and ashamed to hear of the hacking of the phone of Milly Dowler. This, in turn, proved to be part of a wider strategy – a non-aggression pact with everyone. The MPs on the committee; their tormentors on the Guardian; the lawyers who have hauled them through the courts: none were to be attacked. Murdoch Sr sat with head bowed and his hands clasped. Murdoch Jr – whose temper is globally famous – was a model of deference and courtesy.

Only once did Murdoch Sr stray from the pacific script, when he snarled against "all our competitors trying to build up this hysteria". But he soon compensated with two extra PR gambits. He recalled his father as a heroic journalist, who had exposed the truth about Gallipoli (though cynics say Sir Keith fixed the evidence), and then he made a brilliant grab for the friendship of the committee by recommending Singapore's approach to clean politics, which would involve paying MPs $1m a year. They laughed. He smiled. That's PR.

But behind that gloss, there was an intensely serious and carefully organised defence. They allowed some moral blame to get through – hence the humility – but at all costs they had to repel anything that looked remotely like criminal responsibility.

For Rupert Murdoch, this was simple. Essentially, he worked too high up the ladder to see the ground.

And so it was that he had never known that in March 2003 his editor, Rebekah Brooks, had told this same select committee that her journalists had paid police in the past; and he didn't know why no one had investigated this interesting confession; and he had never heard that the judge who presided over Max Mosley's action for privacy in 2008 had accused the News of the World's chief reporter, Neville Thurlbeck, of blackmailing two prostitutes in the case; and he didn't know that his son had authorised more than £1m to be paid to settle the case of Gordon Taylor; and he didn't know that his subsidiary company had authorised another £1m to settle the case of Max Clifford; and he didn't know that last year, this same select committee had accused executives from News International of suffering from "collective amnesia". He couldn't even remember what he had ever discussed with Tony Blair. "We argued about the euro, I think."

For James Murdoch, the defence was more complex. He was not so high up the ladder and was specifically responsible for minding the family business in the region which included the UK. He took a chronological approach, using a different blockade for each phase, to separate himself from culpability.

How could he not have known that in 2007, after the trial of the News of the World's royal correspondent and private investigator, there was evidence that other NoW journalists were involved in hacking? That was easy. He had not been there. But Les Hinton had been there, as chairman of News International (and as Rupert's trusted friend and adviser). What did he know? James didn't know that either. Hadn't he asked Hinton what he knew? No, he hadn't.

But what about 2008, when he personally approved the settlement of the legal action brought by the chief executive of the Professional Footballers' Association, Gordon Taylor, and two associates? "It's a good question," replied James. "I'm happy to discuss the case of the out-of-court settlement with Mr Taylor." This was potentially tricky.

On the one hand, it is a matter of record that the NoW settled the case after a judge ordered police to disclose evidence they held, including an email from an NoW reporter for the attention of Thurlbeck, containing the transcripts of 35 intercepted voicemail messages. This was the smoking gun, which led to the NoW settling the case. On the other hand, James Murdoch's position was that he had not had any evidence of that kind at the time. If he didn't know about the "email for Neville", why did he settle the case? If he did know about it, why didn't he tell the police?

The answer lay with the lawyers, he said. He had been told that the NoW's outside counsel had advised them that they were bound to lose the case – but he had never been told why. He had paid out more than £1m in damages and legal fees without knowing what evidence compelled him to do so.

Beyond this, he insisted, he had known nothing of the illegal activity at the paper until the legal action brought by Sienna Miller in December last year forced the disclosure of paperwork.

Until then, he had relied on the advice of three groups. First, Scotland Yard, which had said repeatedly there was no new evidence and no need to reopen the inquiry. He made no reference to the evidence last week of senior Yard officers who said they had been unable to obtain evidence of the crime at the paper, because News International had lied and obstructed them.

Second, the Press Complaints Commission, which had produced a report saying there was no evidence that anyone other than Clive Goodman had been involved in crime at the NoW. He made no reference to the recent blunt statement by the chair of the PCC, Lady Buscombe, that the News of the World had lied to them. Finally, he cited the report of a highly reputable law firm, Harbottle and Lewis, which had inspected a collection of NoW emails and declared they revealed no evidence of crime. More recently, those emails have been handed to police, and the ex-DPP Lord Macdonald has said they contain evidence of indirect hacking and serious crime. He hadn't known that, he said, until this spring. Two other executives had handled them at the time, but both of them had left.

22 JULY 2011

James Murdoch misled MPs, say NoW executives

News Corp chief may be called back to clarify evidence

22 JULY 2011

Obituary: Lucian Freud

CATHERINE LAMPERT

The original, unnerving, sustained artistic achievement of Lucian Freud, who has died aged 88, had at its heart a wilful, restless personality, fired by his intelligence and attentiveness and his suspicion of method, never wanting to risk doing the same thing twice. The sexually loaded, penetrating gaze was part of his weaponry, but his art addressed the lives of individuals, whether life models or royalty, with delicacy and disturbing corporeality.

Freud had a reputation for pushing subjects to an extreme. But unlike the American painters to emerge in the 1950s, his approach was in the western tradition of working from life and brought about with painstaking slowness, rather than unleashed virtuosity. Photographs taken in the studio by his assistant, model and good friend, the painter David Dawson, show Freud working from a roughly sketched charcoal form, the paint slowly spreading outwards from the head. Some canvases were extended, others abandoned while still a fragment.

Portraits of his maturity drew comparisons with equally shocking works by Courbet, Titian and Picasso, the feelings exposed registering as both brash and profound. The recorded stages of Ria, Naked Portrait 2006-07, his last large female nude, indicate the suspenseful buildup of pigment on her toe and the radiator; heavy incretions represent her curls and flushed face.

By 1987, the critic Robert Hughes nominated Freud as the greatest living realist painter, and after the death of Francis Bacon five years later, the sobriquet could be taken as a commendation, or it could imply an honour fit for an anachronistic "figurative" artist working in London. Art critics since Freud's first shows in the 1940s have had difficulties situating his achievement; the common solution has been to apply adjectives to the painted subjects in a way that reflects little more than personal taste, the writers telling readers whether the person portrayed was bored or intimidated, scrawny or obese, the paint slathered, crumbly or miraculously plastic.

Others, however, eschew this moralising tone and are prepared to be startled. Aidan Dunne, for example, reviewing the exhibition in Dublin in 2007, recognised how a single blonde model, "unmistakably" herself, in 1966 led Freud to push "the bounds of decorum in terms of mainstream depictions of the human body considered not as a generic type but as, to use his own term, a 'naked portrait'". Freud painted three versions of this fine-boned young woman on a cream cover, seen from above, each one a masterpiece. Her pictorial availability seems to some degree predicated on the artist's subtle way of incorporating in his paint strokes the upheavals and new perils that would enliven traditional gender relationships.

Freud was born in Berlin, to Ernst Freud, an architect and youngest son of the great psychoanalyst Sigmund, and Lucie Brasch. The family lived near the Tiergarten, with summers spent on the estate of Freud's maternal grandfather, a grain merchant, or at their summer house on the Baltic island of Hiddensee.

Realising the Nazi threat to Jews, his parents, Lucian and his brothers – Stephen and Clement – moved to England in the summer of 1933. At Dartington Hall, Devon, and then Bryanston, Dorset, Freud was preoccupied by horses and art rather than the classroom. He enrolled at the Central School of Arts and Crafts, London, in January 1939 but found the laid-back atmosphere repellent and rarely attended classes.

From 1939 to 1942 he spent periods at the unstructured school founded by Cedric Morris and Arthur Lett-Haines in East Anglia, first in Dedham, Essex, and then at Hadleigh, Suffolk. Morris proved a sympathetic mentor, one whose confidence and application gave Freud a sense of what it might mean to be an artist. In March 1941 Freud signed on as an ordinary seaman on the armed merchant cruiser SS Baltrover, bound for Nova Scotia. The ship came under attack from the air and then by submarine, and on the return journey he went down with tonsillitis.

By the age of 18, the charismatic, talented young man with a famous name had attracted friends such as Stephen Spender and the wealthy collector and patron Peter Watson. Freud began visiting Paris, first in 1946 while on his way to Greece, where he stayed for six months, and again in 1947, with Kitty Garman, niece of his previous girlfriend Lorna Wishart, daughter of Jacob Epstein and the subject of one of the first major paintings, Girl in a Dark Jacket 1947. His connections in Paris extended to people linked to the arts in the 1930s, such as the hostess and collector Marie-Laure de Noailles.

The handful of surviving postcards contain no mention of postwar deprivations as he offers Méraud Guinness Guevara witty accounts of the installation of André Breton's surrealist exhibition in Paris in 1947, designed by Marcel Duchamp and Frederick Kiesler, and thanks for her hospitality in Provence. Freud expresses admiration for the "malevolence" the French showed to foreigners.

On familiar terms with Alberto Giacometti and Balthus, and, to some degree, Picasso, the young Freud, one senses, was marked for life by seeing how single-mindedly, and self-critically, these already famous artists pushed forward their art. When he moved in 1943 to Delamere Terrace on the Grand Union canal, the first of five addresses in Paddington, London, several of his Irish working-class neighbours became models, especially the brothers Charlie and Billy. A large picture with a spiky palm tree and a tense, young East Ender, Harry Diamond, comprises a poignant drama about survival, Interior in Paddington 1951.

Paintings of Freud's two wives – Garman (whom he married in 1948 and divorced four years later) and Caroline Blackwood (whom he married in 1953 and divorced in 1957) – and other intimate friends are filled with suspense and pain, apparent in the strands of hair and a hand raised to the cheek as much as the wide eyes. The pearly skin of these subjects becomes more trans-lucent and the detail extra-perfect. In an article written in 1950, the critic and curator David Sylvester questioned the perversity of feeling in Freud's latest portrayals. "It is impossible to say whether this indicates the incipient decline of an art whose talent flow-ered remarkably early or simply that every new departure implies growing-pains."

By the time of the Venice Biennale in 1954 – Freud shared the British pavilion with Bacon and Ben Nicholson – the question of prodigy versus an ultimately significant artist was being argued regularly. Freud's only involvement with the art colleges came though accepting William Coldstream's invitation to join the new staff at the Slade in 1949 (he made occasional appearances in the studios until 1954).

It became convenient to account for shifts in Freud's work by focusing on his early reliance on drawing and to cite the influ-ence of painters from northern Europe such as Jean Auguste Dominique Ingres and Albrecht Dürer, or even to suggest a false comparison with the Neue Sachlichkeit painters (active in Germany in the 1920s but unknown to the young Freud) and overlook others as relevant as Paul Cézanne and Chaim Soutine. The significance of the change from sable to hogs' hair brush and flake white to Kremnitz white in the late 1950s was exagger-ated. Freud was attracted to Bacon's merciless wit and risk-taking, admiring his impulsive handling of paint, yet curiously it was Bacon who tried repeatedly to fix an image of his younger friend's physical magnetism.

By the end of the 1950s Freud's fraught personal life contrib-uted to a visual restlessness, and he began standing to paint, letting the raked perspective exaggerate the anatomies of his subjects. A greenish-yellow palette and vein-marked skin made the subjects, such as Woman Smiling 1958-59, superficially less attractive; the paintings exhibited at the Marlborough Gallery in London in 1958 and 1963 were harder to sell.

Freud's obsession with gambling on horses and dogs brought on debts and dangerous threats, although many of the most singular paintings are of fleshly men within the racing fraternity. The journalist Jeffrey Bernard, describing Freud's afternoons in the betting shop and evenings with the rich and distinguished (including "Princess Margaret's set"), wrote admiringly: "He has cracked the nut of how to conduct a double life." The artist's slightly leering face and naked shoulders appear between the fronds of a giant Deremensis, Interior with Plant, Reflection Listening 1967-68. A superb, dangerously over-worked, standing self-portrait, Painter Working, Reflection 1993 portrays the ageing artist wearing only unlaced boots, holding a palette and knife (he was left-handed), addressing the viewer like a silent actor; invariably paint applied imaginatively to the planes of walls and floor reads as though a leitmotif for the prevailing mood. Each millimetre, he insisted, had to become essential to the whole.

In the 1980s the bodies of the nudes pressed into the surrounding space, their three-dimensionality and almost modelled impasto describing deeply contoured forms like those within Freud's favourite bronzes by Rodin – Naked Balzac and Iris. Freud spoke of his curiosity about "the insides and undersides of things".

The reserved Bella Freud placed diagonally on a red sofa (1986) is one of the artist's masterpieces. Leigh Bowery and Freud had a mutually sustaining friendship that went on until just before the performance artist succumbed to an Aids-related illness at the end of 1994. Bowery's "wonderfully buoyant bulk was an instrument I felt I could use in my painting"; "yet it's the quality of his mind that makes me want to portray him". In front of Titian's Diana and Actaeon in 2008, he explained: "When something is really convincing, I don't think about how it was done, I think about the effect on me."

Several paintings approach allegory revisited as parody, beginning with Large Interior, W9 1973 (his mother and his lover), and the heavily promoted Large Interior W11 (After Watteau) 1981-83, with its awkward (and memorable) conjunction of five people from the artist's intimate life. Sitters sometimes came separately, as with Evening in the Studio, where the model Sue Tilley sprawls on the floor in the pose of seaside postcards with captions such as "Roll over Betty". The shuttered interior in Freud's house in Notting Hill was recorded in several large paintings, one now in a Dallas museum: a long-time friend, Francis Wyndham, sits reading in the foreground, whippet at his feet, and in the space beyond, a hybrid Jerry Hall/David Dawson nurses her son.

Annabel Mullion was painted with her shaggy-haired dog Rattler and reappears seven years later with a pregnant belly in Expecting the Fourth 2005 (only 10x15cm), and in a larger etching, limbs still like a thoroughbred, as described by one of Freud's favourite authors, Baudelaire: "vainly have time and love sunk their teeth into her".

Freud's exceptional ability to convey tactile information is evident in early drawings, especially those of gorse sprigs, a dead heron and a bearded Christian Bérard in a dressing gown. A similarly heightened, highly poetic sensibility invades the etchings that began in the 1980s, black whorls and stippled textures fanatically worked, the artist relishing the "element of danger and mystery" that accompanies slipping a heavily worked plate into acid.

International exposure increased after the 1974 Hayward exhibition, nurtured by Freud's admirers, particularly William Feaver, curator of a Tate retrospective in 2002, and the dealer James Kirkman. The revival of interest in painting that emerged around 1980 led to outstanding British artists being ringfenced with an inappropriate label, the School of London. Freud thought his close friend Frank Auerbach the best British painter of his lifetime. Auerbach understood how no original concept or idiom could be credited with the mesmerising reality of art: "I think of Lucian's attention to his subject. If his concentrated interest were to falter, he would come off the tightrope. He has no safety net of manner."

A retrospective organised by the British Council reached Washington, Paris, London and Berlin in 1987-88, and the "recent work" exhibition created by the Whitechapel Gallery in 1993 drew crowds in New York and Madrid as well as the East End. Freud's representative from 1993, William Acquavella, had a buoyant, unwavering reckoning of the artist's worth – in other words in the league of 20th-century masters. In 2007 the Museum of Modern Art in New York organised an exhibition with great impact, titled The Painter's Etchings, Freud's place in postwar art history admitted through a side-door rather than placed in the canon.

The completion of a single picture turned into a newsworthy event. In 1993 a Daily Mail front-page headline asked: "Is this man the greatest lover in Britain?" A disconcerting recent painting, the artist working while "surprised by a naked admirer", fed readers' curiosity about the octogenarian's love life. The rather sensational Benefits Supervisor Sleeping (1995) achieved a record auction price for a living artist in May 2008, £17m, by which time Russian oligarchs had joined the wealthy North American collectors who had already replaced upper-class British patrons. The promotion of pictures at auction sometimes gave unfortunate prominence to the failures, notably the truncated picture of a pregnant Kate Moss.

The artist related his acceptance of honours – the CH in 1983 and the OM in 1993 – to his family's debt to Britain, the country that allowed them naturalisation in 1939. Freud described the move to England as "linked to my luck. Hitler's attitude to the Jews persuaded my father to bring us to London, the place I prefer in every way to anywhere I've been."

Queen Elizabeth II sat for a small portrait in 2001 which Freud donated to the Royal Collection. He selected the pictures for the important Constable exhibition that opened in Paris in 2002, respecting the artist's "truth-telling. The way he used the under-growths to suit himself – things being soaked in water and so on – was a way of looking at nature that no one had really done before."

The portraits Freud made of his mother, beginning in 1972 and ending with a drawing from her deathbed in 1989, are a remarkable elegy of ageing and depression. When his children (15 or so were recognised) began leading independent lives, most of them came to sit for him and he was proud of their talents. Bella Freud is a fashion designer and four others are successful writers – Annie Freud, Esther Freud, and Rose and Susie Boyt. Contrary to what has been written about anonymity, the identities of at least 168 sitters have been revealed in various interviews, commentaries and published information.

Thinking about the women who were closest to him for the longest duration, one realises how reticent they preferred to be, particularly Baroness Willoughby d'Eresby and Susanna Chancellor. Any biography of the artist that is written with the claim to analyse character or feelings is doomed.

The list of those he knew and affected would be enormous (and incomplete), the narratives lopsided, with anecdotes and memoirs exaggerating their author's familiarity. Freud's own, sharp recollections are both exciting and skewed. He recently spoke of how it amused him to hold the heads of schoolmates under water, but his occasional violence was countered by a precise, rather Germanic use of language and good manners.

An admitted control freak, who lived alone and liked to use the telephone but not give out his number, Freud kept relationships in separate compartments. He lived with the same aesthetic as that of his work – fine linen, worn leather, superb works of art (and a few cartoons), buddleia and bamboo in the overgrown garden and the residue of paint carried down from the studio. In this setting, he sustained until the end his ability to make portrayals of many of the people and animals who mattered to him (the one still on the easel, Portrait of a Hound), paintings that face-to-face are all-consuming and oddly liberating.

Lucian Michael Freud, artist, born 8 December 1922; died 20 July 2011

25 JULY 2011

A losing game

ALEXIS PETRIDIS

Perhaps the most startling thing about Amy Winehouse's death was how startled people were by it. She was a drug addict whose crack use had, her father claimed, given her emphysema. She was a drinker who, by her own admission, "didn't know when to stop". And, as she frequently pointed out, she "didn't give a fuck".

It's the kind of story that usually only ends one way, and yet the reaction to her death, my own included, was one of shocked disbelief. Perhaps it's because the chaos of her life had been lived in full public view: it was hardly the first time that an ambulance had been called to her flat because of an overdose, but she'd always somehow survived. Perhaps it's because she had already turned an excess of drink and drugs and emotional devastation into a remarkable album: in the back of your mind lurks the belief that she would somehow do that again, that her talent was such that it couldn't actually be overwhelmed by her excesses, however much horrible evidence there was to the contrary.

Or perhaps it's because, despite all the talk of her "rock'n'roll" lifestyle, Amy Winehouse wasn't rock'n'roll. She was a mainstream pop star, stage-school educated and discovered by Simon Fuller of S Club 7 and Pop Idol fame. Her records got played on Radio 2 and tangoed to on Strictly Come Dancing. She was a global superstar who sold millions and millions of albums at a time when album sales were apparently in terminal decline, whose celebrity hadn't waned despite the fact that she hadn't released anything new for five years. At the most cynical level, perhaps her death came as a surprise because people thought that someone, somewhere would do anything to protect their investment and succeed.

Almost as startling is how much impact she made with so little music. You can listen to literally everything she recorded in a couple of hours. Her posthumous reputation ultimately rests on even less than that: one 11-track album, and a scattering of covers – the Zutons' Valerie, a reggae take on Sam Cooke's Cupid, a handful of songs made famous by the Specials – all of them released in barely 12 months, between 2006 and 2007.

There was a debut album, 2003's Frank, but it was part of a glut of MOR-ish female singer-songwriter albums that appeared in the early noughties: a bit jazzy, a bit neo-soul, a touch of hip-hop about the beats, the songs bolstered by the attentions of writers for hire who had worked with the Sugababes and Kylie Minogue. In truth, it was more interesting than that billing suggested. The voice was obviously there, and even if it hadn't quite found the songs to match it, there was a scabrous wit fuelling the lyrics of

Fuck Me Pumps or Stronger Than Me. There was a hint of something dark about songs like What Is It About Men? and I Heard Love Is Blind and, indeed, about the way she seemed to deliberately align herself with the late Billie Holiday: she claimed her big influence was Sarah Vaughan but there was no mistaking where some of her vocal tics had been borrowed from.

At a time when record companies had begun to surgically deprive mainstream artists of their personality via media training, journalists who met her came back a little startled by how charismatic and funny and candid she was. She told them she didn't particularly care for her debut album, which she claimed she had never bothered to listen to all the way through and didn't even own a copy of. She offered some fairly blunt assessments of her own record company: "I hate them fuckers, man ... they know they're idiots ... I have no respect for them whatsoever."

She already had a reputation as a handful, a prodigious weed-smoker and drinker who occasionally seemed rather the worse for wear during interviews and on stage. "Shut up! I don't give a fuck!" she famously yelled at Bono during an awards ceremony. She wasn't the first person in history to be gripped by an uncontrollable urge to tell the U2 frontman to put a sock in it, but the latter part of her heckle seemed to pertain less to his acceptance speech than herself and have a genuine and slightly troubling ring of truth about it. She clearly wasn't Dido, but Frank was still the kind of album that got advertised in home-furnishing magazines, the implication being that it was the musical equivalent of a scented candle, something that would waft discreetly around the room.

Certainly, nothing about it could prepare people for the album she released three years later. She reappeared virtually unrecognisable, emaciated, covered in tattoos, dressed like a cartoon of a 60s girl group vocalist in the throes of a breakdown, complete with a vast, chaotic Ronnie Spectorish beehive that she claimed rose or fell in height according to the bleakness of her mood. If nothing else, her visual overhaul told you she was still not an artist in thrall to the usual record company machinations. She now had the most striking and instantly recognisable image of any pop star of her era. Within a year Karl Lagerfeld was copying it on the catwalk, within two it was being parodied in the spirit-sappingly unfunny Hollywood film Disaster Movie. But no stylist would ever have suggested she look like that.

The change in her music was equally arresting. Her words had sharpened into a style that was by turns quietly beautiful – "all I can ever be to you is a darkness that we know" – and earthily funny: "he left no time to regret, kept his dick wet".

Initially at least, the single Rehab seemed less personal than witty and topical – a lot of high-profile stars had made a big show of entering The Priory or Clouds – but more noticeable than the lyrics was the music. On one level, it trod a fairly well-worn path – the 60s soul pastiche has been a touchstone in pop for decades – but it didn't feel that way. Producer Mark Ronson's arranging of Winehouse's influences was so brilliantly done that it would change pop music in its wake. Five years on, the charts are still filled with records made in Rehab's image. They're not as good, partly because, however straightforward it seemed, the trick Ronson pulled off was remarkable – he managed to make a record that was smart and knowing without seeming dry or academic; instantly familiar without seeming tired – and partly because Rehab was a brilliantly written pop song, something conspicuous by their absence from her debut album.

But mostly it's because they're not sung by Amy Winehouse. Released from the affectations of her debut album – the samples of crackling vinyl and bursts of scat singing that thumpingly sign-posted her jazz heritage – it turned out she could take a bright, commercial pop song and lend it a depth and an edge. She did it on Rehab – even if you thought the song was simply poking fun at the excesses of celebrity culture, rather than detailing an incident from her own life, there was a raw, screw-you defiance about her performance that gave you pause – and she did it again on Ronson's version of Valerie. Winehouse declined to amend the song to accommodate the change in vocalist's gender: the lyrics were pretty vague, and in another female vocalist's hands it might simply have been transformed from a lovelorn lament into a song bewailing the end of a friendship. But Winehouse sang it with a sleazy urgency, a wilfully suggestive crackle absent from the original and at odds with the upbeat, northern soul backing. It suddenly sounded filthy.

The production and songs on Back to Black were so unfailingly brilliant that it's tempting to think anyone could have had a hit with them; certainly, they've spawned a mini-industry of cover versions, from Prince to Elbow to Wanda Jackson. But it was her voice that made it phenomenal. Even if you had known nothing about Winehouse, even if she hadn't been so candid about her songs' inspiration or chosen to illustrate them with videos that depicted her singing in front of a grave with her name on it, you could have guessed something was up just from listening to her sing Love Is a Losing Game, or Tears Dry On Their Own.

Plenty of female singers were making records with the jazz and retro soul affectations around the same time as her, and plenty more would afterwards, rushing into the void that had been created by the fact that she was unable to play live or complete another record: there was a public demand for music that sounded like Amy Winehouse, whether or not Amy Winehouse was capable of providing it. But for the most part, they sounded like people trying on a vogueish style, doing something they thought would sell. Winehouse's performances, on the other hand, were so heartfelt they chafed against the knowingness of the arrangements, the clever stylistic references in Back to Black's sound. They made you think of Tony Wilson's assessment of Joy Division: "Every other band was on stage because they wanted to be rock stars, this band was on stage because they had no fucking choice." That wasn't why it was a hit – 10 million people don't go out and buy your album because they think you really mean it, any more than they go out and buy your album because you're in the tabloids thanks to your drug problems – but it explains why Back to Black has maintained its impact, despite five years of ubiquity.

A year after its release, she performed at the Mercury prize ceremony. Her personal life had gone haywire in full public view, although much worse was to come. Beforehand, people doubted whether she'd even show up: there seemed to be a general belief that, whether they wanted to or not, the judges couldn't give her the award, not least because her parents had recently turned up in the press demanding that people stop buying her records and giving her awards, thus funding her increasingly dissolute lifestyle. But she did turn up and sang Love Is a Losing Game. You can find a video of it on YouTube, which is worth doing, not least because it counters all the other videos you can find on YouTube, of her staggering and incapable on stage.

What's striking is how unshowy it all seems, the exact opposite of the vocal gymnastics and expressive hand gestures that The X Factor propagates as the apotheosis of great live performance, nothing to do with the spectacle of a big rock show. She just stands there and sings. The audience – cynical, drunk, music industry types – fall eerily quiet: she's silenced them with her talent alone. It tells you more about why Amy Winehouse was famous than any amount of tabloid headlines or terrible cameraphone footage of her drunk and lost at gigs she shouldn't have been performing in the first place. It was because she had talent to burn, not because she burnt it.

26 JULY 2011

Letter: Graven images

DAVID HOCKNEY

I missed Jonathan Jones's piece on the spraying of the Poussin (18 July), but I'd advise him to read The Power of Images by David Freedberg. There is an interesting account of a previous attack on that painting. He does point out it's no accident that they slashed the Golden Calf, the source of all imagery, hence Moses carried on the tablets the commandment not to make any graven image of anything that is on the earth and the sky above the earth and the sea below the earth. It wasn't any old painting that was slashed, it had a big meaning to the slasher. I have often pointed out it's the commandment that is never discussed by anybody. What did Moses know that we don't?

David Hockney
Bridlington, East Yorkshire

28 July 2011

Doctors relieved as Ed nose day passes without a hitch

PATRICK WINTOUR

An expectant cluster of doctors, of both the medical and spinning variety, gathered around a bedside in Grays Inn Road, London, yesterday morning to await an event that could determine the outcome of the next general election.

It was Ed nose day at the Royal National Throat, Nose and Ear hospital.

Ed Miliband had been asleep for an hour, recovering from an operation his team ludicrously continued to insist was solely about tackling a deviated septum in his nose, so making it easier for him to sleep, and possibly for his wife Justine to be spared the odd snore.

The Labour leader's spin doctors continued to blather on about how obstructive sleep apnoea is a respiratory condition, leading the throat to repeatedly narrow or close during sleep. This meant air did not get into Miliband's lungs properly, so waking him in the middle of the night, leaving him with nothing to do but think about the future of European social democracy – a subject that would make most people lapse back comatosed, but has an enlivening effect on a Milimind.

But everyone knew that all this medical detail was spin doctor obfuscation. In reality, the hour-long operation was a giant gamble. No one knew whether when he awoke the sound of Miliband's voice would be transformed. Would the new Bold Ed of recent weeks, willing to tear down the Murdoch empire, be given a voice to match – a lustrous blend of Laurence Olivier, Barry White and

Kathleen Turner? Or would it resemble a squeaky chainsaw liable to make voters run screaming from the room?

As research has shown the sound of a voice is worth more votes to politicians than the content of their speeches, the operation was no trivial matter. Many British politicians, including George Osborne and Lady Thatcher, have undergone coaching to deepen the timbre.

However, Labour voters hoping that the operation would have some magical oratorical impact have been disappointed. Those who have spoken to Miliband (no audio is yet available) say he sounds the same. "It did not change his voice, and nor was it intended to," said his office. He will now spend some "slow time" in his north London home before heading off on holiday to Devon with his family.

With his poll ratings well out of the emergency ward, he will be able to sleep easier before the haul towards his autumn party conference speech, an event that makes the most equable personality wake in the small hours in a cold sweat.

28 JULY 2011

MI5 was right to spy on my father, but why were Tootles and I in their files?

MARTIN KETTLE

I was two years old when my activities first came to the attention of MI5. In 1952, nothing if not thorough, a security service officer carefully filed a copy of an article written by my father in the Daily Worker about the books good Communists should encourage their children to read. The answer, my father wrote, was complicated by the age factor. "My son (aged 2½) adores Tootles the Train but would scarcely enjoy Kidnapped yet."

And there the truth about Tootles and me might have remained. But someone in MI5 decided last year it was time to place 12 files of surveillance records on my father, covering the years 1938 to 1960, in the public domain. Why his files were released, I have no way of knowing. But they are in the National Archives and I have read them. They reveal lots about my parents. But they also say lots that is freshly topical this week about the logic and limits of attempts to monitor political threats.

It was never a secret that my father, Arnold Kettle, was a Communist. He joined the Communist party in 1936 as an undergraduate at Cambridge and he was still a member when he died 50 years later. He spent most of his life as a university English teacher, wrote Marxist books on the novel, and was on the CP's inner executive committee. All this was public knowledge. But my father was also a member of the 1930s Cambridge Apostles, along with the spies Anthony Blunt and Guy Burgess, both of whom he knew, and he made occasional visits behind the Iron Curtain after the war. Was there, perhaps, more to his political activities than he ever admitted? Was he even in some way a spy?

Arnold was certainly a secretive man. And a disciplined one. His loyalty to the Communist party rarely wavered. Only after he died, for example, did I discover that, as a member of the CP executive in 1956, he had voted in a minority of two to condemn the Soviet invasion of Hungary. But the vote went against him and, as he believed in party discipline, he never referred to it again.

But the most striking aspect of the MI5 records on him is paradoxical. They are simultaneously thorough and inadequate, a point echoed in recent criticisms of the service today. Arnold's files are full of carbon copies of innumerable memos and reports. But he was a medium-sized target in a huge operation. By 1952, according to Christopher Andrew's history, MI5 knew the names of 90% of the CP's 35,000 members – not least by bugging the party's Covent Garden headquarters, but above all because they had acquired the party membership lists.

My father first crops up in MI5's files in 1938 in what now seem romantic circumstances, a member of a student delegation to Barcelona during the Spanish civil war. During the second world war, he applies to work in intelligence, but is rejected as "highly undesirable". When he goes for officer training, MI5 keeps in touch with his officers. "I have observed no evidence of anything subversive in his conduct ... Kettle is not a striking figure physically," one of them writes back.

After the war, his marriage to my mother is noted – "she is an ardent communist and seems to be present when anything of note is taking place in the left-wing world in London" – and they move to Leeds. His mail is opened, and there are phone intercepts whenever he contacts the CP headquarters or stays with prominent Communists during London visits. His bank accounts are monitored. In 1952, with Doris Lessing and others, he visits the Soviet Union. An MI6 report describes him as "an intellectual with a clever approach to communism when talking to the unconverted, in that he appears to ask searching or suspicious questions concerning the regime in the USSR but sees that the answers are always favourable to the Soviet side". That gets it about right.

Sometimes the reports widen into less conventional subjects. Cambridge police report to MI5 about a meeting "at which Dr Arnold Kettle will speak on Hamlet". An intercepted letter, carefully filed for posterity, asks for Arnold's views on Shelley. A note reveals that Arnold has defended EP Thompson's views on

William Morris in a party meeting. A party official asks why Arnold's new book is "imbued with the Leavis critical approach" and contains "nothing approaching Marxist criticism". In 1958, Arnold writes a letter to the party urging them not to denounce Boris Pasternak's Doctor Zhivago, "a work of great genius by a man of extraordinary intelligence and honesty". John Berger writes back, intercepted again, to congratulate him.

Occasionally, there is something more serious. An invitation from party HQ to take part in a meeting on "the development of automation and automatic devices which are substituting larger numbers of clerical and accounting workers" leads to him being tailed across London by the legendary Jim Skardon, interrogator of Kim Philby. Then, during a 1958 visit to Leeds, the Communist party leader John Gollan, who is being tailed, gives him a box, thought by MI5 to contain money, which he places in his bank for a year, before giving it back to Gollan. It looks as though Moscow gold passed through our house. Certainly many Indian and African students did so; "they all appeared to be intellectual types", a watcher reported.

On a personal level, these 12 files are of course hugely fascinating to me. But what wider lessons, if any, do they contain? I think MI5 was right to try to monitor the Communists. At least in its early days, the CP wanted to overthrow capitalism and transform the British state – and it was being financed by a hostile power to do so. MI5 could hardly look in the other direction, even when it was clear, as it certainly was by the 1950s, that the CP wasn't going anywhere as a revolutionary force and was increasingly looking for democratic and liberal legitimacy. My father was a small part of that, not a spy, but some monitoring of our lives made sense.

Maybe there are more damning files elsewhere. In their absence, though, the picture in these documents is of someone who was not so much wicked or threatening as wrong. "Nobody any longer believes socialism won't work," Arnold is reported to MI5 as saying in 1959. Half a century on, plenty of people believe the opposite. My father got a lot of the individual issues – Spain, Hungary, Stalin, Pasternak and certainly Hamlet – right. But he and his comrades got the big call very wrong indeed. Reading these files does not make me shocked so much as sad.

Ironically, my father did have a real secret. His family have known it for years. Doris Lessing wrote about it in her autobiography. And MI5 knew about it too. "It has been suggested from a somewhat doubtful source that Dr Kettle may have homosexual tendencies," they noted in 1953. The source was right. Five years later, the watchers reported: "Kettle attends meetings of the political committee in London on the second Saturday in each month, following which he makes contact with homosexual friends in St Martin's Lane and Soho."

Half a century on, much of the technology of surveillance has changed out of recognition from those distant days. So have the threats. But the pressure to monitor the potentially dangerous is just as great as it was in the cold war era. I want MI5 to protect us from bombers like the 7/7 jihadis or butchers like the Norwegian racist. I'd like to think they have become better at sorting out the lethal from the harmless and the public from the private. "It is a wonder that you can pick as many locks leading into the hearts of the wicked men as you do," Oliver Cromwell's son wrote to England's spymaster John Thurloe. Then as now, the effort comes at a high price.

8 August 2011

Unedited extract from @PaulLewis Twitter feed, 8.33pm to 11.05pm

PAUL LEWIS

8.33pm	Police car containing solitary office just attacked by a dozen youths with bricks and sticks #Pembury #Hackney
8.34pm	The car windows smashed in seconds; officer only managed to escape crowd. #Hackney #Pembury
8.35pm	More police now being chased away from #Pembury #Hackney
8.35pm	Two fortified police vans have fled #Hackney #Pembury
8.41pm	#Hackney Youth: "I wanted to see us do this to the fucking Feds for years."
8.42pm	People ripping off tree branches to attack police. This is all Three Sisters Church #Hackney
8.42pm	Police now battling riot police with sticks and bricks. Hand-to-hand fighting. #Hackney #Pembury http://yfrog.com/h85cvzlj
8.42pm	Police officer isolated, tripped. Mobbed with bricks and sticks. Colleagues rescued him in about ten seconds. #Hackney
8.50pm	Mounted police charging through #Hackney Downs park http://yfrog.com/h3bzdyoj
8.51pm	City of London Police officer: "You're not a fucking journalist. Do you want some." #Hackney

9.08pm   Here is my Audio report from #Hackney #Pembury
         http://bit.ly/qkxoJW

9.12pm   My audio report from #Hackney #Pembury http://bit.
         ly/qkxoJW

9.13pm   I don't want to say this, but seeing pictures of Croydon
         from a pub. People might die tonight. #londonriots

9.24pm   About to go on BBC Five Live #Hackney

9.41pm   I'm writing: Can people tell me precisely what time
         violence started in #Hackney?

10.19pm Can someone monitoring #Londonriots in detail tell
         me where best to head in east/north London?

10.26pm I will be on live (on the phone) to BBC Newsnight in 30
         mins #londonriots

10.39pm Violent clashes now on Kingsland Road, Hackney,
         as hundreds of Turkish men attack others youths
         #Hackney

10.40pm Kingsland Road chaotic as Turkish men attack other,
         predominantly black, youths with sticks, metal barri-
         cades and bricks. #Hackney

10.43pm Turkish man: "We're protecting our homes. This is
         war." #Hackney

10.48pm Man with stick: "This is Turkish Kurdish area. They
         come to our shops and we fight them with sticks."
         #Hackney

11.05pm I'm headed to #Camden. Any *specific* directions?

10 AUGUST 2011

Everything must go

ZOE WILLIAMS

The first day after London started burning, I spoke to Claire Fox, radical leftwinger and resident of Wood Green. On Sunday morning, apparently, people had been not just looting H&M, but trying things on first. By Monday night, Debenhams in Clapham Junction was empty, and in a cheeky touch, the streets were thronging with people carrying Debenhams bags. Four hours before, I had still thought this was just a north London thing. Fox said the riots seemed nihilistic, they didn't seem to be politically motivated, nor did they have any sense of community or social solidarity. This was inarguable. As one brave woman in Hackney put it: "We're not all gathering together for a cause, we're running down Foot Locker."

I think it's just about possible that you could see your actions refashioned into a noble cause if you were stealing the staples: bread, milk. But it can't be done while you're nicking trainers, let alone laptops. In Clapham Junction, the only shop left untouched was Waterstone's, and the looters of Boots had, unaccountably, stolen a load of Imodium. So this kept Twitter alive all night with tweets about how uneducated these people must be and the condition of their digestive systems. While that palled after a bit, it remains the case that these are shopping riots, characterised by their consumer choices: that's the bit we've never seen before. A violent act by the authorities, triggering a howl of protest – that bit is as old as time. But crowds moving from shopping centre to shopping centre? Actively trying to avoid a confrontation with police, trying to get in and out of JD Sports before the "feds" arrive? That bit is new.

By 5pm on Monday, as I was listening to the brave manager of the Lewisham McDonald's describing, incredulously, how he had just seen the windows stoved in, and he didn't think they'd be able to open the next day, I wasn't convinced by nihilism as a reading: how can you cease to believe in law and order, a moral universe, co-operation, the purpose of existence, and yet still believe in sportswear? How can you despise culture but still want the flat-screen TV from the bookies? Alex Hiller, a marketing and consumer expert at Nottingham Business School, points out that there is no conflict between anomie and consumption: "If you look at Baudrillard and other people writing in sociology about consumption, it's a falsification of social life. Adverts promote a fantasy land. Consumerism relies upon people feeling disconnected from the world."

Leaving Baudrillard aside, just because there is no political agenda on the part of the rioters doesn't mean the answer isn't rooted in politics. Theresa May – indeed most politicians, not just Conservatives – are keen to stress that this is "pure criminality", untainted by higher purpose; the phrase is a gesture of reassurance rather than information, because we all know it's illegal to smash shop windows and steal things. "We're not going to be diverted by sophistry," is the tacit message. "As soon as things have calmed down, these criminals are going to prison, where criminals belong."

Those of us who don't have responsibility for public order can be more interrogative about what's going on: an authoritarian reading is that this is a generation with a false sense of entitlement, created by the victim culture fostered, and overall leniency displayed, by the criminal justice system. It's just a glorified mugging, in other words, conducted by people who ask not what they can do for themselves, but what other people should have done for them, and who may have mugged before, on a smaller scale, and found it to be without consequence.

At the other end of the authoritarian-liberal spectrum, you have Camila Batmanghelidjh's idea, movingly expressed in the Independent, that this is a natural human response to the brutality of poverty: "Walk on the estate stairwells with your baby in a buggy manoeuvring past the condoms, the needles, into the lift where the best outcome is that you will survive the urine stench and the worst is that you will be raped ... It's not one occasional attack on dignity, it's a repeated humiliation, being continuously dispossessed in a society rich with possession. Young, intelligent citizens of the ghetto seek an explanation for why they are at the receiving end of bleak Britain, condemned to a darkness where their humanity is not even valued enough to be helped."

Between these poles is a more pragmatic reading: this is what happens when people don't have anything, when they have their noses constantly rubbed in stuff they can't afford, and they have no reason ever to believe that they will be able to afford it. Hiller takes up this idea: "Consumer society relies on your ability to participate in it. So what we recognise as a consumer now was born out of shorter hours, higher wages and the availability of credit. If you're dealing with a lot of people who don't have the last two, that contract doesn't work. They seem to be targeting the stores selling goods they would normally consume. So perhaps they're rebelling against the system that denies its bounty to them because they can't afford it."

The type of goods being looted seems peculiarly relevant: if they were going for bare necessities, I think one might incline towards sympathy. I could be wrong, but I don't get the impression that we're looking at people who are hungry. If they were going for more outlandish luxury, hitting Tiffany's and Gucci, they might seem more political, and thereby more respectable. Their achilles heel was in going for things they demonstrably want.

Forensic psychologist Kay Nooney deals impatiently with the idea of cuts, specifically tuition fees, as an engine of lawlessness. "These people aren't interested in tuition fees. In constituency, it's most similar to a prison riot: what will happen is that, usually in the segregation unit, nobody will ever know exactly, but a rumour will emanate that someone has been hurt in some way. There will be some form of moral outrage that takes its expression in self-interested revenge. There is no higher purpose, you just have a high volume of people with a history of impulsive behaviour, having a giant adventure."

Of course, the difference is that, in a prison, liberty has already been lost. So something pretty serious must have happened in order for young people on the streets to be behaving as though they have already been incarcerated. As another criminologist, Professor John Pitts, has said: "Many of the people involved are likely to have been from low-income, high-unemployment estates, and many, if not most, do not have much of a legitimate future. There is a social question to be asked about young people with nothing to lose."

There seems to be another aspect to the impunity – that the people rioting aren't taking seriously the idea it could rebound on them. All the most dramatic shots are of young men in balaclavas or with scarves tied round their faces, because it is such a striking, threatening image. But actually, watching snatches of phone footage and even professional news footage, it was much more alarming how many people made no attempt at all to cover their faces. This could go back to the idea that, with the closure of a number of juvenile facilities and the rhetoric about bringing down prison populations, people just don't believe they'll go to prison any more, at least not for something as petty as a pair of trainers. I feel for them; that may be true on a small scale, but when judges feel public confidence seriously to be at issue, they have it in themselves to be very harsh indeed (I'm thinking of Charlie Gilmour). But there is also a tang of surreality around it all, with the rioters calling the police "feds", as though they think they are in The Wire, and sending each other melodramatic texts saying: "So if you see a brother ... SALUTE! If you see a fed ... SHOOT!"

Late on Monday night, news went round Twitter that Turkish shopkeepers on Stoke Newington Road in Dalston were fighting off the marauders with baseball bats, and someone tweeted: "Bloody immigrants. Coming over here, defending our boroughs & communities." And it struck me that it hadn't occurred to me to walk on to my high street and see what was going on, let alone defend anything. I was watching events on a live feed, switching between Sky and the BBC, thinking how interesting it was, even though it was audible from my front door, and at one point, when I couldn't tell whether the helicopter noise was coming from the telly or from real life, it was because it was both.

The Dalston clashes remind us, also, that it wasn't just JD Sports, even though the reputation of that chain is, for some reason, the most bound up with everything that's happened. Smaller, independent corner shops, the kind without a head office in Welwyn Garden City, that aren't insured up to the teeth, were ransacked as well, for their big-ticket items of booze and fags. When a chain is attacked, the protection of its corporate aspect means that, while we can appreciate the breakdown of law and order, we do not respond emotionally. When a corner shop is destroyed, however, the lawlessness has a victim, and we feel disgusted. That's what drags these events into focus: not the stuff that was stolen, but the people behind the stuff.

13 AUGUST 2011

The week that shook Britain

PAUL LEWIS

For me, it started when I saw a man walking through an estate in Tottenham, north London, carrying a flat-screen TV.

It was 10.30pm last Saturday, and I was checking out reports of fires and clashes with police.

Riot police had formed a cordon around the south end of the road. It was like an artificial boundary, separating a quiet north London suburb from another, unrecognisable world.

Tottenham, the scene of a peaceful protest against the police shooting of Mark Duggan five hours earlier, had erupted into a riot.

It dawned on me in stages. Two older women hurried past with a suitcase. Then other men and women came running past, looking terrified.

I turned the corner on to the High Road, and found a police car ablaze, and boys, some who looked as young as 10, ransacking a music shop. Inside the next store, a travel agent, a desk was on fire.

It had taken 48 hours and a host of unanswered questions for the ripples of anger from the fatal shooting of Duggan, 29, to lead to civil unrest in Tottenham.

From that point on the contagion would spread with breathtaking speed, igniting riots and disorder in towns and cities across England.

By the end of the week, five people would have been left dead from the disturbances, and more than 1,500 arrested.

Tottenham was the start of a five-day journey in which my colleague, film-maker Mustafa Khalili, and I would record similar destruction in dozens of suburbs in places as varied as west London and Gloucester, in what felt like a country at war with itself.

The first portal for communicating what we saw was Twitter. It enabled us to deliver real-time reports from the scene, but more importantly enabled other users of Twitter to provide constant feedback and directions to troublespots. While journalists covering previous riots would chase ambulances to find the frontline, we followed what people on social media told us. By the end of the week, I had accumulated 35,000 new Twitter followers.

At 1.30am on Sunday, I had returned home assuming the rioting had died out. Then someone sent me a picture of an Aldi supermarket on fire. The BBC and Sky had been ordered out because it was too dangerous, with reports emerging of trouble in Wood Green, two miles west of Tottenham. Around 2.30am I decided to head back, this time wearing a hoodie and riding a bicycle; to blend in, and because no one could have got through in a car. On the approach, roads were blocked with burning barricades. Mostly the streets were filled with bystanders. But in places there were men, some in balaclavas, guarding the streets as shops were looted.

A minicab was driving erratically down a quiet residential street. As it passed, a wide-eyed teenager stared out. He looked 14.

The looting on nearby Wood Green's main high street was brazen, and was still going on around sunrise at 5.30am. That Sunday afternoon I toured Tottenham Hale retail park. I found people peering into the smashed stores: Boots, JD Sports, O2, Currys, Argos, Orange, PC World and Comet.

Everyone was asking the same questions. How had police lost control? And was it going to happen again?

It was just before 9pm on Sunday when I saw hundreds of youths head to the G Mantella jewellery store on Enfield high street, six miles north of where the disturbances had begun.

Police had earlier warned residents that the suburb would be on the "frontline" that night and filled a Tesco car park full of police horses in anticipation.

By late afternoon, a police car had been attacked in Enfield, and a handful of shop windows broken. The attack on the jewellers was over in seconds.

Minutes later I was stood on a side street, where young men were knocking down garden walls and collecting bricks to hurl at police. I used my bottled water to wash the bleeding hand of a boy who looked about 12.

This was the opening salvo in what would turn into the second night of disturbances. But Sunday was not, as was reported, a night of worsening riots. The disorder in Enfield, Hackney and Brixton was smaller in scale than the previous night, and felt like organised theft.

I was shown the BBM – BlackBerry Messenger – broadcast circulated hours earlier, announcing Enfield as a target.

It called on everyone in nearby boroughs to "start leaving ur yards" and bring "bags trollys, cars vans, hammers the lott!!!". It warned against passing the message to "snitch boys" (police informants) and said the aim was to "just rob everything".

There was one line – "dead the fires though" – that seemed to discourage arson.

I saw only one fire that night, as I followed in the wake of the looting, through debris-strewn streets.

In Ponders End, a suburb east of Enfield, Tesco workers told me how dozens of youths had made away with TVs and alcohol. "The windows smashed and they just came pouring in from all four sides," one said.

Minutes later I came across a group of teenagers huddled by Edmonton Working Men's Conservative Club. Most of them were girls, and in a state of panic. I saw they were holding a topless boy, who looked about 17. "He's been stabbed," one said.

As soon as he was in the ambulance, his friends fled, telling police they did not want to talk to "feds" (slang for the police). One screamed: "We hate you." Another shouted: "You're the reason this is happening."

Three teenagers cycling past stopped to look at the blood-splattered pavement. One looked at me and said: "Bruv, you the man from Twitter?"

He said he had been following updates from journalists about the riots, and told us to head to Edmonton Green, where there was a plan to attack shops at midnight.

As it turned out, lines of riot police protecting shop fronts appeared to have thwarted that plan. At 4am, as I drove home along Hackney's Kingsland Road, the scene of minor looting hours earlier, I saw pavements still filled with police.

They had rows of young men and women lined up against the walls, queueing for their stop and search.

Twelve hours later, it was reportedly a stop and search about half a mile away, on Mare Street, that ignited more violent scenes in Hackney.

In truth, it was more likely the "copycat" contagion that would make Monday night the worst by far for unrest in London, with disorder spreading to cities such as Birmingham, Nottingham, Liverpool and Bristol.

I arrived at Hackney's Pembury Estate around 6pm, following the large plumes of smoke that could be seen from most of east London, to see a white van which had been rammed into a wall and set on fire.

Next a motorbike was turned on its side and set alight, followed by two cars; each time the crowd waited nervously for the fuel tank to explode, and then added fuel to the burning barricades that blocked all roads into the estate.

This was not looting, but a return to a visceral desire to fight police that was first seen two days earlier in Tottenham.

There was an excited, frenzied mood. There appeared to be more older people and particularly more women taking part, many helping carry fuel debris for the fires.

Some rioters turned on people taking images on mobile phones. I saw one press photographer pulled to the ground and beaten with sticks.

It took police three hours to retake control of the estate. One telling incident occurred when youths started attacking a patrol car with bricks. It was only when the car reversed that the crowd realised there was an officer inside.

Around 10 men instantly sprinted towards the car, pelting it with bricks and blocks of concrete. One tried frantically to open the car door.

Unable to see through his smashed windows, the officer accelerated his vehicle into the crowd, almost crashing into traffic lights. "I've been wanting to see us do this to the feds for years," said one man, in his 30s, looking on.

I took shelter in a pub on the outskirts of the estate that – remarkably – was still open. The TV was showing helicopter images of a fire in Croydon, south London, where Trevor Ellis, 29, would be shot dead in the midst of the riots hours later.

That night I would see a rapid series of incidents that was almost impossible to compute. On Kingsland Road, groups of shopkeepers, many of them Turkish Kurds, sprinted past our car as they chased looters away.

An hour later, and further west, I was in Chalk Farm to see men armed with scaffold poles attack passing motorists and smash their way into shops.

When the windows were broken, people of all backgrounds surged in to help themselves to the free goods.

Khalili and I were pretending to be part of the crowd, with hoodies pulled tight over our heads. A man in a balaclava came up to me and gave us a hard, searching stare.

He walked away, and spoke to a friend who returned seconds later, asking us for a cigarette. We left soon after.

Later that night, as we headed to the scene of what was possibly the largest fire of the riots – at a Sony distribution centre near the M25 – we suspected we were being followed by a car with a smashed windscreen, forcing us to accelerate through a red light.

It was not until around 3am that we arrived at the west London suburb where Khalili lives: Ealing looked worse than anywhere else we had seen.

It was here that Richard Mannington Bowes, 68, was reportedly killed as he tried to put out a fire. There were parts of Ealing where every single shop had been attacked, and every car set on fire.

When we arrived the disturbances had died down, the streets almost empty.

I spoke to an eastern European builder who had just boarded up his friend's ransacked wine bar. He could not keep his eyes away from a burned-out buggy in the middle of the road which reminded him of a war zone.

"Surreal is a good word I think for this," he said. "Hollywood does not know what can happen in real life." Like almost all the looting victims I spoke to, the builder asked: "Where were the police?"

The expectation that lawlessness would prompt communities to defend themselves in what could spill into vigilantism was well-founded.

The fear that it could turn into something far worse – racial conflict – did not transpire, despite pockets of far-right activity in parts of London. I saw one worrying development in Enfield on the fourth night, Tuesday.

As we drove north up Hertford Road, we came across more than 70 white males, in their 30s and 40s, running in unison down a street shouting "get the Pakis", "get the blacks".

They looked drunk, and people told us they had been chasing black teenagers. I reported the incident as a "minor skirmish", but my reports quickly became viral and, taken out of context, were being used to stoke fears of imminent racial conflict.

Worse, some took the report to be a misleading reference to a peaceful gathering of citizens who had come together to defend their community elsewhere in Enfield. It was a sobering reminder of the power of social media. The streets were in chaos, but so too was the internet, which was both the fastest source of reliable news and, unchecked, a means of spreading panic.

Tuesday turned out to be relatively quiet in London. I headed to Birmingham, to see yet more scenes of looted shops and torched cars.

Elsewhere, Manchester and Salford witnessed widespread looting, with shops attacked in Liverpool, Leicester, Bristol, Leeds and Nottingham, where a police station had been firebombed.

But the most tragic incident occurred in Birmingham, when three men guarding a petrol station – Haroon Jahan, 21, and brothers Shazad Ali, 30, and Abdul Musavir, 31 – were killed in an apparent hit-and-run incident.

Around 3am, as rumours circulated about their deaths, we began to receive reports of a major fire in Gloucester.

We arrived in the small city at dawn, to see there had been a riot there, too. The damage was not on the scale of bigger cities, but in places it appeared just as intense. I talked to Dale Millar, 26, who had spent the night photographing the riots. He described bins and bricks being hurled at police, adding: "I heard one little kid, 17, shout out 'I done my job today, I hit a police officer.'"

Four teenagers lingering nearby showed me BBM messages that had been calling on Gloucester to be attacked since Monday. One said: "Pussys stay at home! Bad man dnt come alone. Tell a fren to tell a fren!"

So why did the English riots of 2011 stop? Police chiefs will argue that their strategy, which took three days to formulate, of flooding the streets with riot officers, proved a significant deterrence. The fact that police numbers were bolstered by people determined to protect their own streets must also have had an impact, as did the rain.

But there was also a social pressure at work, and it came from the very same "culture" that David Cameron has blamed for the riots.

I spoke to parents who said they had persuaded their children to stay indoors, and young people who had held back their friends from taking part.

Even in the midst of the seeming immorality of rioting without a cause, there were signs of a moral compass, with young men trying to rein back others they felt were going too far.

In the early hours of Thursday, the first night of calm, I stood at what could have been a flashpoint: the Jet garage forecourt in Birmingham where three Asian men had died the previous day.

The fear that the deaths could trigger retribution against the local black community remained unspoken, but well-founded.

As soon as I arrived on Dudley Road I heard racist language used to describe the three men's killers. Around 300 Asian men – Sikhs and Muslims – had gathered, some in masks. I met Upinder Randhawa, who had spent the previous days using his tiny broadcaster, Sangat TV, to provide gripping live reports from the frontline of the disturbances.

Randhawa was talking hurriedly about shared religious values and the need for unity when a teenager in a mask barged in. "Fuck that, man, I'm gonna get a gun and shoot somebody," he said.

But there were no guns and no shooting, in large part due to the debate that ensued after prayers. They decided collectively to abandon a planned march into the city, and avoid what many felt would be inevitable violence.

If Birmingham was on the brink that night, it was saved by the very same demographic that, elsewhere in the country, has been blamed for causing civil unrest. These were angry young men – many of them poor and the children of immigrants.

Disorder could still break out, but whatever happens in England over the coming days, the debate on that petrol forecourt should serve as a hopeful reminder; of grieving young men who would show restraint in a time of crisis that some would say has eluded politicians, police chiefs and judges.

"We need to tell the media we will not tolerate the tyranny, but we will not react either," said Harpreet Singh, 28. "We are capable, but we will not do it."

15 AUGUST 2011

We've been warned:
the system is ready to blow

LARRY ELLIOTT

For the past two centuries and more, life in Britain has been governed by a simple concept: tomorrow will be better than today. Black August has given us a glimpse of a dystopia, one in which the financial markets buckle and the cities burn. Like Scrooge, we have been shown what might be to come unless we change our ways.

There were glimmers of hope amid last week's despair. Neighbourhoods rallied round in the face of the looting. The Muslim community in Birmingham showed incredible dignity after three young men were mown down by a car and killed during the riots.

It was chastening to see consumerism laid bare. We have seen the future and we know it sucks. All of which is cause for cautious optimism – provided the right lessons are drawn.

Lesson number one is that the financial and social causes are linked. Lesson number two is that what links the City banker and the looter is the lack of restraint, the absence of boundaries to bad behaviour. Lesson number three is that we ignore this at our peril.

To understand the mess we are in, it's important to know how we got here. Today marks the 40th anniversary of Richard Nixon's announcement that America was suspending the convertibility of the dollar into gold at $35 an ounce. Speculative attacks on the dollar had begun in the late 1960s as concerns mounted over America's rising trade deficit and the cost of the Vietnam war. Other countries were increasingly reluctant to take dollars in payment and demanded gold instead. Nixon called time on the Bretton Woods system of fixed but adjustable exchange rates, under which countries could use capital controls in order to stimulate their economies without fear of a run on their currency. It was also an era in which protectionist measures were used quite liberally: Nixon announced on 15 August 1971 that he was imposing a 10% tax on all imports into the US.

Four decades on, it is hard not to feel nostalgia for the Bretton Woods system. Imperfect though it was, it acted as an anchor for the global economy for more than a quarter of a century, and allowed individual countries to pursue full-employment policies. It was a period devoid of systemic financial crises.

There have been big structural changes in the way the global economy has been managed since 1971, none of them especially beneficial. The fixed exchange rate system has been replaced by a hybrid system in which some currencies are pegged and others float. The currencies in the eurozone, for example, are fixed against each other, but the euro floats against the dollar, the pound and the Swiss franc. The Hong Kong dollar is tied to the US dollar, while Beijing has operated a system under which the yuan is allowed to appreciate against the greenback but at a rate much slower than economic fundamentals would suggest.

The system is an utter mess, particularly since almost every country in the world is now seeking to manipulate its currency downwards in order to make exports cheaper and imports dearer. This is clearly not possible. Sir Mervyn King noted last week that the solution to the crisis involved China and Germany reflating their economies so that debtor nations like the US and Britain could export more. Progress on that front has been painfully slow, and will remain so while the global currency system remains so dysfunctional. The solution is either a fully floating system under which countries stop manipulating their currencies or an attempt to recreate a new fixed exchange rate system using a basket of world currencies as its anchor.

The breakup of the Bretton Woods system paved the way for the liberalisation of financial markets. This began in the 1970s and picked up speed in the 1980s. Exchange controls were lifted and formal restrictions on credit abandoned. Policymakers were left with only one blunt instrument to control the availability of credit: interest rates.

For a while in the late 1980s, the easy availability of money provided the illusion of wealth but there was a shift from a debt-averse world where financial crises were virtually unknown to a debt-sodden world constantly teetering on the brink of banking armageddon.

Currency markets lost their anchor in 1971 when the US suspended dollar convertibility. Over the years, financial markets have lost their moral anchor, engaging not just in reckless but fraudulent behaviour. According to the US economist James

Galbraith, increased complexity was the cover for blatant and widespread wrongdoing.

Looking back at the sub-prime mortgage scandal, in which millions of Americans were mis-sold home loans, Galbraith says there has been a complete breakdown in trust that is impairing the hopes of economic recovery.

"There was a private vocabulary, well-known in the industry, covering these loans and related financial products: liars' loans, Ninja loans (the borrowers had no income, no job or assets), neutron loans (loans that would explode, destroying the people but leaving the buildings intact), toxic waste (the residue of the securitisation process). I suggest that this tells you that those who sold these products knew or suspected that their line of work was not 100% honest. Think of the restaurant where the staff refers to the food as scum, sludge and sewage."

Finally, there has been a big change in the way that the spoils of economic success have been divvied up. Back when Nixon was berating the speculators attacking the dollar peg, there was an implicit social contract under which the individual was guaranteed a job and a decent wage that rose as the economy grew. The fruits of growth were shared with employers, and taxes were recycled into schools, healthcare and pensions. In return, individuals obeyed the law and encouraged their children to do the same. The assumption was that each generation would have a better life than the last.

This implicit social contract has broken down. Growth is less rapid than it was 40 years ago, and the gains have disproportionately gone to companies and the very rich. In the UK, the professional middle classes, particularly in the south-east, are doing fine, but below them in the income scale are people who have become more dependent on debt as their real incomes have stagnated. Next are the people on minimum-wage jobs, which have to be topped up by tax credits so they can make ends meet. At the very bottom of the pile are those who are without work, many of them second- and third-generation unemployed.

A crisis that has been four decades in the making will not be solved overnight. It will be difficult to recast the global monetary system to ensure that the next few years see gradual recovery rather than depression. Wall Street and the City will resist all attempts at clipping their wings. There is strong ideological resistance to the policies that make decent wages in a full-employment economy feasible: capital controls, allowing strong trade unions, wage subsidies, and protectionism.

But this is a fork in the road. History suggests there is no iron law of progress and there have been periods when things have got worse not better. Together, the global imbalances, the manic-depressive behaviour of stock markets, the venality of the financial sector, the growing gulf between rich and poor, the high levels of unemployment, the naked consumerism and the riots are telling us something.

17 SEPTEMBER 2011

Met use Official Secrets Act to force hacking disclosure
'Unprecedented' attempt to make Guardian reveal Dowler source

21 SEPTEMBER 2011

Fashion VIPs fill No 10 but it's the MiniCams who steal the show

JESS CARTNER-MORLEY

It is not often that Anna Wintour gets upstaged by a young upstart who is wearing not a single designer label and whose Manolo collection stands at a woeful zero. But at Samantha Cameron's Downing Street reception for the fashion industry last night, the American Vogue editor's entrance on the arm of a hulking bodyguard was comprehensively overshadowed by that of Florence Cameron, who made a cameo appearance on the hip of her babysitter, who also happens to be the prime minister.

Wintour, famously, never stays at a party longer than 20 minutes. Florence, along with her older brother and sister, made her excuses after 15. Game, set and match to the MiniCams.

The question on everyone's lips was, of course, what is she wearing? The smart money had Florence in White Company, Arthur in Gap Kids and Nancy in Boden, though at press time the Minister for Pyjamas was not returning calls.

At the now regular Downing Street receptions for fashion, Samantha Cameron is unique in being both genuinely at home in the surroundings and entirely au fait with the gossip. Last night she congratulated designers whose shows she had seen, while confidently debating contrasting brand-building strategies among the designers and the strictly off-the-record matter of whose star is on the wane and whose on the rise.

While David Cameron's three young children gave him an excuse for an early exit, George Osborne's small talk was put to rigorous test. Jeremy Hunt, in an Aquascutum suit with a London 2012 badge, was keen to stress the importance of fashion: "We need to start talking about what is great about contemporary Britain, and fashion is important in that. It's that mix of ancient and modern excellence that is unique about Britain."

As the champagne flowed, the party divided into factions. The lemon drawing room was where retail moguls (Philip Green) and the seriously wealthy and well-dressed (Heather Kerzner) hung out. The salmon pink sitting room next door, meanwhile, was the place to be for the designers, stylists and It kids. ("This lot are the people who dance in the kitchen at parties," as one famous British model put it.)

Sam Baker, editor of Red magazine, noted how the shared excitement made accessible human beings of even the most aired-and-graced fashionistas. "I love how happy everyone is to be here. Designers who can seem quite intimidating are very human in this context."

On Twitter, she continued: "Everyone tries to get you to steal some loo paper. You have to explain that they get their loo paper the same place the rest of us do." But the imposing dimensions of Downing Street did, it seem, break through even the icy fashion demeanour. "The big windows are fantastic," one mogul mused.

"Wouldn't this be a marvellous place for an after-show party?"

21 SEPTEMBER 2011

Met abandons fight to force Guardian to reveal its sources

Action against reporters who broke hacking stories dropped after CPS intervention

ACKNOWLEDGMENTS

I would like thank Alan Rusbridger, editor-in-chief of the Guardian, for the opportunity to edit this volume and Katie Roden for being a supportive publisher, astonishingly calm as deadlines came and went. Felicity Ward delved into the archives producing files and cuttings, Fiona Shields and Roger Tooth lent me their expertise for the selection of photographs, and previous Bedside Guardian editors Chris Elliott, Martin Kettle and Hugh Muir offered gratefully received advice. Rory Foster, a terrific colleague, was the text editor who actually assembled the book but also did so much more: his considered opinions were always spot-on, his ability to spot howlers was vital. And I'd also like to thank Nuala, Jamie and Niamh for putting up with weekend after weekend in a house that resembled a newspaper recycling plant.

Paul Johnson, September 2011